ENCYCLOPEDIA OF
CATS

ENCYCLOPEDIA OF
CATS

Candida Frith-Macdonald

PaRragon

Bath · New York · Singapore · Hong Kong · Cologne · Delhi · Melbourne

First published by Parragon in 2008

Parragon
Queen Street House
4 Queen Street
Bath BA1 1HE, UK

Created and produced by

13 SOUTHGATE STREET WINCHESTER HAMPSHIRE SO23 9DZ

DESIGN Sharon Rudd
EDITORIAL Jennifer Close

ISBN: 978-1-4075-2442-9

Printed in China

CONTENTS

ABOUT THIS BOOK

The cat has lived alongside us for several thousand years. In all that time, it has probably never changed so much or so rapidly as it has in the last hundred years. Of course, the basic feline physique, habits, and instincts remain much as they have been since the days of ancient Egypt, but our view of the cat, how we treat it and breed it, have changed radically.

THE FELINE PAST
Thanks to DNA analysis, we have a better idea than ever of where the domestic cat fits into the feline family, and when and where the most sociable and adventurous of wildcats began to hunt agricultural pests until a new type of cat, able to live in colonies and alongside another species, emerged. This change was largely psychological: the domestic cat brought its magnificent senses and abilities into our homes intact.

THE FELINE PRESENT
After centuries in which it has been revered and protected, reviled and persecuted, and immortalized in pictures and prose, the cat has conquered every continent. Today, there are many cats that still come and go as they please and live partly on handouts, partly by their own skills, but the way we keep our cats has changed. Most now live into their late teens, due to vastly improved healthcare. But when the cat overtook the dog in popularity, many still really wanted a dog-like pet, so there is a growing tendency to treat cats like dogs, and behavioural problems are on the rise.

THE FELINE FUTURE?
As the cat's popularity has risen, the kind of cat we own has become more important to some people. In most countries, pedigree cats are a tiny percentage of all pet cats, but in some places, primarily North America, they make up a substantial proportion of all cats owned. Here, the amateur world of the cat fancy is beginning to look highly professional, and attracting ever more controversy through breeds with curly ears, short legs, and wild feline blood. When the first GM cat appears, the fur will really fly.

SYMBOLS IN THIS BOOK

Symbols in the breed profiles give a quick-reference guide. Build is not always apparent under an abundant coat; types are explained on pages 174–77. In temperament, cats generally vary between self-contained and dignified to chatty, 'look-at-me' types; this is often classed as a Western/Oriental split, but breed origins are not always a guide. Coat care depends on more than coat length: the hairless breeds need more care than many longhairs. The swatches on profiles show a representative spread of popular colours.

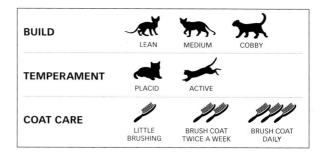

BUILD	LEAN	MEDIUM	COBBY
TEMPERAMENT	PLACID	ACTIVE	
COAT CARE	LITTLE BRUSHING	BRUSH COAT TWICE A WEEK	BRUSH COAT DAILY

COAT COLOURS

 BLACK SELF

 WHITE

 BLUE SELF

 BLUE SELF (LONG)

 RED SELF

LILAC SELF

 BLACK & WHITE

 BLUE & WHITE

 RED & WHITE

 BROWN CLASSIC TABBY

BROWN STRIPED TABBY

 RED STRIPED TABBY

 CREAM STRIPED TABBY

SILVER TABBY

 SILVER STRIPED TABBY

 LILAC STRIPED TABBY

 BLUE SILVER TABBY

 BROWN TICKED TABBY (LONG)

 BLUE TICKED TABBY

 RED TICKED TABBY

 BROWN TICKED TABBY

 BLACK SMOKE

 CHINCHILLA

 SILVER SHADED

 TORTIE

 TORTIE & WHITE

 TORTIE TABBY

 TORTIE TABBY & WHITE

 BLUE TABBY & WHITE

RED STRIPED TABBY & WHITE

 BROWN TABBY & WHITE

 BLUE TORTIE & WHITE

 BLUE TORTIE TABBY & WHITE

 LILAC CREAM TORTIE

 SEAL POINT

 BLUE POINT

 RED POINT

 LILAC POINT

CARAMEL POINT

CREAM POINT

 CHOCOLATE POINT

FAWN POINT

 SEAL TABBY POINT

 BLUE TABBY POINT

 RED TABBY POINT & WHITE

 LILAC TABBY POINT

HAIRLESS BREED COLOURS

 BLACK SELF

 LILAC SELF

 BLACK & WHITE

 TORTIE

 TORTIE & WHITE

 BLUE TORTIE & WHITE

 SEAL POINT

 BLUE POINT

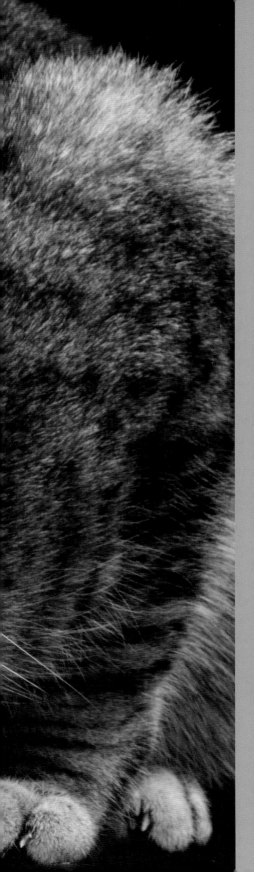

THE NATURE OF THE CAT

Across five continents, wild cats have evolved into predators of unrivalled speed and efficiency abilities. From tigers to tiny sand cats, they are the ultimate solitary hunters, ranging alone through their territories, killing enough to satisfy one stomach, and fighting off all comers. The journey from this wild beginning to the genial domestic cat purring on the sunniest seat in the house has been a long one in human terms, but an evolutionary blink of the eye. Our pet cats still carry within them the physiological and psychological needs of their wild cousins – truly 'tigers on the hearth'.

FAMILY FEATURES The cat carries in miniature a remarkable array of traits found throughout the feline family. How that family colonized the world and eventually our homes is now known in more detail than ever before.

EVOLUTION OF THE CAT FAMILY

Traditionally the modern cat family has been divided into the big cats, which can roar but not purr, and the small cats, which can purr but not roar. The finer details of their relationships and when species appeared are hard to ascertain. Only recently has science revealed a fairly firm family tree and reliable dates for feline evolutionary history, with a major genetic study published in 2006.

WHY GENETICS?

There are several problems with tracking feline evolution through the traditional evidence of fossils: there aren't many fossils, and those that exist are often very similar.

Genetic studies look at the DNA, in chromosomes inside each cell, that provides a code for building an individual of any species, unique to that species. Most of the DNA is 'reshuffled' in each new generation, mixing the genes of the two parents, but not all of it. Mitochondrial DNA, or mtDNA, is stored outside the nucleus of the cell and does not change; it is handed down from the female side, with mtDNA from the male parent being destroyed. Variations and mutations occur, however, at a fairly constant rate. So looking at just how different the mtDNA of two species is tells scientists how long ago they diverged.

DEAD END Sabre-toothed predators evolved separately, several times, but all were superseded by nimbler predators tens of thousands of years ago.

THE EARLIEST BEGINNINGS

The first carnivores that resembled cats appeared some 35 million years ago. *Proailurus*, from Europe, was not much bigger than a modern domestic cat, and may have lived in trees. About 20 million years ago it gave way to *Pseudaelurus*, found across Europe, North America, and Asia. This was about the size of a cougar by the time it disappears from the fossil record. Neither ancestor was as impressive as the huge Machairodonts, such as the 'sabre-toothed tiger' Smilodon. The name is misleading: they developed completely separately from modern tigers or

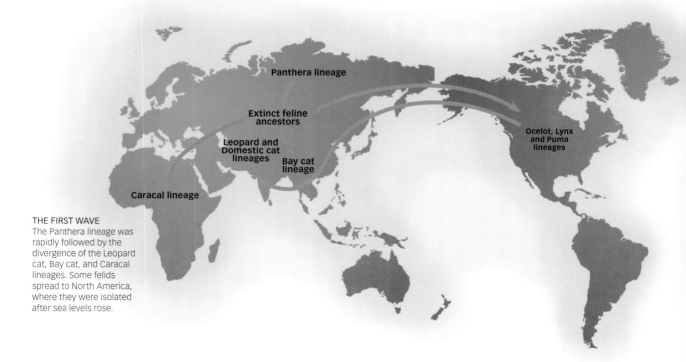

Panthera lineage

Extinct feline ancestors

Leopard and Domestic cat lineages

Bay cat lineage

Caracal lineage

Ocelot, Lynx and Puma lineages

THE FIRST WAVE
The Panthera lineage was rapidly followed by the divergence of the Leopard cat, Bay cat, and Caracal lineages. Some felids spread to North America, where they were isolated after sea levels rose.

any other cats. They vanished some 10,000 years ago, a dead end in the family tree with no surviving descendants.

The story of the modern cat begins in the late Miocene, about 11 million years ago. There was a burst of diversification into many different branches or 'lineages', lasting until about 6 million years ago, followed by a second burst about 3 million years ago. The early feline species crossed back and forth over the land bridge from Asia to North America in a complex network of development covering several continents.

THE FIRST WAVE

The first modern cat lineage, the Panthera or big cats, diverging from a common feline ancestor in Asia 10.8 million years ago, followed by the Bay cat lineage, also in Asia, about 9.4 million years ago. The next lineage to split was the Caracal, migrating to Africa 8.5 million years ago.

At this time, low sea levels allowed animals to move from the far eastern point of Asia across to North America over the Bering land bridge. Cats crossed to North America and diverged into the Ocelot, Lynx, and Puma lineages between 8 and 6.7 million years ago. The final first-wave divergence was the start of the Leopard cat and Domestic cat lineages 6.2 million years ago. None of these lineages necessarily looked like their modern forms (see pp 12–13): but these are the points at which they started down their separate genetic paths.

Lands without cats

During their evolution, cats spread to every part of the globe except for Antarctica and the Australasian ecozone of Australia, New Zealand, New Guinea, and their associated small islands. These lands had all split away from the rest of the world's landmasses by 45 million years ago, long before the appearance of cats and many other mammals. While local species did evolve to fill the niche of the small, agile predator, none was quite like the cat. This is one reason for many recent campaigns to constrain or even cull Australian domestic cats, perceived as an unnatural threat to the unique local wildlife, although how much the cat is to blame and how much it is a scapegoat for damage caused by human development and road traffic remains disputed.

THE SECOND WAVE

A second spread of lineages occurred within the last 5 million years, in the late Pliocene and Pleistocene. The Panthera lineage in Asia spread to Africa and over the Bering bridge to North America and on to South America. The Lynx and Puma lineages crossed back from North America to Asia and Europe, and the Puma lineage spread to South America and Africa. And the final piece in the jigsaw that leads to the cat in our homes, the Domestic cat lineage, spread westwards and into Africa.

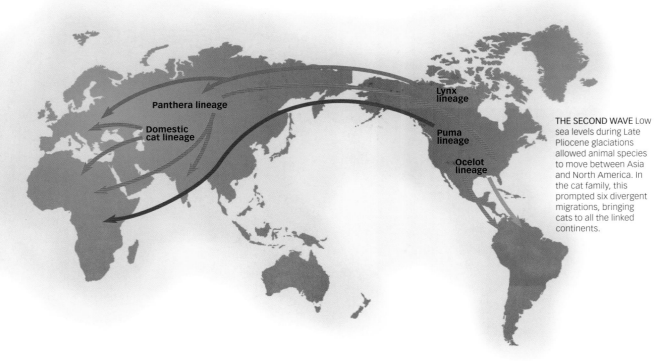

Panthera lineage

Domestic cat lineage

Lynx lineage

Puma lineage

Ocelot lineage

THE SECOND WAVE Low sea levels during Late Pliocene glaciations allowed animal species to move between Asia and North America. In the cat family, this prompted six divergent migrations, bringing cats to all the linked continents.

THE CAT FAMILY TREE

Today we have a fairly robust family tree of the modern cat species, although it does not look like the traditional family tree, with ancestors linked and their offspring converging down to one present-day individual. Instead, closely related species are clustered into family branches or lineages. The most recent developments are the hardest to be certain of. This might seem paradoxical, but in these smaller timeframes a single atypical piece of data can skew the whole picture.

EARLY FELIDS

LION

PANTHERA LINEAGE
Lion *Panthera leo* (*see* p 14)
Jaguar *Panthera onca* (*see* p 14)
Leopard *Panthera pardus* (*see* p 14)
Tiger *Panthera tigris* (*see* p 15)
Snow leopard *Panthera uncia* (*see* p 15)
Clouded leopard *Neofelis nebulosa* (*see* p 15)

CARACAL

CARACAL LINEAGE
Caracal *Caracal caracal* (*see* p 22)
African golden cat *Caracal aurata* (*see* p 22)
Serval *Caracal serval* (*see* p 23)

ASIAN GOLDEN CAT

BAY CAT LINEAGE
Bay cat *Pardofelis badia* (*see* p 24)
Asian golden cat *Pardofelis temminckii* (*see* p 24)
Marbled cat *Pardofelis marmorata* (*see* p 25)

OCELOT

OCELOT LINEAGE
Ocelot *Leopardus pardalis* (*see* p 20)
Margay *Leopardus weidii* (*see* p 20)
Andean mountain cat *Leopardus jacobita* (*see* p 20)
Pampas cat *Leopardus colocolo* (*see* p 20)
Geoffroy's cat *Leopardus geoffroyi* (*see* p 20)
Kodkod *Leopardus guigna* (*see* p 21)
Tigrina *Leopardus tigrinus* (*see* p 21)

In recent years, genetic studies have been instrumental in rewriting the cat family tree. Advances in science have thrown out the old scientific names for the cats that you may find in older books. All species are named according to a convention that puts their genus first, followed by their species. Until quite late in the 20th century, cats were divided simply into the cats that could roar but not purr, and those that could purr but not roar. The former were mostly in the genus *Panthera*, and this group becomes the 'Panthera lineage' in the new classifications. But most of the smaller, non-roaring cats were grouped together in one vast genus of *Felis* in most listings. This has gone, to be replaced by over ten smaller genera. The names and lineages shown here are those suggested by an international genetic study led by Dr Warren Johnson and published in 2006 (*see* p 370). This approach has revealed some surprises. The cheetah (*Acinonyx jubatus*), for example, was an oddball of the cat family, with a natural range in Africa but characteristics unlike any other cat there. It was hard to place by conventional means, but the DNA showed it to be a far-flung arm of the Puma lineage.

LYNX LINEAGE
Iberian lynx *Lynx pardinus* (*see* p 24)
Eurasian lynx *Lynx lynx* (*see* p 24)
Canadian lynx *Lynx canadensis*
  (*see* p 18)
Bobcat *Lynx rufus*
  (*see* p 18)

CANADIAN
LYNX

LEOPARD CAT LINEAGE
Pallas cat *Otocolobus manul* (*see* p 25)
Rusty-spotted cat *Prionailurus rubiginosus* (*see* p 25)
Leopard cat *Prionailurus bengalensis* (*see* p 25)
Fishing cat *Prionailurus viverrinus* (*see* p 25)
Flat-headed cat *Prionailurus planiceps* (*see* p 25)

PALLAS CAT

PUMA LINEAGE
Puma or cougar *Puma concolor*
  (*see* p 19)
Jaguarundi *Puma yagouaroundi*
  (*see* p 20)
Cheetah *Acinonyx jubatus*
  (*see* p 23)

PUMA

DOMESTIC CAT LINEAGE
Domestic cat *Felis catus*
  (*see* p 28)
European wildcat *Felis
silvestris* (*see* p 26)
African wildcat *Felis libyca*
  (*see* p 27)
Chinese desert cat *Felis bieti*
  (*see* p 27)
Desert cat *Felis margarita*
  (*see* p 27)
Black-footed cat *Felis nigripes*
  (*see* p 27)
Jungle cat *Felis chaus*
  (*see* p 27))

EUROPEAN
WILDCAT

BIG CATS

The oldest feline lineage, Panthera, is found across Africa, Asia, and the Americas. Despite their evolutionary success and a long history in human art and religions, almost all big cats are on the international Red List of species under threat. Most are solitary predators, but this group also includes the only co-operative hunter of the cat family, the lion. Big cats live into their teens in the wild, but can live into their twenties in captivity.

POTENT SYMBOLS

Big cats are often found in art and legend, from Ancient Greece to South America. Sadly, they have also been a high-status hunting quarry. Assyrian sculptures portrayed the king hunting lions, and vast numbers were killed by 19th-century Europeans seeking an impressive trophy. Under added pressures on habitat and prey from human development, big cats still live on a knife-edge of survival.

LION – *PANTHERA LEO*

Lions today survive only in sub-Saharan Africa and one small forest sanctuary in northwestern India. Their natural habitat is open savannah, where their tawny yellow coats provide good camouflage. This is the only cat species with a visible difference between the sexes, the females being noticeably smaller. The mane of the male lion is affected by temperature, growing thicker in cooler climes.

Lions live in prides of up to thirty females and cubs, with one male. The male protects the pride, while the females hunt. They work co-operatively to bring down large game, a style suited to their open habitat, which means that each pride must defend a large hunting area.

LEOPARD – *PANTHERA PARDUS*

This is the most widespread of the big cats, found from Africa to eastern Asia, in terrains ranging from swamp and forest to open semi-desert. A long tail and body on short legs give the leopard a low-slung appearance. It has rosettes of dark spots on a golden ground; a 'black panther' is a leopard with a very dark melanistic coat.

The leopard is expert at living undetected close to humans. It takes a range of prey from antelopes to rodents, and will often drag its kill up a tree. Leopards are superb climbers, able to scale vertical trunks and descend head-first.

JAGUAR – *PANTHERA ONCA*

The only big cat in the Americas, the jaguar ranges from Argentina to Mexico; some survive in Arizona and possibly elsewhere in the United States. They prefer densely wooded terrain close to water. The coat is rosetted, and melanistic black jaguars with 'ghost' markings occur.

Most active around dusk, jaguars are solitary hunters of large game. Equipped with the most powerful jaws of all cats, they strike at the top of the head to deliver a killing blow straight to the brain. They are accomplished swimmers, and can tow heavy prey through the water.

TIGER – *PANTHERA TIGRIS*

Tigers live in jungles and forests from India to Siberia. Tigers on Bali and Sumatra, and the Caspian tiger, were hunted to extinction in the 20th century. This is the largest cat, and there are several subspecies, larger in the north than in the south. The only striped cat, it bears bands of brown to black on a generally orange coat.

Tigers defend large territories, hunting wild boar and cattle, stalking before charging or leaping. Loss of habitat, competition for resources, and hunting for trophies and Chinese medicine have reduced numbers to under 2,500.

LION Although mature adults have a uniform, tawny coat, lion cubs have spots that persist until they are quite well grown. These help to camouflage them when they are young and relatively defenceless.

SNOW LEOPARD The snow leopard's tail is one of the longest in proportion to the body to be found in the cat family. It is essential for balance in the rugged mountain terrain the species inhabits.

JAGUAR The beautiful coat of the jaguar was one of the most popular for fur coats, with tens of thousands killed before the trade was banned. Now, reduced habitat has become a greater threat.

SNOW LEOPARD – *PANTHERA UNCIA*

These cats live in mountain ranges from Afghanistan to China and Mongolia. They stay above the treeline in summer, descending into forested areas in winter. The long, insulating coat is a soft, pale grey, with rosettes on the body and solid spots on the extremities, and turns white in winter. Dense fur on the undersides of the paws makes effective 'snowshoes'. They are among the smallest of the big cats.

Their main prey includes wild sheep or goats and small game, taken with a pounce from above if possible. Living in harsh climates, they mate in late winter, and cubs are born in spring. Hunting for fur and for Chinese medicine has helped to put this cat on the endangered list.

CLOUDED LEOPARD – *NEOFELIS NEBULOSA*

Living at low altitudes and in evergreen forests, this cat is also sometimes seen in mangrove swamps and open scrubland. It is found from Nepal through southeast Asia to Sumatra and Borneo. This is the smallest of the Panthera lineage. Its name comes from its distinctive coat markings: a pale-golden ground bearing darker patches edged with black. It has very long canines, reminiscent of sabre-toothed prehistoric felids.

The clouded leopard spends much of its life in trees, and is an excellent climber. It appears to be active during the day as well as the night, and, although reclusive and hard to observe, is thought to prey on tree-dwelling mammals.

LEOPARD Leopards are completely at home in trees, storing their kills in them and sleeping deeply stretched on their branches, often with their tails or limbs hanging down. They hunt mainly at dusk and night, and rest during the day.

SMALL CATS IN THE AMERICAS

The small, or non-roaring, cat species found in North, Central, and South America belong to the Ocelot, Lynx, and Puma lineages (*see* pp 12–13). Of these, the Ocelot lineage, composed of cats found almost exclusively in South America, is the oldest, while the Lynx and Puma groups diversified into the species seen today much more recently.

STRUGGLE TO SURVIVE

These cats have suffered great losses in numbers at the hands of human hunters, mostly following European colonization. In North America the puma, lynx, and bobcat have been trapped for their skins and regarded as a threat to livestock, while the spotted cats of Central and South America have been extensively hunted for the fur trade.

CANADIAN LYNX – *LYNX CANADENSIS*

This cat is found across Canada, with pockets within the United States. It has dense fur – reddish-brown in summer and silvery in winter – with a black-tipped tail, tufted ears, and often a ruff at the neck. Furred feet act as snowshoes, and long legs help it move through deep snow.

This nocturnal cat breeds in spring, and needs a large hunting territory. Although it hunts rodents and birds, and sometimes deer, the Canadian lynx specializes in hunting snowshoe hares, and the two species show matching fluctuations in their populations. Lynx populations are also threatened by habitat loss and trapping for fur.

BOBCAT – *LYNX RUFUS*

This smaller relation of the Canadian lynx is found farther south, in southern Canada, the United States apart from

CANADIAN LYNX Although it was regarded by some as the same species as the Eurasian lynx (*see* p 24), this species is smaller and more closely resembles the bobcat.

PUMA Although the largest cat in the Americas, the shy puma avoids human contact. However, pressure on wild habitat makes human encounters more likely.

BOBCAT Although it is the smallest member of the lynx genus, the bobcat has been known to take small deer in winter when other prey is scarce.

areas of the Midwest, and northern Mexico. It is adaptable and will live in wooded areas, semi-desert, swamps, and even close to humans. It takes its name from its stubby tail which, uniquely in the lynx family, is white underneath. The coat is brown to grey, with black bars on the forelegs and tail, and variable spots, and the ears have distinctively tufted tips. The bobcat is twice as large as a house cat.

Bobcats are most active around dusk and dawn, when they hunt anything from deer to small rodents, with a preference for rabbits or hares. They are good climbers and they are also able to swim, but avoid water if they can.

PUMA – *PUMA CONCOLOR*

The puma is also known as the cougar or mountain lion. It has been widely called 'panther', a name that can lead to confusion with the *Panthera* big cats (*see* pp 14–15). Its range, the largest of any wild cat, extends from the Rocky Mountains in Canada to the southern reaches of the Andes in South America; it was wiped out in eastern North America by European settlers. Pumas can adapt to almost any habitat and, while they prefer dense brush and rocky cliffs, they will live in forests and mountain or lowland deserts. These large, powerful cats are reddish-brown to silvery grey in colour; although pumas are called panthers, US sightings of 'black panthers' are most likely to be jaguars (see p 14) or melanistic bobcats (see pp 18–19).

Pumas are active at dusk and dawn. They climb well, and can swim if necessary. Prey varies from large deer in North America, where the puma competes with the wolf, to smaller mammals and birds or reptiles in South America.

JAGUARUNDI – *PUMA YAGOUAROUNDI*

This unusual cat lives near water in dense undergrowth and ranges from Mexico southwards to Argentina, with small populations in southern regions of the United States. It weighs 4–6 kg (9–13 lb) and although fairly closely related to the puma, it resembles an otter more than a cat, with short legs, a long tail, and rounded ears. The coat, which is without distinctive markings, may be a greyish brown or a chestnut brown; this rather dull appearance has protected it from the attention of the fur trade. Depending on habitat, jaguarundis are active at twilight or after dark, and hunt mainly on the ground, taking small mammals, reptiles, fish, and birds.

OCELOT – *LEOPARDUS PARDALIS*

Found from Texas through to northern Argentina, the ocelot lives in a range of habitats from dense forest to coastal marsh, but never in open country. It is the largest South American feline. It was hunted near to extinction for its handsome, blotched coat, once popular in the fur trade, and was also captured and kept as an exotic pet. Trade is now banned and populations have recovered. Ocelots are largely nocturnal, and hunt prey mostly much smaller than themselves, such as rodents, fish, and birds.

MARGAY – *LEOPARDUS WEIDII*

This cat ranges from Central America to southern Brazil, and is only found in forest habitats. It is well adapted to living in trees, with a long tail and the ability to rotate its legs and climb down trunks head first. It is smaller than the ocelot, but has a similar coat with black rosetted marks on a tawny ground, and was also hunted for its fur. It spends most of its life in trees and hunts small prey.

ANDEAN MOUNTAIN CAT – *LEOPARDUS JACOBITA*

This cat is rare and even more rarely seen. It is thought to live only in the high Andes in South America, and has been sighted above the treeline: it may follow a lifestyle

OCELOT The ocelot's fur was valued because it resembled the jaguar's (see p 14). Its name comes from the word *ocelotl* in the Nauhatl language indigenous to Mexico, and even this word referred mostly to the jaguar.

similar to that of the snow leopard (see p 15). It is about the same size as a domestic cat, but has thick fur that may make it appear larger. The coat is sandy and irregularly marked with darker rosettes and spots on the sides and bars on the legs and tail.

PAMPAS CAT – *LEOPARDUS COLOCOLO*

Also known as the colocolo, this cat may be split into three distinct species across its range, which covers western South America as far north as Equador. The split is suggested on the basis of differences in the coat length and the details of the pattern: cats from the Andes have shorter coats that are greyish and more strongly patterned than Argentinian and Brazilian individuals, and Brazilian males have longer hair on their backs. All are about the size of a domestic cat. As the name suggests, the Pampas cat lives in grasslands, but also humid forests. It is probably nocturnal and preys on small ground-dwelling mammals.

GEOFFROY'S CAT – *LEOPARDUS GEOFFROYI*

Named after the 19th-century French zoologist, this cat is found in Argentina and Chile, in habitats from dense grassland and woodland to mountain deserts, but not rainforest. It is one of South America's most common wild cats, although it was in the past hunted for its fur, which has an all-over pattern of black spots on an ochre to greyish ground. Melanistic individuals are quite common. It is about the size of a domestic cat, and it is a nocturnal hunter, preying on small mammals, fish, and reptiles.

KODKOD – *LEOPARDUS GUIGNA*
Limited to a small range in the Andes mountains, this cat is elusive and little is known about it. It is the smallest of the American cats – smaller than most domestic cats. The appearance is similar to the closely related Geoffroy's cat, with a brownish, heavily spotted coat; melanistic individuals are common. It is a good climber, and preys mostly on rodents and birds, including domestic chickens.

TIGRINA – *LEOPARDUS TIGRINUS*
Also called the oncilla, this cat is found from Venezuela to Paraguay. It appears to prefer forests and scrubland at high altitudes, and has been seen as far up as the snowline. Slightly larger than a domestic cat, it is more lightly built. It has been widely hunted for its coat, which is a rich colour bearing dark-ringed spots with lighter centres. A nocturnal hunter, it is thought to live alongside ocelots and margays, and to avoid competition by taking smaller prey, such as birds, small mammals, reptiles, and insects.

GEOFFROY'S CAT The ground coat colour of this species varies with location: it is more often a warm yellowish-brown colour in the northern part of the range, and greyish further south.

MARGAY This beautiful cat is one of the smallest in the Americas, and was one of the most popular in the fur trade in the 1980s. A high proportion of individuals, perhaps as much as one in five, are melanistic.

SMALL CATS IN AFRICA

One of the earliest migrations of the cat family occurred when the ancestors of the caracal, serval, and African golden cats moved from Asia to Africa some 8.5 million years ago. They had the evolutionary stage to themselves until the much later arrival of the lion (*see* p 14), the cheetah, and closer relations of the domestic cat (*see* pp 28–29) within the last 3.1 million years.

ADAPTATIONS

African cats are very well adapted for drought, being able to survive without drinking for long periods because they obtain the water they need from their prey. Like others in the family, these cats are solitary and territorial, fiercely defending their hunting patch against competition.

CARACAL – *CARACAL CARACAL*

This is a cat of open, semi-desert habitats, although it will also live in savannah, scrub, and woodland. Primarily African, its range includes western Asia. The name comes from the Turkish 'karakulak', meaning black ear. This is amongst the heaviest of the small cats, but slender and long-legged, giving it a lithe appearance. The fur varies from reddish to sandy or even grey, with a pale, spotted belly and black ears sporting long, distinctive tufts of hair on the tips. Melanistic or black caracals do occur.

SERVAL The serval is superbly adapted for savannah hunting. Long legs and neck enable it to see over tall grass, while the large ears can pick up even the sound of rodents burrowing under the ground.

CARACAL The caracal's ear tufts are not just for decoration: they help to pinpoint the origin of sounds, allowing more efficient stalking. Even domestic cats tend to have longer hair on the tips of their ears.

The caracal generally hunts small game, such as hyraxes, but it will take larger gazelles and readily attacks prey larger than itself. It was in the past tamed and kept for catching birds in Iran and India, but today it is more likely to be persecuted for taking domestic poultry.

AFRICAN GOLDEN CAT – *CARACAL AURATA*

This rare and secretive cat lives in the moist equatorial forest habitats of west and central Africa. It resembles the Asian golden cat (*see* p 24), although the two are not closely related. The fur is plain or sometimes spotted, with two distinct colour variations: cinnamon or reddish and a less common grey, and black individuals also occur. Although it can climb, the African golden cat hunts mainly on the ground, preying on small to mid-sized mammals such as tree hyraxes, rodents, birds and monkeys. It is active at twilight and during the night.

SERVAL – *CARACAL SERVAL*

Servals are found across sub-Saharan Africa, with small populations in southwest Africa. They prefer moist, grassy habitats, near watercourses; they will not live in arid areas unless they have to. Pressure on habitat and hunting for the beautiful skin have reduced numbers. Servals are slender with unusually long legs and a small head bearing large, upright, black ears. The fur is usually tawny with black spots.

Although it can climb and swim, the serval hunts primarily on the ground, feeding on small mammals and taking small birds out of the air. Its exceptional hearing allows it to stalk prey in long grass by sound, only using sight for the final pounce.

CHEETAH – *ACINONYX JUBATUS*

The cheetah is found in Africa. It prefers semi-desert, prairie, and thick brush habitats. It has a greyhound-like, long-legged body and a small head. Its short coat is tan with small, round, black spots and a white underside, and the tip of the tail often carries a white tuft. Black 'tear marks' from the corner of its eyes down the sides of the nose to its mouth distinguish it from the leopard (*see* p 14).

The cheetah's semi-retractable claws give grip in high-speed chases. It can reach speeds of more than 105 kph (65 mph) and accelerate from 0 to 110 kph (70 mph) in three seconds, using its tail as a rudder. Its prey is mainly small antelopes, hares, and guinea fowl, taken in the early morning or late evening. The cheetah is not very adaptable and is difficult to breed in captivity; once hunted for its fur, it is still threatened by loss of habitat.

CHEETAH Although physically a 'big' cat, the cheetah's ability to purr makes it an oddity and, together with its unusual claws, kept it out of the *Panthera* genus. It may not look like a puma (*see* p 19), but that is its lineage.

EUROPEAN AND ASIAN SMALL CATS

The widest variety of cats is found in Asia, where the common ancestor of all modern felines is thought to have lived. These cats live in a wide variety of habitats from jungle to desert, and so a range of sizes and coats reflects their different environments. They have the common characteristics of solitary lifestyles and nocturnal or twilight stalking of their prey. Most of them are 'vulnerable' or worse on the international Red List of endangered species.

EURASIAN LYNX – *LYNX LYNX*
This species prefers mountainous and forested terrain. It once ranged from China and Siberia across Asia, Europe, and Scandinavia. By the mid-20th century it was extinct in most of western Europe, but reintroduction schemes have had success in some areas. It is the largest lynx, but it is shy and may live unseen near humans. The fur is reddish to greyish with variable dark spots. It takes small mammals such as rabbits, and in winter may hunt deer and larger prey.

IBERIAN LYNX – *LYNX PARDINUS*
The world's most endangered cat, this lynx once ranged across all of Spain, but now has only scattered populations totalling around 100. Captive breeding may be the species' only hope. It prefers a mix of open grassland and dense shrubs. It is smaller than the Eurasian lynx, with stronger markings. It preys on rabbits, and occasionally young deer.

BAY CAT – *PARDOFELIS BADIA*
Found only in dense rainforest in Borneo, this rare cat is also known as the Bornean cat. It is about the size of a domestic cat, with a reddish or greyish coat, and is thought to prey at night on rodents, birds, and monkeys.

ASIAN GOLDEN CAT – *PARDOFELIS TEMMINCKII*
Also called Temminck's golden cat after the 19th-century Dutch naturalist, this species lives in forest habitats from Tibet to India and Sumatra. It usually has a plain golden or reddish coat, although it may be black, grey, and even spotted. These are adaptable hunters: not always nocturnal, taking birds, lizards, small mammals, and even small deer.

EURASIAN LYNX Lynx coats may be plain, striped, or spotted. In the past, unpatterned lynxes seem to have predominated, but heavily marked, reddish coats are now more common in reintroduced populations in Europe.

MARBLED CAT – *PARDOFELIS MARMORATA*
Ranging from northeastern India through southeast Asia to Borneo and Sumatra, this rarely seen cat likes dense forests. It resembles a miniature clouded leopard (*see* p 15), with blotched greyish to reddish-brown fur. It lives in trees, hunting mammals, birds, and reptiles.

PALLAS'S CAT – *OTOCOLOBUS MANUL*
This species lives in the Central Asian high steppes and is named after the 18th-century German naturalist. Its long ochre-brown coat has stripes. It has short legs, a flat face, and low, rounded ears. It hunts rodents, pikas, and birds.

FLAT-HEADED CAT The large eyes and webbed feet of the flat-headed cat are perfect adaptations for a secretive nocturnal predator of waterways. It was believed extinct in the 1980s, but was then rediscovered in the 1990s.

PALLAS'S CAT Pallas's cat was once hunted for its thick, plush fur, but is now protected. Because it preys on small rodents that are agricultural pests, it is generally regarded more favourably than larger wild cat species.

RUSTY-SPOTTED CAT – *PRIONAILURUS RUBIGINOSUS*
This cat lives in dry forests and dry grasslands in India and in rainforests in Sri Lanka. It and has a greyish coat with reddish spots. Living partly in trees it hunts small mammals, lizards, and birds at night.

LEOPARD CAT – *PRIONAILURUS BENGALENSIS*
Found in forest and scrub close to watercourses across southeast Asia, this cat's appearance varies across its range. About the size of a domestic cat, it has yellow fur in the south and silver-grey in northern areas, marked with spots or rosettes. A good climber, it is an ancestor of the Bengal (*see* pp 362–67).

FISHING CAT – *PRIONAILURUS VIVERRINUS*
This cat is found in wetlands from Pakistan to Sumatra and Java. It is variable in size, with olive-grey fur with parallel rows of dark spots and a fairly flat face, with short, rounded ears. The claws of the slightly webbed paws do not fully retract. It is a skilful swimmer, living mainly on fish but taking other aquatic animals like frogs or crayfish, as well as rodents and birds.

FLAT-HEADED CAT – *PRIONAILURUS PLANICEPS*
This cat lives in the Malaysian peninsula and Sumatra and Borneo in swampy areas and close to water in forests. It has a dark reddish-brown coat, with some spots on the throat and the short legs. It is lighter on the head, which is flat and long, with small, round ears. The paws are webbed and the claws do not retract fully. This nocturnal cat hunts fish, shrimp, and frogs.

THE CAT'S CLOSEST RELATIONS

A genetic study published in 2007 shows that the domestic cat is descended from the African wildcat, putting an end to any lingering disputes over the possible input of other species. Among the other members of the domestic cat's most immediate relations there is 'relatively low resolution' on the evidence considered so far: further studies may reveal which are the closest. One common characteristic of this group of cats is that their ears do not bear white blotches on the back. Known as 'ocelli' or eyespots, these are found in many of the other small cats.

EUROPEAN WILDCAT – *FELIS SYLVESTRIS*

This secretive wildcat is native not only to Europe but also to the western part of Asia. Across its range populations are scattered and isolated. The coat is typically grey-brown and similar to a striped tabby domestic cat, but with fewer stripes, and with a thick, blunt tail. It hunts small mammals, birds, and other creatures of a similar size. Genetic evidence suggests that wildcats occasionally interbreed with domestic cats along the edges of their ranges, where wild mates are hard to find; the offspring are always wild.

EUROPEAN WILDCAT Although a protected species, the European wildcat is still sometimes shot by gamekeepers. It is larger and more furry than a domestic tabby, but similar markings make long-range identification tricky.

AFRICAN WILDCAT This small, sandy-coloured species could be called the most successful member of the cat family. While others face possible extinction, the descendants of this cat are cared for in homes worldwide.

AFRICAN WILDCAT – *FELIS LYBICA*

This cat has sometimes been considered a sub-species of *Felis sylvestris*, sometimes a species in its own right. Its range extends from Africa across the Middle East, and it is also known as the desert cat, although it is found in a range of habitats from steppe to savannah. It is smaller than European wildcats, and has shorter fur. The coat is yellowish-brown to grey in colour, with stripes on the legs and tail and variable striping or spotting on the body. The main prey is rodents and other small mammals, but it also takes birds, reptiles, and insects.

CHINESE DESERT CAT – *FELIS BIETI*

Also more appropriately known as the Chinese mountain cat, this species lives in western China and Mongolia in forests, shrubby areas, and rarely deserts. The long, dense coat is sandy with whitish underparts, bars on the legs and tail, and sometimes faint vertical stripes. At night it hunts rodents, rabbit-like pikas, and birds.

DESERT CAT – *FELIS MARGARITA*

Also commonly known as the sand cat, this small cat lives in the Sahara, the Arabian Desert, and the deserts of Iran and Pakistan. It is well adapted for these arid areas, with long hair on its paws to protect them from hot sand, large ears, and sandy fur bearing faint stripes and just a black tip to the tail. During the day it escapes the heat by resting in the shade of rocks, and at night it hunts rodents, lizards, and insects. It obtains all the water it needs from these, and can go for long periods without drinking.

BLACK-FOOTED CAT – *FELIS NIGRIPES*

Living in open, grassy savannah and semi-desert, this cat ranges from South Africa into Namibia and Botswana, with scattered populations through the Kalahari desert. It is one of the smallest cat species. The coat is a warm buff colour, with dark spots and bands on the legs and tail, and the undersides of the paws are black. During the day it rests out of the sun under rocks or in empty burrows. By night it hunts rodents and birds, usually smaller than itself, both by stalking and by waiting to ambush them outside burrows.

JUNGLE CAT – *FELIS CHAUS*

The jungle cat's other common name, 'swamp cat', is perhaps more appropriate, because this species is found from Egypt eastwards to India and Sri Lanka in reeds along the edge of water, and in grasslands, scrub, or forests, but not in jungles. It is a long-legged cat, with a reddish to yellowish-brown coat marked with bars on the legs and tail. Unusually, it hunts in the daytime, preying on small mammals, birds, and fish, which it will swim to catch, and is less solitary than other cats, living in small family groups. Jungle cats have been crossed with domestic cats to produce the Chausie breed (*see* p 369).

JUNGLE CAT The jungle cat has a wide range, and the wild population was until recently not thought to be under particular threat. Numbers are falling, however, largely due to progressive destruction of their wetland habitat and loss of prey.

THE DOMESTIC CAT

So just when, where, and how did the domestic cat emerge from the wild feline family? Many theories, some of them quite far-fetched, have been advanced over the centuries, but archaeological finds and more recently DNA studies have begun to provide concrete answers.

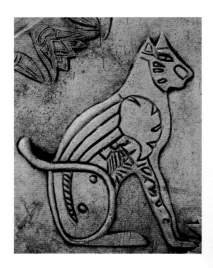

HARD EVIDENCE
Many of the early records of the modern domestic cat are found in Egyptian art, where the cat was a popular element. .

EARLIEST EVIDENCE

It is usually said that the ancient Egyptians domesticated the cat, and that this happened by 2000BC. The date is based on the many images of cats and the large numbers of feline remains found in ancient Egyptian sites, but the cat was not wild one day, or century, and tame the next: it took thousands of years, and the Egyptians may not have been the only ancient civilization to invite cats in.

The oldest remains of a cat buried with a human so far were found in 2004 at Shillourokambos, near Limassol, on the island of Cyprus, and date from 9500BC. No wildcats lived on Cyprus, so this cat was almost certainly brought there deliberately by the Neolithic settlers. It appears to

be a large African wildcat, and seems to have been tame and regarded as a possession, because it was buried with a human body, but it is unlikely that cats were ensconced as pets at this time. Other finds of feline remains include a tooth from 9000BC from Jericho in Israel, and remains from around 4000BC found near Harappa in the Indus valley.

CATS AND AGRICULTURE

Genetic analysis shows our cats are descended from middle-eastern wildcats; the closest matches were found in the deserts of Israel and Saudi Arabia. If domestication began here with the start of agriculture 10,000 to 12,000 years ago, it has left little trace. The earliest remains of a cat buried with a human in Egypt date from around 4000BC, when a workman was buried in Mostagedda, or An Nazlah al-Mustajiddah, with a gazelle and a cat: probably intended as a meal and companionship for the afterlife.

This is about the time when Egyptians began to cultivate grain crops, and rodent-hungry felines prowling around the grain stores would clearly benefit both the cats and the farmers. Many early Egyptian paintings show cats, but it is impossible to say whether they are wild or domesticated: the ancient Egyptian word for cat, *miu*, simply means 's/he that mews' and was applied to all cats.

After about 2000BC, the cat appears in hieroglyphics and paintings that show that it has been fully domesticated. The earliest firm evidence is in a painting from around 1950BC in the tomb of Baket III at Beni Hasan in Middle Egypt, in which a domestic cat faces down a rat. From this time, on the cat appears increasingly in domestic

Coat colours

The range of coat patterns and colours in the domestic cat has led some to believe that it interbred with other wild species as it spread around the globe. This view was held by no lesser an authority than Darwin, but genetic evidence discounts it. Given the diversity within the cat family, from white tigers (*below*) to black jaguars, and piebald lynxes to tabby leopards, it is perhaps not so surprising that the potential for such a range could lurk in the domestic cat, emerging when freed from the need to blend into a dusty desert.

scenes. They were also venerated (*see* pp 122–23) and mummified in vast numbers.

WHICH ANCESTOR?

It was long disputed whether the African wildcat, *Felis lybica* (*see* p 27), or the jungle cat, *Felis chaus* (*see* p 27) gave us our modern domestic cat. Ancient Egyptian paintings of domestic cats show the long, ringed tail and striped coat typical of the African wildcat, rather than the short tail and ticked coat of the jungle cat, which is also seen in some early marsh hunting scenes. Genetic evidence confirms that the domestic cat is descended solely from wildcats, but the jungle cat is a close relation.

So why was one domesticated and not the other? The two wild species have quite different personalities. The jungle cat is too wary to live in close quarters with humans; the more adaptable personality of the African wildcat was better able to exploit this new niche. The most amenable cats probably moved in around the grain stores, and over succeeding generations the most tractable offspring stayed there. At some point, the wild and domestic cats stopped interbreeding regularly, and the domestic cat was born.

NEBAMUN'S 'RETRIEVING' CAT This scene, painted around 1450BC, appears to show a cat participating in a hunt. However, no written evidence supports this.

FERAL CATS

Estimates of the numbers of feral or escaped domestic cats are variable, and often influenced by the sentiments of those doing the estimating. Broadly, there are thought to be 40 million ferals in the United States, around 1.2 million in the United Kingdom, and perhaps 12 million in Australia, where they were released into the wild to kill rabbits and rats.

FAMILY GROUPS Litter survival rates are higher among urban than rural ferals, as food supplies tend to be more plentiful. It is not unusual for related females from the same group to share suckling and caring duties.

THE CAT THAT WALKS BY ITSELF?

Cats lack the close pack mentality of dogs, and the convention down the years has been that the cat, like many of its wild family, pleases itself and feels only 'cupboard love' for its owners. Many cat owners tell a different story, and studies of feral cats do too.

Most domestic cats live fairly solitary lives, sharing their core territory (*see* pp 38–39) with human companions and perhaps one other cat, interacting only occasionally with others. If they are one of the increasing number of cats living an indoors-only existence, they may never meet another cat at all. Studying feral cats shows us just how far this is from the lifestyle cats choose when left to their own devices.

The availability of food influences the sociability of cats. In the countryside, there simply isn't the food to support dense populations of cats; instead, rural ferals will hunt and scavenge over a personal territory of perhaps 10 hectares (25 acres), and may congregate in small groups around farms. This is not so dissimilar from wild felines, who have to defend a hunting territory to survive. But where humans supply plentiful food from waste, colonies can accumulate at 20 times this density. In some places local people will even feed feral cats. Opportunistic from the start, and now rendered more tolerant of company and less territorial through thousands of years of domestication, the supremely adaptable cat simply squeezes into whatever niche it can.

FAMILY GROUPS

Large colonies are often made up of overlapping smaller groups of a few dozen related cats. Within these groups, observation shows that cats do not congregate randomly, but have favourite companions. Gender does not seem to be important, but in at least one study these preferences have been found to be familial, with female cats four times more likely to sit with their female relations as with other females. Female cats have also been seen to give birth close to related females raising young kittens, and to feed and wash each other's kittens indiscriminately. Females leave colonies for new haunts more than males; and it may be that competition for kittening sites drives them out.

FEEDING FERAL CATS Dedicated cat lovers in cities worldwide devote time and energy to providing food regularly for stray and feral cats. Even without this boost, modern urban centres offer rich pickings of waste food.

These family relationships can often be seen in the cats' coat colours, the most visible guide to their genetic make-up. While overall the most common coat colour for feral cats is the dominant pattern of a brown tabby, the cats in some areas have their own distinctive appearance. An example is the high proportion of black-and-white cats reported in London, in the United Kingdom.

FERAL PROBLEMS AND CONTROL

While the average life of a feral cat is estimated to be just two years, females can become sexually mature by six months of age and raise two litters of kittens a year. Although one study found that 75% of kittens died or disappeared by six months of age, populations grow as much as circumstances allow. Large, unmanaged colonies can become a source of disturbance and disease, and in almost all circumstances human intervention is inevitable.

Policies aimed at trapping and euthanizing ferals prove surprisingly unsuccessful, due to the 'vacuum effect': if there is a vacant habitat, new cats will move into it. Some attempts to eradicate ferals by these means on islands – for example, Ascension Island in the south Atlantic – have been successful, however.

Such a complete removal of a feral colony is rarely possible. More successful are management schemes, in which cats are trapped, neutered, and released, with an ear tip clipped to show their sterile status. The neutered cats defend their territory against new arrivals, and numbers

CLIPPED EARS In areas where a capture-neuter-release programme is in operation, feral cats that have been re-released are often marked with a clipped tip to one ear to keep track of their status.

drop overall to more acceptable levels. These schemes can have a significant impact if they outpace feline reproduction, and unless humans remove the food sources that sustain urban ferals, they seem to be the best available option for both the cats and their human neighbours.

TOUGH LIFE Feral cats are vulnerable to sickness and injury; roundworm and tapeworm infestations are common. Feline immunodeficiency virus (FIV), which is spread through fights, is common in older unneutered males.

THE FELINE LIFECYCLE

There is no simple correlation to make along the lines of 'one human year equals six cat years'. Cats mature quickly: at three months of age they are still playful and kittenish, but by one year they may have produced their own kittens, and would be late adolescents in human terms. After this, they could be said to slow down, reaching middle age sometime around six years. By about ten years, they will have reached old age.

EARLY PROGRESS

The early period of family life is the most important time of a cat's life. It is when cats are most accepting of new experiences and their minds are most able to learn, which they do by watching their mothers (*see* pp 50–51).

In feral cat colonies (*see* pp 30–31), suckling may continue for months as a way of reinforcing family bonds, and families stay close for six months or more. But in most

LEARN WITH MOTHER The bond between mother and kitten is vital for the kitten's development. Kittens learn discipline, hunting skills, and essential life skills from the example of their mother's behaviour.

NOT YOUR CHAIR NOW All cats will have their favourite resting places, and visit them often to renew their scent. Once a cat has made its choice and staked its claim, it will be very reluctant to change its behaviour.

domestic situations, the mother begins to tire of feeding when the sharp teeth appear around five weeks, and as her milk dries up, she pushes the kittens to greater independence in all aspects of their lives. Domestic cats are ready to leave their family from around the age of 12 weeks.

A PLACE OF THEIR OWN

Once settled into a new home (*see* pp 84–85) a cat will pick its favourite spots and return to them. Cats are comfortable in the places where they find their own scent, so strongly scented substances such as citrus and herbal essential oils are useful repellants, and washing a cat's favourite cushion will not earn you its gratitude.

Farther afield, a cat will reconnoitre and mark every scrap of its new territory (*see* pp 38–39). Any interesting-looking room, shed, or even car has to be investigated, and many a 'lost' cat has turned up close to home, shut behind a rarely opened door. The size of the territory will vary depending on local conditions and the individual cat.

Cats are naturally cautious and conservative animals, disliking too many changes or surprises. Variety is not the spice of a cat's life: house moves, new companions, or other changes in their environment can all cause stress. As long as they have plenty of scope for natural behaviour such as hunting or play-hunting (*see* pp 40–41), a steady routine suits them best.

SEXUAL MATURITY

Cats can produce kittens from the age of about six months. With many unwanted cats, there is a strong drive from animal welfare charities to spay or neuter all pet cats at

WELL-EARNED REST As your cat approaches old age, its behaviour and needs will subtly alter. Many cats enjoy the switch to a more relaxed lifestyle, with even more frequent catnaps.

Social animals

The cat's adaptability has made it hugely successful as a pet, but some things do not change. Healthy young cats are playful, and cats that do not hunt continue to use play to fulfil their need for activity. Cats also need to socialize, and how they do this depends on their individual personality more than age. Some more reserved individuals and breeds are content with brief physical contact and then simply curl up in the same room as their feline or human family, while the more demonstrative types want to sit on their owners' laps, or even stand on their shoulders and chat to them.

this age. Apart from the population issue, there are good behavioural reasons for this: 'fixed' cats of both sexes spray less or not at all, roam less, fight less, and so tend to live longer, healthier lives. Neutered females have a lower risk of cystic ovaries and potentially fatal uterine infections, while neutered males suffer less from fight injuries and feline immunodeficiency virus (FIV, *see* p 112).

DECLINING YEARS

The average lifespan of a domestic cat is somewhere around 12 or 13 years. Of course some cats live longer than this: many live into their twenties, and a few into their thirties. As cats age, they tend to slow down like all animals. Joints begin to lose their legendary elasticity and muscles their strength, and white hairs can appear. Caring for an elderly cat (*see* pp 100–101) means keeping a look-out for failing faculties, but many age gracefully and are still active and healthy to the end. In contrast, the life of a feral cat may be over in just two years, due to poor diet, infectious diseases, and the physical dangers of street life.

CAT COMMUNICATION

Cats communicate more subtly than our other favoured pets, dogs. They have no wagging tail, less mobile faces, and less of a tendency to bounce or jump up in greeting. Their reputation for holding aloof from the world is at least in part a consequence of our lack of skill in reading their signals.

VOCAL COMMUNICATION

Cats have a wide repertoire of sounds. The classic mewing sounds are used only by kittens in wild cat species, but in domesticating the cat we have perpetuated infant behaviour into adult life. As an infant sound, mewing is used primarily to ask for things: attention, food, comfort, or a door to be opened. The tone and intensity of the sound indicate what the cat wants, although interpretation takes some practice.

Purrs and quiet 'chirrups' generally indicate contentment. They are used to settle or encourage kittens – or owners! Sometimes, injured or frightened cats will purr, apparently

WARNING HISS This cat feels angry but is not spoiling for a fight: it is crouched rather than standing with an arched back. In extreme fear, the ears are held entirely flat and the cat cowers.

in an effort to keep their spirits up. A cat communicates displeasure with an array of sounds, all coming from the throat. These include low growls, grunts and grumbling, snarls, higher pitched yowls, and screams. Hissing and spitting are the final escalation before an attack begins.

JUST PRACTISING These young cats are acting out the clawing and yowling of a real fight, but the claws are likely to remain sheathed. Littermates often take part in rough play to practise their fighting skills.

EVER ALERT Even a laid-back and contented cat is likely to keep its ears pricked. Combined with a relaxed posture and purring, this is the sign of a cat interested in its surroundings, but not feeling under threat.

But perhaps the loudest and most distinctive sound of the feline vocabulary is the wild 'caterwauling' of a female in heat or during mating. This sound is penetrating because it needs to carry through the surrounding area, bringing as many potential mates as possible (*see* pp 46–47).

BODY LANGUAGE

A cat uses every part of its body from whiskers to tail to communicate. Facial expressions and movements are used for close-up conversations, while postures and body movement are used to communicate over greater distances or send louder messages.

A cat's ears are a good indicator of how relaxed it feels. Pricked to catch every sound, they indicate tension or excitement, perhaps focused on potential prey or an unfamiliar sound. Folded flat against the head, they indicate fear or readiness to fight, because in this position they are best protected from injury.

Eyes are also informative. Half-closed eyes do not necessarily mean sleepiness, but security and contentment. A direct stare is challenging to a cat, so when it looks down or away, appearing dismissive, it is actually just avoiding confrontation. Cats that look away all the time, and accompany it with a yawn, are nervous individuals. Fear will make the eyes dilate, taking in all possible visual clues as to what might happen next.

A relaxed cat looks just that: the body moves fluidly or sprawls as if its bones were made of rubber. The tail is down and moves only to balance the body. An interested and alert cat sits or moves with its head and tail up; little twitches or flicks of the tail indicate anything from interest

to irritation, and the more the tail moves, the more it means anger. At the extreme is the 'Halloween cat' posture of arched back and bottlebrush tail. This is the classic fight-or-flight stance. Everything about it aims to make the cat look bigger than it is, and the cat often turns sideways to present an even larger, more imposing view. Conversely, a cat crouching down is fearful and trying to make itself as small as possible, but remains ready to lash out if appeasement is unsuccessful. And when it rolls over onto its back, it is not showing submission but preparing to defend itself: in this position, four of its five extremities are equipped with razor-sharp claws, ready for use.

TOUCH AND SCENT

Touching is an important part of feline social behaviour. Cats greet each other with head bumps and nose touches, lick each other, and if friendly will often curl up and sleep against each other into adulthood. They do the same to us, although they may have to content themselves more often with ankles and being tripped over. While cats clearly enjoy this contact, it also marks out companions as part of their group. Cats have scent glands concentrated on the face, shoulders, and rump, and contact with these areas leaves a scent marker on another cat or owner.

All animals also have ways of leaving messages for others. With cats, these markers may be visual and scent-based, and scratch marks, faeces, urine, and spraying are all used primarily in defining territory (*see* pp 38–39).

TOUCHING NOSES This form of greeting is common among cats as a way of sharing information about each other through scent. Owners will be used to having a cat's nose pushed against their hands as a form of this gesture.

KITTEN BEHAVIOUR To a kitten, the whole world is both a playground and a classroom. They are allowed to roam through adults' territories and take all sorts of liberties as they learn about their environment.

TERRITORIAL BEHAVIOUR

When territorial behaviour appears in a cat, it often surprises or irritates us. Owners can interpret it as a fault in the cat, even vindictiveness, when really it is the expression of a natural instinct that has not been accommodated in the home.

TERRITORIAL DISPUTES Border disputes are rarely full-blooded fights. In this encounter, as one cat approaches, the other is already backing away with its tail lowered: a serious scrap is unlikely.

FLEXIBLE TERRITORIES

All wild animals defend a territory. In the cat family, a male's territory may overlap with those of several females, with obvious mating advantages, but territories are not usually shared with the same sex. One reason for the cat's successful domestication is its willingness to share and shrink its territory until it fits into our lives. Cats adapt to living at very high densities in feral colonies (*see* pp 30–31), but cats in the home face different territorial pressures.

WALKING THE BOUNDARIES A fence makes a perfect boundary for this outdoor cat, because everything on either side can be seen clearly from the top. As it patrols, the cat's paws leave scent marks on the palings.

In a normal suburban situation, cats will have to share outdoor space. They often accomplish this with little strife, and some studies suggest that one reason for this is that a territory has several zones of different importance. High fences along which they can patrol with a view to all sides are very useful boundaries, so the core of a cat's territory is likely to be its owner's garden. This core territory may be vigorously defended against all comers. Beyond this are zones that cats are more content to share.

Cats within a house share their territories even more intimately, in a way akin to feral cats. Even within the confines of a house, individual and overlapping territories are maintained. Dominant cats have larger territories, and, while kittens are allowed to go anywhere, their movements become more restricted as they mature. Favourite spots are 'timeshared', with any disputes settled verbally.

ON PATROL

All cats look after their territory in a number of ways. They patrol regularly, looking, listening, and sniffing to pick up information about what has happened since they last passed by. They might find the scent markings of other cats, new prey, or other sources of food.

As cats patrol, their paws leave a scent trail. When they rub their heads against tree trunks and posts, their faces

Scratching

The most common territorial behaviour is scratching, and this can cause real trouble. One problem is that to indicate their territory, cats want to scratch in a highly visible, busy spot, but a scratching post is not their owner's idea of attractive furniture, so it is tucked away in a corner. Frustrated owners may even resort to having their cat's claws surgically removed or the tendons that extend them cut, leaving a cat with no defences or needing a lifetime of regular clipping because they can no longer look after their claws themselves. This practice is banned in some places as cruel and unnecessary treatment of an animal that we have voluntarily chosen to bring into our homes.

leave more scent. Boundary markers, showing the limits of a cat's terrain, need to be reinforced, but scent marks are also left in other places. Two cats marking the same area are not necessarily in conflict: the marks may be in a shared area, and they are just showing other cats in the area that they are around.

Scratching also leaves a clearly visible sign that a cat regularly uses a particular area, together with scent from its paws to say just who that cat is.

Faeces, which are not always buried by dominant cats, are doused with scented secretions as they leave a cat's body, and also mark territory. They tend to be left at the edge of a cat's territory, away from the core area, which is why an outdoor cat annoys the neighbours more often than it soils its owner's garden.

MARKING INDOORS

Many behaviour problems perceived by owners are linked to territorial behaviour, particularly in indoor cats. These cats have the same needs as their free-roaming counterparts, but a smaller range in which to fulfil them.

Spraying is partly territorial but is also affected by sexual hormones, and is most effectively prevented by early spaying or neutering. Once a cat has begun to spray, smelling its own scent on places where it has sprayed triggers the same response in future, as it instinctively reinforces its presence.

PUNGENT MARKERS This intact male cat will not only rub against vertical surfaces to mark them, but also spray. He stands in the typical posture, with a raised tail that quivers as he sprays.

HUNTING

All cats hunt in one way or another. Hungry rural cats hunt to eat, well-fed family cats hunt through instinct, and indoor cats hunt toys or their owners' passing feet. A trait that we have valued for thousands of years is now one that many cat owners prefer not to think about.

THRILL OF THE CHASE Well-fed domestic pets often make more successful hunters than hungry and undernourished ferals. They will even devote time and energy to chasing nutritionally unrewarding insect prey.

ANCIENT PURPOSE

The ability to dispatch vermin brought the cat into our lives. One of the first Egyptian illustrations of a domestic cat shows it confronting a rat. Once domesticated, the cat was carried on around the world, taken to protect vital ships' stores from rats on board. At the destination ports, cats were welcomed for the same reason.

Today, however, the cat is villified as a predator of wildlife under pressure, and owners are more squeamish than previous generations about their pets' gifts of dead rodents.

HOW CATS HUNT

Cats are opportunistic and adaptable in their diet. They often scavenge, which takes less energy than hunting. Well-fed cats will hunt more successfully than hungry cats, and at least one study has found that mothers are better hunters than non-mothers. While cats are normally most active at dawn and dusk, they will hunt through the night when days are hot, and in the day during winter when the nights are too cold for good pickings.

Not all cats are good hunters. How well they hunt and what they hunt are governed largely by what their mothers taught them. The prey also depends on local availability, but tends to be largely small mammals such as rodents and rabbits. Some cats develop a taste for birds, and stranger prey includes insects such as moths, and spiders. Frogs and toads may be killed, but rarely eaten.

The cat will often wait in ambush, rather than stalking. When it detects a well-used path or area by scent, the cat settles down and waits for the prey to come to it. A jack-in-the-box spring will bring it down directly on top of its prey. If the cat is hungry, the prey is killed with a swift bite to the neck and eaten on the spot. When hunger is less urgent, a cat may bring prey home to present to its owner, like a parent providing for its young. Sometimes a cat carries live prey home and appears to play with it before killing it; this is seen more often in pet cats than in

those living by their wits. An indoor cat needs plenty of play to fulfil its natural hunting instinct (*see* pp 70–71).

THE IMPACT ON WILDLIFE

Recent years have seen much debate over the threat cats pose to wildlife. In restricted areas where cat populations grow too large, damage is undoubtedly done. A single lighthouse keeper's cat hunted the Stephen's Island wren to extinction in 1894. Elsewhere the evidence is less clear.

UNDESIRABLE PREY Nobody likes to see cats killing birds, but they will not understand why owners praise mouse corpses but not bird bodies. Restricting the daylight freedom of outdoor cats at fledging time may help.

PREFERRED PREY Small mammals are the cat's most typical prey, with mice at the top of the list. Rats will be killed, but less often consumed unless the cat is hungry, and rural cats often specialize in rabbits.

Australia, where cats were released into the wild in the 19th century to control rabbits and rats, was the centre of this debate in the 1990s. Early in the decade, studies seemed to show that cats were responsible for devastating numbers of wildlife kills, but these findings have since been discredited. They led to calls for cat curfews and even culls, but to clear a continent of cats is an impossible task.

Studies that look at one species, however, miss the big picture. Australia had cats for 200 years before it began to worry about wildlife populations, and critics argue that road building, deforestation, urban sprawl, and habitat fragmentation are more significant threats to wildlife there. Stopping these activities would be uncomfortable, and the cat is a convenient scapegoat. In Britain, the bird that has suffered the most catastrophic fall in numbers is the house sparrow. Recent studies show that it stays lean in the winter, the better to avoid predators like the cat,

but leaving it vulnerable to food shortages that are caused by human activity, such as intensive farming. However efficient the cat is as a predator, humans are far ahead in number of kills.

BELLS AND WHISTLES Because cats sit in wait and pounce, bells are ineffective in cutting bird predation. Collars or sonic devices that emit a regular beep have been shown to work better.

ACTIVITY AND SLEEP

The domestic cat seems to sleep more than any other animal. This is one reason for their popularity as pets: at the sight of a sleeping cat, humans tend to relax too. Things do not work out so well, however, if the cat wakes up and wants to hunt in the early hours.

SERIOUS SNOOZING

The adult cat sleeps between 12 and 20 hours out of every 24. All members of the cat family have high sleep demands, dictated by their diet and lifestyle. While a herbivore needs to graze steadily for hours to meet its energy requirements, a cat feeds itself by brief bursts of hunting, followed by a protein-rich meal. Feline hunting is particularly energy-consuming and intensive, and it makes sense for cats to conserve their strength as much as possible between pursuits. Additionally, small animals tend to sleep more than large ones. Their higher metabolic rates may take a greater toll in wear and tear to cells. This necessitates more repair work, which is carried out during sleep.

SLEEP PATTERNS

There are two basic kinds of sleep. Rapid eye movement or REM sleep is so called because the eyes move in response to spikes of activity in the brain, while the rest of the body is deeply relaxed. Non-REM sleep, also called slow

VITAL SLEEP A cat dozing in the sun is not the picture of indolence it seems. Frequent naps are part of its hunting lifestyle, and its muscle type and inability to sweat make strenuous activity in hot weather inadvisable.

wave sleep, has slow brain activity, some muscle activity, and is generally considered a lighter kind of sleep.

Settling down for eight hours of deep sleep would be a bad idea for a small predator. Instead, cats sleep in several periods through the day. They start in lighter, slow wave sleep, moving on to REM sleep. In humans, sleep cycles of the two last 90–110 minutes, and REM makes up 20–25% of our sleep. Cats, by contrast, have a cycle of periods of light sleep lasting about 25 minutes, followed by six or seven minutes of REM sleep and then either wakefulness or another period of light sleep. In laboratory studies, cats were found to spend 35% of their time awake, 50% in light sleep, and only 15% in REM sleep. During the periods of lighter sleep a cat can wake and move very quickly: these are the 'cat naps' for which they are famed.

NIGHT VISION Cats' senses are designed for hunting in near dark, especially their eyes. Here, the tapetum lucidum, the reflective surface that intensifies light inside the eye, can be clearly seen.

THE FUNCTIONS OF SLEEP

Sleep seems to be used both to repair the body and to reorganize the brain. Growth hormones are released during sleep, particularly in kittens. Disturbance of REM sleep during kitten development has also been found to cause abnormalities in their visual systems. A study of kittens in 2001 seems to show that sleep is also important to brain 'plasticity' or adjustment to new environmental challenges. The kittens had one eye covered for six hours, after which the electrical activity of their brains was recorded and they were allowed to sleep for six hours or kept awake. The level of changed activity doubled in the kittens who were allowed to sleep, but did not increase in the kittens kept awake.

DAILY CYCLE

Cats are governed by the same circadian rhythm of 24 hours as all animals, with preferred times for sleeping and activity. They are by nature crepuscular, most active at dawn and dusk. But a cat's sleeping and activity patterns are moderately flexible, changing to suit their circumstances. Some studies have found that barn cats sleep less than pet cats, perhaps indicating that when there is more going on, cats are more alert, but they curl up to sleep when life offers no excitement or threats.

Indoor cats are the most dependent on activity in the household: they may sleep the day away and come to life when their owners return. Cats that are asleep alone in a house all day may revert to their 'default' pattern of activity, waking their owners some hours before dawn.

EVER ALERT This outdoor cat has plenty in its surroundings to keep it alert and busy, and it is likely to sleep less than a relaxed indoor cat that has no other cats to interact with.

GROOMING

A cat's coat is its first line of defence against cold, heat, and injury, and also gathers vital information through sensitive hairs, while teeth and claws are vital for defence and hunting. Meticulous routine maintenance is clearly a necessity for cats, not vanity. An owner's intervention may be needed to help with some aspects of grooming.

COAT CARE AND HAIRBALLS

Cats shed hair all year round. Hair grows on a two to three-month cycle (see pp 54–55) and old hairs must be removed from the coat constantly. The barbs on the tongue that scrape the meat from the bones of their prey (see p 63) tug on hairs, pulling out those that are loose, scrape off loose skin cells, and clean dust from the coat. Pests or debris are dealt with by small bites. Cats can reach almost all parts of their body, and clean their heads and faces by licking a paw and rubbing it over in circular motions. Licking also leaves saliva on the coat. This evaporates to cool a cat, which does not sweat.

Because the barbs on a cat's tongue point towards the throat, there is only one way for the hair to go: down. Moderate amounts of hair usually pass through the digestive system. Problems arise for cats moulting heavily when they shed a winter coat in spring or, more often, for those with long hair. Long hair is a mutation that is not present in wild cats, so it is not surprising that the digestive system of a Persian (see pp 258–61) is not equal to the task of processing its coat. The hair builds up in the stomach, trapping fat and debris until it forms a hairball. If this moves on through the intestines it can form a blockage; more often it is regurgitated in a fit of hacking spasms.

Hairballs can be tackled by giving anti-hairball cat foods. Some of these are high-fibre, to ease hairballs through the intestines, while others contain substances to dissolve the fat and shrink the hairballs. A better approach is to groom cats prone to hairballs (see pp 90–91), especially in spring.

CLEAN IN TOOTH AND CLAW

Cats have an advantage over other mammals in that they cannot appreciate sweet foods (see p 63). This means that their natural diet does not encourage plaque bacteria, and decay. However, teeth need to work to keep them firmly rooted, with healthy gum and bone, and regular scraping to remove any plaque that does build up. Stripping meat from the bones of prey cleans their teeth naturally. Without this action, dental problems can develop. Dried foods are of variable value, as some cats will swallow them whole, and even when chewed they tend to shatter, so do not provide whole-tooth cleaning. If cats do not hunt or have access to meat on the bone, regular tooth-brushing (see pp 90–91) may be the only solution.

GROOMING KIT Kittens start to groom themselves quite early, and are fairly adept at the task by six weeks of age. The backwards-pointing barbs on the tongue (inset), called papillae, contain higher levels of keratin, the horny substance that makes up cats' claws.

Cats' claws are constantly growing (see p 55), rather like nails, and need regular care. The worn, outermost layer of the tip must be removed to reveal the fresh, razor-sharp layer underneath. The natural and necessary way for a cat to do this is by scratching. The ideal surface for scratching is firm enough to grip the sheath and pull it off, but with enough surface give to allow the claws to be embedded in the first place. Outdoors, trees are the abundant, ideal solution; indoors, unfortunately a wide variety of household furniture and some wall coverings make acceptable substitutes. Early introduction of an acceptable scratching post (see p 92) is essential.

Scratching serves several purposes in the life of a cat. As well as renewing the claws, it provides a muscular exercise and stretch that keeps the upper back strong and flexible, relaxes a stressed cat, and leaves territorial marks (*see* pp 38–39). The drive to scratch is so strong that even declawed cats go through the motions, raking their useless paws over surfaces.

The comfort of grooming

While grooming clearly serves important practical purposes, it also has psychological benefits. A cat may groom to calm down or distract itself from something upsetting. Everyone has at some time seen a cat that comes off worse in a staring contest busily grooming itself, and cats often groom after a chase or active play. The cooling effect may also be important here. The psychological benefits of grooming go back to kittenhood, when a mother grooms her kittens not only to clean them but to promote bonding (*see* pp 48–49). This continues through life, with cats licking each other as a regular part of social contact: in one study, 64% of interactions between cats in a feral colony involved licking. Grooming may be the most natural way of bonding with a cat.

SCRATCH AND STRETCH The ideal scratching post offers a firm base with a slightly springy, resilient surface layer. A tree with living bark is ideal, and also allows enough height for the cat to get a good stretch.

FELINE REPRODUCTION

Cats have among the noisiest and most promiscuous sex lives of the animal world. The reasons for this are intricately bound up with how the members of the cat family live and associate, and even their basic biology. Committed relationships don't suit hunters who compete with their partners for prey.

CALL OF THE WILD Wild cats are more scattered than domestic cats, and potential mates far less abundant. When in heat, females like this bobcat must find a high point and call males from far and wide.

INDUCED OVULATION

Male cats are always ready to mate, but female cats come into heat on a regular cycle of roughly every three weeks, and their cycle is moderated by daylight hours. When days are short, they do not come into heat, but as daylength increases in spring, they come into cycle.

Females across the cat family ovulate only after repeated mating. The end of a male cat's penis is covered with barbs all pointing back towards his body. When he withdraws from the female, her vulva is painfully abraded. The pain is a stimulus that sends a hormonal signal to the brain to trigger the release of eggs. The more matings take place, the higher the chances of a plentiful litter of kittens. Because the cat family is by and large solitary, a female might waste eggs if no males are in the vicinity when she is in heat. Eggs that are only released after several matings, on the other hand, are almost certain to be fertilized.

CALL OF THE WILD

When a female cat, or queen, comes into heat, oestrogen in her urine leaves a pungent scent trail wherever she goes, to advertise her status to any toms in the vicinity. A female cat in heat not only urinates more frequently, but also sprays. She calls to advertise her exact location, and may roll on the floor or drag herself along by her forelegs, pace, demand affection, and wander in search of males. Keeping an unspayed female inside when in heat needs constant vigilance about open doors and windows.

JUST ROLLING? Not all queens in heat are highly vocal and demonstrative. Affection, mewing, and rolling can be restrained enough to look like normal behaviour; and a first heat may go unnoticed until a queen is pregnant.

PROSPECTIVE FATHERS

Domestic and feral queens live at unusually high densities, and may attract several males. These sometimes fight for the right to mate, but usually disputes are settled with more sound than fury. It is not even that unusual to see toms in a feral colony forming an orderly queue near the queen, hoping she may mate with more than one of them. Mating can continue for some days, and as the first male tires, others are in with a chance of siring kittens.

A queen that mates with several toms can bear a litter of kittens of mixed parentage. Litters from free-breeding cats sometimes show obvious evidence of multiple fathers. With multiple matings females are maximizing their chances of a successful pregnancy each cycle.

MATING CHOICES

Although a queen will often mate first and most frequently with the most dominant tom, this is not invariably the case. In free-breeding feral colonies, behaviourist Roger Tabor observed less dominant males courting a female before she came into heat, so winning a place in her favours.

Other studies show that when feral females in a colony all come into heat at the same time, as often happens, a wider spread of males sire kittens, as the dominant males cannot be everywhere at once. Multiple matings and natural synchronization of heat cycles help to ensure that a colony remains genetically diverse rather than inbred.

COURTSHIP PAYS In urban feral colonies, females disperse at breeding age, while males stay put. Together with female willingness to mate with the less dominant males that court them, this helps to ensure genetic diversity.

PICK AND MIX With the genes for pointing, long hair, tabby, tortoiseshell, and white spotting all present, there is no guessing the parentage of these kittens, but more than one father may well have been involved.

KITTENING

Cats are famed for the ease with which they produce their young, and the ferocity and self-sacrifice of a mother cat. Most cats make naturally good mothers, even those who were hand-reared themselves. Feline pregnancy and parenting are driven by deeply rooted instinct.

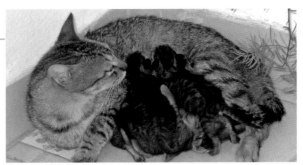

KNEAD TO FEED Instinct and sense of smell guide a kitten to the nipples. They knead their mother's flank with their paws to stimulate the release of milk – a behaviour that often continues into adult life.

FOETAL DEVELOPMENT

Mating (*see* pp 46–47) stimulates the release of eggs from the ovaries for fertilization within 24 to 48 hours. Before these bundles of rapidly dividing cells become implanted in the walls of the uterus, at about day 12 of the pregnancy, they are very vulnerable to attack by disease or chemicals. Any damage or mistake in cell duplication at this stage is usually fatal. Most organs and structures are formed between implantation and day 24, and damage at this time results in congenital defects. Cats have a relatively low level of birth defects in comparison with other domesticated animals, but they do occur, with cleft palates and umbilical hernias among the more common. By day 24, the foetus is about 1 cm (½ in) long. From this time until birth, which happens 60 to 70 days after mating, it is mainly increasing in size and is generally less vulnerable to damage.

MATERNAL BEHAVIOUR

During the first half of pregnancy, the cat is physically not hampered and acts as normal. By about half way through the pregnancy her behaviour changes noticeably. As the growing kittens become heavier and bulkier, she slows down and rests more. A few days before the kittens are due, she will seek out a secluded nesting spot and spend time there. This ensures the nest is full of her scent. When birth is imminent, she usually loses her appetite and may become restless. In the last day or so of pregnancy her temperature will drop by about 1°C (2.7°F).

When labour begins, the contractions can be seen and felt along her sides. Most cats purr during labour, but they may also cry out. Amniotic fluid is expelled first, and the first kitten is usually produced within 45 minutes. Each

PERSONAL CHOICE You may provide a cat with the ideal birthing place, secluded, warm, and soft, but still find that when the time comes she chooses your wardrobe or a corner of the sofa.

kitten is enclosed in its own amniotic sac. The mother breaks open the sac and licks the kitten, drying the fur and stimulating breathing. She bites through the umbilical cord, and may eat the placenta. The kitten begins to suckle, stimulating the release of milk. The rest of the kittens are born at intervals of between 15 minutes and over an hour. The feline uterus is divided into two long, slender 'horns', and once all the kittens from one horn are delivered, there can be a break of a few hours with no contractions before the kittens from the other horn start to emerge.

The mother may move the litter shortly after birth, an instinctive behaviour to protect the kittens in the wild predators attracted by the smell of blood at the birthing site. She will consume all their waste, again to conceal the presence of vulnerable young from predators.

THE YOUNG FAMILY

When a kitten is born, it is deaf and blind, with only its sense of smell to guide it. Many reactions to the world are present – the closed eyes twitch in response to light as if to blink, and the ears move – but the senses are not properly developed. The eyes open when kittens are about nine days old, and vision gradually clears and improves until they have full binocular vision at around 47 days. The ears progress faster, with kittens reliably turning towards the sounds of their family by about seven days, and being able to pin down the source of a sound by 16 days.

Unable to move around or even regulate their temperature, kittens are completely dependent on their mother for the

CARRYING KITTENS Mother cats carry their kittens by the scruff of the neck. When her mouth closes on the loose skin, kittens instinctively relax and hang passively while they are moved; never try to lift an adult cat this way.

first few days of life, but develop quickly from this early helplessness. Fed on high-fat, high-protein milk, they can move about within a few days, and if they wander from the 'nest' will find their way back by smell. By two weeks of age they begin to play with their littermates, and by three weeks they are standing, walking, exploring, beginning to groom themselves, and can start to use a litter tray. At this age they have a mouth full of teeth and can also start to eat solid food, although they continue to suckle for at least another three weeks. Kittens need to stay with their mother for at least three months.

Kitten development

① At birth, kittens' eyes and ear canals are not yet open. They fit in the palm of a hand, and their umbilical cords remain attached for a few days.

② By two weeks, the eyes are fully open, but vision remains blurred. The kitten is growing fast and becoming aware of its surroundings.

③ Over the next week or so, kittens start to move around, pulling themselves forwards on unsteady legs. Their ears are erect and open.

④ By four weeks of age, a kitten can stand and walk, in a wobbly fashion. It begins to explore and may use a litter tray.

⑤ By five weeks a kitten will be washing itself and exploring boldly. As the teeth are now coming in, the weaning process has already begun.

HOW CATS LEARN

Cats learn most in the first few weeks of their lives, when the brain is said to be most plastic. After this time, cats become more set in their ways, but it is wrong to imagine that they stop learning at all.

EARLY LEARNING

The greatest influence on a cat's behaviour is its mother's example, but kittens of wild feral mothers can become loving household pets if they are accustomed to people from birth. The power of early conditioning in cats was demonstrated in the early 20th century by a study in which kittens were raised with rats. For the rest of their lives, the cats would never attack that type of rat.

ADDING VALUE Kittens that are handled daily for at least 15 minutes are not just better socialized. They are more playful, explore more, and even develop larger brains and learn faster than kittens that are not handled.

HOME SCHOOLING Between 7 to 14 weeks of age, kittens are most open to learning adult skills by copying their mothers.

Cats become markedly less receptive to change after infancy, giving them a reputation for intractability, but learning does continue. Studies in the late 1970s found that testing hunting skills in kittens at three months is not necessarily a good predictor of skills at six months; kittens that lag can learn and catch up.

HOW INTELLIGENT ARE CATS?

The problem with assessing intelligence is how you test it. Cats are not pack animals, and so have little innate desire to please. They can be very unco-operative test subjects, unless the reward is very strong.

The environment of a test has a strong influence on the result with cats. When trained to find a food reward by distinguishing dissimilar objects on covered bowls, cats sitting in cages were found to perform just as well as monkeys. When the bowls were placed in a larger room, however, cats always tended to head for the bowl straight ahead. Cats have well-developed strategies for remembering and negotiating spaces, and these seem to override the pattern-matching skills they were taught in the trial.

Some studies seem to show that cats have good long-term memory, but other tests to find hidden objects have shown that cats have relatively poor short-term or working memory. This short-term memory is the ability to remember and manipulate information such as signs we have just seen, and it drops off steeply within a minute in cats.

HOW CATS LEARN

Humans develop theories of what may happen because we have an insight into why things happen. Cats, on the other hand, learn primarily from observing and imitating. They also learn through experimentation, committing to memory the strategies that work. This was shown in a famous series of experiments by American psychologist Edward Thorndike. He timed how long it took cats to

USING A CAT FLAP To teach your cat to use a cat flap, prop it open. When the cat is used to going in and out through the hole, let it close; the cat will nudge it open again.

escape from puzzle boxes, theorizing that if they gained an insight into how the boxes worked, the time they took to escape would drop suddenly. In fact, their times improved gradually and steadily the more often they escaped from the box, indicating that they learned by trial and error.

This method can be very effective, as anyone whose cat has learned to open cupboards and food packets can attest. But it means that cats live very much in the here and now, with little or no concept of their actions having wider consequences. This has profound implications for anyone wanting to train their cat (*see* pp 96–97) or confronting behaviour problems (*see* pp 102–103).

LEARNING TOLERANCE Although cats have an instinct to chase anything that looks like prey, it can be overridden by early experiences.

CATS IN MOTION

Cats are creatures of apparent extremes. At one moment a loose, languid assembly of floppy fur, they can within an instant become a tightly coiled bundle of sprung muscle and alertness.

BRED IN THE BONE

Cats' almost liquid flexibility is built into their very bones. They have 30 vertebrae between the skull and the hips, the same as a dog and a few more than a human. What makes the cat different from either dogs or humans is the cartilaginous joints between these bony discs. They are far looser in the cat, allowing the spine to bend and twist to an extraordinary degree. This may save the Munchkin (*see* pp 354–57) from the back problems that can plague similar short-legged dogs, whose spines are strained by the abnormal flexing caused by short legs and a long body.

Unlike the human collarbone, fixed at each end and holding the shoulders out, the cat has a floating collarbone,

THE HIGH LIFE Although a cat stuck in a tree is traditionally rescued by firefighters with long ladders, in truth they rarely need help. Coming down is harder than going up, but cats are well able to manage.

a vestigial sliver of bone held in the muscle. The front paws can be placed directly in front of one another when walking, and the shoulders can squeeze through the narrowest gap. The paws can also be turned sideways to some degree, giving the cat a great dexterity when manipulating

LONG JUMPS Cats can jump six times their own length, vertically or horizontally. They use visual cues and their balance organ (*see* p 61) to tell them when to tuck in their tails and prepare for landing.

The feline skeleton

The feline skeleton seems to be remarkably resistant to change. Dogs have been bred in many shapes and sizes, but the domestic cat seems to come in 'one size fits all'. There is some variation between the largest and the smallest breeds, but it is relatively minimal. While oddities in bone and cartilage formation have given us some quirky breeds (*see* pp 330–59), tales of giant cats and miniature cats have so far proved to be just that. One way that the shape of a cat can be influenced is through neutering: cats neutered early tend to grow longer leg bones. This is good news in breeds whose standard calls for a supermodel build, but some breeders of cobby types prefer to neuter their cats later.

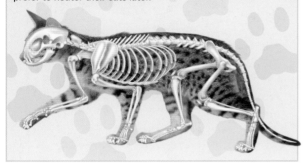

FULL STRETCH Cats can make high leaps without any warm up, probably due to their fast-twitch muscles. But like any good athlete, they often execute full-body stretches starting from this 'play-bow'.

objects and even a limited ability to climb downwards head first, but this is never as graceful as their ascent.

TALL TAILS

The cat's tail has 14 to 28 flexible vertebrae. The primary purpose of the tail is to balance the movements of the body. It is held out behind when running to act as a rudder in turns, and upright when taking off into a jump, swinging down as the hind legs are curled under the body to land.

The genes that control the formation of the tail seem to be a 'hotspot' for mutation, and there are some famous breeds with incomplete tails, such as the Manx (*see* pp 332–37) and the Japanese Bobtail (*see* pp 340–41). While these cats do not seem to suffer any great handicap through the loss of their tails, they have not become widely established except where there are relatively restricted breeding populations, such as on islands.

Full-length but kinked tails are more common. They usually have no more than a hook in the end, which may not be visible but can be felt. Kinks are considered a serious fault in show cats, because of concerns that they might indicate other skeletal problems, but they continue to occur in ordinary domestic cats with no apparent ill effects. The Siamese (*see* pp 220–23) was particularly noted for this trait when it was introduced.

BUILT FOR SPEED

Cats are the sports cars of the animal world, with superb acceleration, power, and responsiveness. They can jump to several times their own length, and run at about 50 kph (30 mph), but all this comes at a cost. The cat has poor endurance: although it can outrun a dog in a sprint, it will lose in a trotting race over any great distance. The reason for this lies in its muscle type. There are three kinds of muscle fibre: fast-twitch fatiguing, fast-twitch fatigue-resistant, and slow-twitch. A cat has primarily fast-twitch muscles, excellent for rushing and pouncing but tiring very quickly, rather than slow-twitch muscles like the dog. When a cat runs, its heart rate and temperature will rise rapidly, and as the muscle fibres tire, it must stop.

The other factor in speed and reactions is nerve fibres. The speed at which information travels along nerves to and from the brain is strongly influenced by the thickness of the myelin sheath that surrounds them. Feline nerves are particularly well-coated with layers of myelin, enabling them to pounce faster than their prey can react.

LEAPS AND BOUNDS
A cat runs in a series of leaps. It pushes off with its hind legs and its whole body becomes airborne until the forelegs touch down.

COAT AND CLAWS

Luxurious feline fur, with its many colours and patterns, is not just ornamental. The cat's skin and coat keep it warm, help it to cool down, protect it from injury, and leave scent markings, while tough paw pads and sharp claws ensure that a cat is ready for anything.

SKIN DEEP

The cat has layers of skin, constantly shedding cells and replacing them from below. The outermost or cornified layer is dead cells bound together by sebum, an oily substance produced in the skin. Below this is the living basal layer or epidermis, which constantly makes new cells; these take about three weeks to work their way to the surface. The skin is home to a mix of fungi and bacteria.

TRUE COLOURS The pigmentation that produces a cat's coat colour is also present in its skin. Hairless breeds like the Sphynx (*see* pp 326–27) show this colouring well.

LUSTROUS LONGHAIR Whether a cat is shorthaired or longhaired is determined by a single gene, with two longhaired cats always producing longhaired kittens. Length and thickness are controlled by a range of genes.

Resident skin bacteria attack alien bacteria that land on the skin, and are generally beneficial. The salinity of sweat helps to keep them confined to the surface, and even bacteria that will cause infections if the skin is broken can be carried apparently without harm.

Below these protective layers lies the dermis. This layer is richly supplied with blood vessels, and contains nerves, glands that produce lubricating oil and sweat, insulating fat, and the roots of the hair.

Feline sweat removes waste products from the blood, keeps bacteria in check, and carries scent. The scent glands are particularly concentrated around the genitals, but also in the paws, to leave a scented trail, and in the face, shoulders, and rump.

GROWING THE COAT

Human hairs grow singly, each from its own root sheath or follicle, but in cats, a follicle usually produces a tuft of hairs. There will be several primary or guard hairs, which are the strongest and longest, and carry the coat colour. These are accompanied by finer awn and soft, wavy down hairs. All are pulled upright in response to cold, trapping a layer of warm air and increasing insulation.

head and body can fit. They allow cats to find and investigate things or navigate without sight. Whiskers are also used in hunting, because when the prey is too close for a cat to see it, the whiskers are pulled forward around it, allowing the cat to feel where to bite. Cats with damaged whiskers are less likely to make a clean kill.

PAWS AND CLAWS

Cats normally have five toes on their front feet and four on the hind, although some cats have more, a condition known as polydactyl (*see* pp 358–59). The paw pads are tough skin, and there is an extra carpal pad on the back of the front legs. This plays no part in normal walking or running, but may provide a cushion or a brake in climbing or touching down from a jump.

The razor-sharp claws are formed from tough protein called keratin, and grow from the last bone of the toe. This bone is anchored with elastic ligaments, which hold the claw retracted to protect it when at rest, and become taut to extend it when needed. Claws have a protective outer layer covering a living substructure, called the quick, and like skin, the surface is constantly shed through scratching (*see* p 45) and renewed from beneath.

WARNING WHISKERS The sensory hairs on a cat's face are more prominent than those elsewhere on the body. Those around the mouth are used actively; the 'eyebrows' alert the cat to obstructions and protect the eyes.

Hairs are constantly replaced. They go through a stage of growth lasting two to three months: the length of a cat's coat is determined genetically by the speed at which it grows in this phase. This is followed by a resting phase of no more than two months, after which the dead hair is pushed out by new growth. Light influences this cycle, with longer daylight hours in spring stimulating a heavy moult.

Climate has affected the evolution of different cats and provided the basis for many of today's breeds. Harsh winters favoured longhaired cats and gave us breeds like the Norwegian Forest (*see* pp 268–73). Conversely, hot climates favoured short, fine coats, like that of the Siamese (*see* pp 220–23), which lacks insulating down.

SPECIAL HAIRS

Some hairs in the cat's coat are produced singly. These are the sensory hairs, also called vibrissae or tylotrich hairs. They are longer and stiffer than the rest of the coat, and serve as the outermost sensory detectors. The most obvious are of course the whiskers concentrated on the face, primarily on the cheeks and over the eyes, but sensory hairs are also scattered across the body and legs.

The roots of these hairs are surrounded by both nerves and a blood capsule that responds to the slightest stimulus. They are exquisitely sensitive, even reacting to changes in air pressure. Tip to tip, the whiskers on the face measure the width of a gap through which the cat's

ESSENTIAL KIT Cats use their claws for defence, climbing, stretching, grooming, and even when walking. Although normally retracted, to keep them sharp, they are extended when a cat feels the need for extra grip.

HEALTH AND BEAUTY When a cat is healthy, it shows in every aspect of its body. A cat in top condition has a coat that is glossy and smooth, bright and clear eyes, and a clean nose.

CATS' EYES

What exactly a cat sees can mystify its owners. Sometimes cats will pounce on a tiny object that we barely notice, apparently seeing it perfectly out of the corner of their eyes, while at others they will appear to look straight through an object right in front of them.

THE ANATOMY OF THE EYE

The eye is roughly spherical, filled with fluid, and has a pupil at the front through which light enters, protected by the cornea. The light passes through a lens, which focuses it on the retina at the back of the eyeball. Here, rod and cone cells detect light and colour respectively, and the optic nerve feeds the information to the brain. Refinements to this design account for the differences in vision between species, and in the cat all the adaptations are geared towards optimal hunting in low light levels.

MAXIMUM EXPOSURE Even in moderately dim light a cat's pupils open wide. In near darkness, the whole visible part of the eye may be pupil, allowing cats to see with seven times less light than we need.

SUN PROTECTION The ability of the pupil to narrow to a slit gives greater depth perception, and protects the eye from an overload of light; the tapetum lucidum, which improves night vision, is a liability in bright daylight.

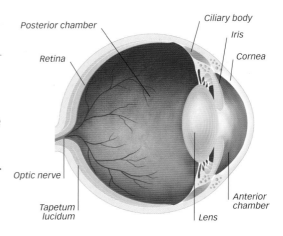

PARTS OF THE EYE At the front of the eye, the clear cornea covers a fluid-filled bulge. Behind this, the iris controls the amount of light passing through the lens and eyeball to the retina, and so to the brain.

SEE THE LIGHT

Cats are far more sensitive to light than we are, and are able to detect it at levels seven times below our threshold. A large cornea lets in as much light as possible; the vertical slit pupil can open wider than a round pupil to admit more light; and the lens is large and set relatively far back in the eye, maximizing the brightness of the image on the retina.

In the retina, light-sensitive rod cells predominate, and the feline form of rhodopsin, the pigment that responds to light, is effective for twice as long as the human form. The retina is backed by a reflective layer called the tapetum lucidum, which amplifies the light that strikes it.

COLOUR OR MOVEMENT?

Although cats have relatively low levels of colour-sensitive cone cells, studies suggest that they do have a limited capacity for colour vision if the coloured objects are large and differ greatly in colour. The higher proportion of rod cells enables cats to detect movement in dim light far better than us. The area of their peripheral vision is large, but cats react to moving objects more than stationary ones.

FIELD OF VIEW AND DEPTH PERCEPTION

Like most predators, cats have eyes that face forwards, giving good depth perception rather than a wide field of vision. They have about 200° of vision, slightly more than our 180°, and a smaller overlap in the images from each eye, or binocular field, than we do.

Another difference is that humans have cells concentrated into one area, the fovea, giving us excellent vision in the centre of our field. Cats, however, have a visual streak, a band of better vision optimized for a hunter on the move.

ALL IN THE DETAIL

The adaptations that give the cat excellent night vision cost dearly in clarity. The large lens is hard to focus, especially on close objects; anything nearer than about 25 cm (10 in) is probably blurred, and cats tend to use smell, touch, or taste to investigate items at close range. The position of the lens in the eye means that images on the retina are smaller, and so contain less detail. In the retina, the cat has four times as many cone cells 'reporting' to the same nerve connection as in humans, resulting in a grainy image. Lastly, the tapetum lucidum, which intensifies light by bouncing it around inside the eye so that it strikes the retina more than once, also seems to have a slight negative effect on the crispness of a cat's vision.

Normal visual acuity in humans is described by the term 20/20, or its metric equivalent 6/6. This means the subject can discern at a distance of 6 m (20 ft) the details of a test image that 'good' sight should see at 6 m (20 ft). When tested at this distance, cats only seem to be able to distinguish details that normal human vision can make out at 30–60 m (100–200 ft). So if a cat seems unsure if something is right in front of it, that may just be the case.

SPECIALIZED VISION Everything about a cat's eyes, from positioning to internal design, is aimed at facilitating nocturnal hunting.

CATS' EARS

As many owners will attest, cats can detect and recognize the opening of a food packet from the other end of the house or garden, but seem unable to hear their own names being called. Is this selective deafness real, or feigned?

ANATOMY OF THE EAR

The cat's outer ear flap or pinna is cup-shaped, to capture sound waves and funnel them down to the middle and inner ear. The pinnae are highly mobile, and swivel to point sideways and even backwards, capturing sounds from all directions. Each is controlled by 20 muscles, and can move independently. Cats locate the source of a sound by turning their ears towards it, and can pinpoint it within 7 cm (3 in) at a distance of 1 m (3 ft).

From here the sound travels down the ear canal to vibrate the eardrum. Behind this, in the inner ear, three bones called the ossicles pick up the vibration and pass it on to the inner ear. Here, sound passes into the cochlea, a coiled, hollow chamber of bone filled with fluid and lined with hair cells that 'hear' the sound and pass it on to the brain.

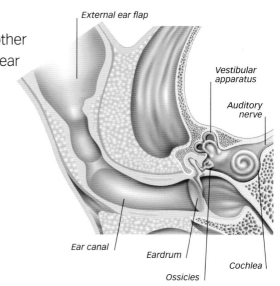

External ear flap

Vestibular apparatus

Auditory nerve

Ear canal

Eardrum

Ossicles

Cochlea

PARTS OF THE EAR The ear is a device for passing vibrations from the air to the brain. They are funnelled down the ear canal, passed through the ear drum, and transferred through the ossicles to the cochlea and brain.

HEARING RANGE AND DISCRIMINATION

All animals hear a of different pitches or frequencies: beyond this range are sounds that are too high or low in frequency for us to detect. The limit of a cat's hearing for low-frequency sound is similar to ours, which is around 20 Hz. We can hear high-pitched sounds up to about 20,000 Hz, and dogs can hear up to 45,000 Hz, but cats top this with hearing that goes up to 64,000 Hz. This range covers noises made by mice and rats, allowing the cat to detect the squeaks made by its prey.

Hearing is also biased towards certain frequencies. Our greatest sensitivity is around 3,000 Hz, which is the pitch of the human voice, while in cats it is around 8,000 Hz. There is also discrimination, which is how well the brain can separate and identify different sounds. The cat's ability to discriminate has been found to be much more limited than ours. This means that a cat inhabits quite a different world of sounds from us. If they jump at nothing, they are often responding to sounds that we cannot hear, and some music or the sound of a household appliance can be unbearable to them. Most words sound like meaningless babble to a cat, and using a short name and raising the pitch of your voice really does make a cat more likely to notice.

KEY ROLE Although their sense of smell will guide them to where prey might be found, and their keen sight is essential for the final pounce, cats often first locate a mouse or other creature by sound.

crucial. Also known as the organ of balance, this consists of three fluid-filled loops of hollow bone that detect movement of the head in different directions.

This structure works in the same way in all mammals: fluid in the loops, each of which is oriented in a different direction, acts like an organic spirit level to give a three-dimensional picture of the head's position. But the apparatus is particularly well-developed in some animals, especially predators. It is responsible for the way a hawk can keep its head perfectly still in flight to watch prey, and in land-based animals it is seen at its best in the righting reflex that allows a falling cat to land on its feet. The very first thing a falling cat does is right its head; it then pulls the rest of its body round, from the shoulders to the tail. When the twist is complete it is perfectly positioned to land: paws outstretched, back arched, and legs ready to bend and absorb the impact of landing, its tail acting as a rudder to keep the legs in line. The whole movement can be accomplished in just 60 cm (2 ft). This extraordinary ability evolved in the wild, but has saved many domestic cats from falls from high windows, and even from persecution (*see* pp 126–27).

SUREFOOTED A cats' vestibular apparatus, or organ of balance, is exquisitely sensitive. Even blind cats can balance proficiently, detecting and correcting any off-balance movement in a fraction of a second.

PERFECT BALANCE

Cats have a sense of balance that a tightrope walker would envy. They seem as comfortable walking along a fence no wider than their paws as they would be on the ground. There are a number of factors at work here: the cat's flexible skeleton, balancing tail, and excellent nervous system (*see* pp 52–53) are important. But the fluid-filled canals of the vestibular apparatus in the inner ear are

HOW EYES AFFECT HEARING Some blue-eyed white cats are deaf, because a layer in the ear vital to hearing, formed of the same stem cells that give eyes their colour, fails to form.

SMELL AND TASTE

These senses are perhaps the hardest to understand in an animal, because it is so hard to interpret their responses to different stimuli. In general, cats' sense of smell is superior to ours, while their sense of taste is less refined, but there are greater differences than this.

SMELL

Feline smell sensitivity is many times greater than that of humans, although it is not as good as a dog's. The smell-sensitive cells are spread over the convoluted inner surface of the nose, giving plenty of opportunity for scent-carrying cells to be picked up. In addition, cats, like many mammals, have a chamber in the roof of the mouth called Jacobsen's organ. Air is drawn into this in a characteristic grimace known as flehming, with the head up and the upper lip raised in a sneer. This seems to be particularly associated with sexual odours, although the exact use of the organ is not fully understood.

FOLLOWING THEIR NOSES Although kittens will still latch on and feed from nipples even if the mother cat is washed and scentless, they seem to find their way to preferred, perhaps more productive, nipples by scent.

WORLD OF SMELL

A kitten uses its sense of smell from the moment it enters the world. The mother's nipples are located by smell, and a kitten can find its way back to the same nipple repeatedly by smell. They can tell whether their mother is present or not by smell, and as they begin to move away from the nest, this is the sense they use to find their way back.

Smell is vital to help cats find prey in the wild, scenting out pathways that are regularly used by small mammals and then lying in wait. Smell remains critically important to cats in their dietary preferences, and often when a cat is off its food it has more to do with smell than taste. It is vital in marking out a cat's territory (*see* pp 38–39) and in attracting and choosing mates (*see* pp 46–47). The scent markings that cats leave are very specific, giving information about the age, gender, and sexual status of the cat.

Cats also use scent for pleasure, in the form of catnip, or more specifically the chemical nepetalactone. This is found in many plants of the genus *Nepeta*, which are commonly known as catmints. The smell of the leaves can send cats (but not kittens) into a euphoric state, without any unpleasant side effects. Chemical evidence suggests that the chemical travels on pathways normally used by feline pheromones or sexual scents.

TASTE

While we might envy cats the harmless intoxication of catnip, when it comes to taste, cats are missing out on a lot. To begin with, they have fewer taste buds than we do – a few hundred in comparison with our 10,000 or so.

POSSESSIVE SCENT When your cat rubs against your legs, it seems like an affectionate greeting, but cats also 'greet' furniture this way. You, like this fence, are being marked as part of your cat's territory.

THE CAT THAT GOT THE CREAM Cats cannot taste the slight sweetness given to milk by the sugar lactose, and adult cats may be lactose intolerant. The texture and fattiness is a large part of milk's appeal to cats.

NATURAL HIGH About two-thirds of all domestic cats are susceptible to the effects of catnip, and the trait is hereditary. Affected cats will be sent into an ecstatic state by the smell of a catnip-stuffed toy.

But there is an even greater difference between the sense of taste in cats and in almost all other mammals. Of the flavour groups, cats seem to perceive salty, sour, savoury, and bitter flavours, but not sweet. While they do have taste buds that it appears ought to detect sweetness, studies have always shown them to be indifferent to sugary foods, and in 2005 a genetic study finally revealed why. The ability to taste sweetness is controlled in mammals by a combination of two genes. In the cat family, one of these genes is faulty, an unexpressed 'pseudogene', meaning that any sweet taste buds they may have on their tongues are redundant. Because this is common to cats from the domestic cat to the cheetah and the tiger, it seems to be an ancient mutation that has helped to shape the evolution and diet (see pp 64–65) of the whole cat family.

THE FELINE DIET

The cat family are among the most specialized eaters of all animal families, feeding exclusively on meat. Their diet is not a result of food availability, but a matter of basic biology, and their needs remain largely unchanged in our domestic pets.

NO SWEETS HERE

At the very root of the cat's evolution is its inability to taste sweetness (*see* p 63). The result is that cats became extremely specialized hunters and carnivores. They had no drive to eat plant matter at all, because much of the taste of plants comes from sugar content; the salty, savoury taste of meat satisfied the feline sense of taste.

In the end cats have become 'obligate' carnivores; this means that a cat cannot survive on a vegetarian diet. Unlike many other mammals, they have no ability to synthesize certain proteins, such as taurine, themselves, and must obtain them from eating meat. Their livers are also programmed for a constant high-protein diet, rather than responding to changes in the diet as the livers of omnivores do, so cats must eat a carnivorous diet.

This need to eat meat is matched by an inability to use the nutrients found in plants. Cats cannot convert plant amino acids into the amino acids they need as building blocks for their own bodies, or beta-carotene to vitamin A, as we can. They also have a low tolerance of sugar in their diet, and too much of it will cause them problems.

The cat is unable to synthesize vitamin D3. We make this in our skin when exposed to the ultraviolet (UV) rays in sunlight, and it was thought that cats

NATURAL DIET We are used to thinking of a well-balanced diet as one that contains a range of foodstuffs. For members of the cat family, however, animal carcasses provide everything they need.

produced it in the sebum on their coats and ingested it when they licked themselves. However, in recent studies, young cats were fed a diet deficient in vitamin D, and either exposed to UV light or kept out of it, with full coats or clipped. In all cases, they rapidly showed vitamin D deficiency. Vitamin D3 is found in animal, rather than vegetable sources, and our ability to make it may be

CONVENIENCE FOOD Dry foods are highly convenient for owners, and many cats seem quite happy with them. If you feed dry food, provide lots of fresh water, and monitor how much your cat drinks.

naturally adjust their diet so that they still get an adequate level of protein. Cats, on the other hand, seem to lack the discrimination to tell what is good for them, and often choose an appealing low-protein food over less palatable high-protein food.

So why does the animal with the most specific dietary needs have the least ability to sense and correct imbalances? The reasons may lie precisely in those specific needs: as omnivores, dogs and wolves need to be able to balance different elements in their diets to remain healthy. The cat, on the other hand, has such a narrow niche in the wild that it has never needed this ability: it eats meat, and that is that. So a cat knows how much meat to eat, but when presented with a wider range of foods, it simply doesn't have a clue.

LIQUID INTAKE

Cats drink very little water. In the wild, they evolved to get the liquid they needed from the bodies of their prey. They can go without drinking water for long periods if their food contains at least 67% water, but if the water content of their food drops, they need extra water or will become dehydrated. This rarely happens in the wild, because a cat's natural prey contains almost all the water it needs. The result is that cats do not have a strong thirst drive, and are not naturally inclined to drink. When the water content of their food drops, or the temperature rises and increases dehydration, cats adjust their water intake in response less rapidly and accurately than other mammals, and can become dehydrated.

MEANT FOR MEAT This mouthful of teeth is designed for a carnivorous diet. The front teeth are used in dispatching prey, the premolars for cutting and chewing meat. The molars are insignificant compared with ours.

an adaptation to an omnivorous diet; analysis of the typical prey of wild felines shows that they can obtain all they need from their exclusively carnivorous diet, and have no need to make it themselves.

PICKY EATERS?

Cats in the wild do not become overweight, even though there might be enough prey available for this to happen, while domestic cats can develop faddy habits and weight problems. Studies show that when dogs are given a choice between foods of differing protein content, they

CATS NEED FIBRE While cats in the wild obtain insoluble fibre from the coats of their prey, cats on a domestic diet need other sources. Fibrous plant matter, like grass, can help.

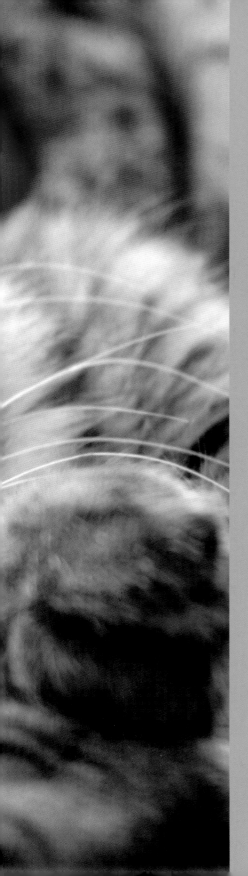

CAT CARE

Why have a pet cat? In fact, why have a pet is a question in itself. Pets are good for people. They improve our mental and physical wellbeing, fulfil our drive to nurture, and bring pleasure to our lives. But why choose a cat? Once, there were 'dog people', sold on big brown eyes and unquestioning loyalty, and 'cat people', captivated by elegance and self-sufficiency. Today, cat owners are more inclined to think of their cats like dogs, as 'fur babies'; while owning a cat is more of a responsibility today than in the past, a cat still has feline needs.

RELAXING SIGHT A contented cat can help make a contented owner, but if you want to get the best out of your relationship with your pet you will need to put in some thought and some work.

OWNING A CAT

You may be acquiring your first ever cat, or the first since childhood. You may be sharing a cat with a partner or family for the first time. Whatever the circumstances, avoid falling for the first ball of fluff you are offered or getting carried away with the idea of an exotic breed until you have established exactly what the cat's role in your life, and your role in its life, will be.

EARNING THEIR KEEP From ancient times to the present, the cat's role in many homes has been that of the working mouser, sharing home and hearth but essentially maintenance-free.

WHY GET A CAT?

For centuries, the cat was seen as an inexpensive, low-maintenance, working pet, not a close companion, but a part of the household. Recently, this image has changed; cats have been perceived and marketed in new ways.

One image is of the cat as a devoted, emotionally supportive, and dependent soul mate – in short, a dog that meows. Much breed information now portrays happy stay-at-homes that just want to be cuddled. Beware of this image. A cat is a cat, not a dog: while selective pressures down the centuries have made them happy in our homes, and recent breeding has modified pedigree cats, they retain unique aspects of their original nature.

Another, almost opposing, image of the cat is the scaled-down big cat, the 'tiger on the hearth' exemplified in the recent trend towards creating hybrids (*see* pp 360–69). Some publicity for these breeds promises glamorous wildcat looks with a lap-cat temperament, but this should be treated with caution. As successive generations move away from the original wild cross, so temperaments become more like that of the normal domestic cat. But domesticating the friendly African wildcat took thousands of years, and so thousands of generations; breeding out to a less tractable species inevitably introduces some less desirable traits, which can surface unpredictably.

HOUSE RULES

Before you get a cat, consider your household and how a cat will change it. Everyone in the home should want a cat (even if some want it more than others), and everyone should agree on the basic rules. If the cat is to be barred

The family pet

Once upon a time, man's best friend was the dog, but substantially more households now own cats than dogs in North American and much of Europe. As pressures of work, urban living, and smaller homes make dogs an impractical option for many people, a cat that needs no nearby park for a run and is inclined to sleep rather than pine and destroy the house in frustration is a sensible choice. In some ways the change has been to the cat's benefit: it is no longer perceived as aloof and independent, but appreciated as a friendly companion, and made part of the family.

NEW DANGERS The cat's nocturnal tendencies may not disturb its owner if it is allowed to roam outdoors. However, free-ranging cats are more likely to be killed in road accidents at night than during the day.

from certain rooms or particular items of furniture, and put out at night or kept permanently indoors, everyone should agree on these matters and treat the cat the same way. Confusion is not fair on the cat.

Consider the things that could go wrong. The ideal cat sleeps when you are out or asleep, plays when you feel inclined to play, lets you read your newspaper in peace, never lays claws on the furniture or flowerbeds, never sheds a hair or leaves its scent on your dry-clean only furnishings, and does not exist! There will be issues over clawing of furniture and housetraining, or trespassing and arguments with neighbours. How patient are you able to be when the inevitable problems arise?

MUTUAL SUPPORT

Studies over the years have shown that pets have a calming effect on their owners. They lower blood pressure, increase lifespans, and improve survival rates after heart attacks. Cats fulfil our need to nurture, but nurturing is a commitment. A cat needs feeding, worming, flea treatments, vaccinations, and other routine veterinary care. A cat also needs time: it may not need the hours of walking that a dog demands, but it does need to be played with every day.

Cats also need to have a stable territory, because they derive much of their security and happiness from their surroundings rather than from their owners. If you are moving in the near future, leave the acquisition of a cat until you are in your new home. Lastly, a cat needs a daily routine to feel secure. If you live a topsy-turvy life with frequent travel and little fixed routine, you will not make the kind of owner cats would choose.

KING OF THE CASTLE Cats need high places to survey their territory. If you want a pet that will not climb on the furniture, get something else.

INDOOR CATS

Although historically cats have been free-ranging pets, there are increasing numbers of indoor-only cats today. While this trend has not made a great impact in European countries, a range of concerns make it some owners' choice, particularly in North America and Australia. Some breeders will now sell pedigree cats only to those who promise to keep them inside.

SLOW STROLL Some owners take their indoor cats for walks on a lead, providing fresh air, interesting scents, and a change of scenery under close control. If you do this, be prepared to go at the cat's pace.

WHY HAVE AN INDOOR CAT?

One motivation is to protect cats from vehicles, fights, disease, predators, and poisons in the world outside. How serious these dangers are depends on where you live, but diet, neutering, and veterinary care are greater influences on lifespan than the choice of an indoor or outdoor life.

Another motivation is to protect the outside world from the cat. Keeping a cat in at night protects nocturnal mammals, but keeping it indoors all the time is the only way to guarantee that it can't hunt birds.

When choosing to have an indoor cat, remember that this is not the natural life of a cat: instinctive drives must be fulfilled. Cats can adapt, but owners must take trouble too; to give a cat a long, dull life is not a kindness.

An adult outdoor cat asked to adapt to an indoor life may be unhappy and destructive. The decision should be made in kittenhood, when the mind is most adaptable (*see* pp 50–51). An indoor cat is also in considerable danger should it get outside by accident. It will be at a disadvantage with local cats to whom it is a stranger, and will not know about hazards like traffic. Indoor means indoor for life.

ACCOMMODATING AN INDOOR CAT

An indoor cat has a very small territory, shared at a very high density with humans and often other pets. This can be stressful, so be sure there are quiet spots for retreat. Cats also naturally patrol their territories from high places,

VITAL EQUIPMENT A scratching post is not just a grooming tool, it is a feline gym. When cats scratch, they work and stretch a whole series of muscles down their torso. No other exercise gives quite the same effect.

ALONG FOR THE RIDE Those who feel their cat needs fresh air or a change of scenery might take this novel approach to excursions. Whether this does as much for the cat as for the owner is debatable.

Passive smoking

Owners may keep their cats indoors to protect them, but there are dangers in the home as well. Everything from household cleaning fluids and hanging cables to the owners' habits is important. A veterinary study carried out in the 1990s found that indoor-only cats belonging to smokers were at least twice as likely to develop feline lymphoma as those belonging to non-smokers. Candles and incense are also known to cause problems in humans, and the air in a house can be far more laden with pollutants than the air outside. For a cat that never leaves the home, these are serious considerations.

PROVIDING ENTERTAINMENT

Many owners know the 'mad half hour' in the evening, when their cats chase non-existent prey or enemies around the house, attack furniture, rugs, or ankles, and run up the curtains. To an indoor cat, this is a substitute for the exploration and hunting it would be doing outside: those drives are built in.

Indoor cats need exercising with their owners, even in two-cat households. A sensible owner provides a range of toys (see pp 92–93) and a good chunk of time to play with the cat evening and morning. An owner who does not is asking for their cat to wake them at three in the morning or destroy the furnishings. Play should be part of the daily routine; cats need routine, and an indoor cat is utterly dependent on its owner to provide it.

so an indoor cat may find it very hard to keep off the work surfaces and the back of the couch. Territorial spraying is a 'hard-wired' behaviour, so intact indoor cats are a recipe for a very smelly house. The only sure way to prevent it is to neuter both sexes before sexual maturity.

There will be some essential purchases. Scratching is instinctive, and physically and mentally necessary; even declawed cats go through the motions. A scratching post (see pp 92–93) is a must. Indoor cats of course need litter trays (see p 92). Fortunately they prefer out-of-the-way areas at the edge of their territory. A covered box just inside the back door is usually ideal; never put it near the feeding area.

An alternative to a completely indoor life is a screened enclosure outside, accessible through a catflap. This increases the cat's territory, providing a retreat when the home is busy, and allows it to spend time outside chasing insects when owners are out. It may even be preferable to put the litter tray in a corner outside.

ENTERTAINING EACH OTHER Toys are an essential part of the indoor cat's world. It is far safer to play with your cat using toys than just your bare hands, especially for children.

OUTDOOR CATS

For millennia, cats have lived out of our homes as much as in them, coming and going as they please. A cat's 'right to roam' is even recognized by most legal systems. This makes them a relatively low-maintenance pet, able to amuse themselves for much of the time. In a more crowded world with new dangers and changing lifestyles, however, the choice of an outdoor cat merits more thought.

MODERN DANGER In a quiet area with sparse or slow-moving traffic, cats have a high chance of survival to old age. Busy roads, high-speed traffic, and dark nights all increase the risk of accidents.

WHY HAVE AN OUTDOOR CAT?

An outdoor cat can patrol and mark its larger territory without upsetting its owner, and it can interact with other cats. If neighbours have cats, the cat-free household in the street is likely to see most toileting activity by those cats; a cat that uses the garden as its core territory can reduce this.

Where outdoor cats are usual, the question is more often why not have an outdoor cat, and some believe it is cruel to keep a cat inside. But while outdoor cats are easier to keep happy, owners cannot just open the door and forget them.

PROTECTING AN OUTDOOR CAT

Cats do face risks outdoors. Most cats develop good road sense, and their fast

OLD FASHIONED Farm cats live the most traditional feline lifestyle: hunting rodent pests, their diet supplemented by humans, socializing, and organizing their own daily routine. It is sometimes a short life, but may be a very contented one.

reflexes mean that road deaths are relatively low, but they happen. Cats probably learn most from watching the reactions of other cats to traffic.

Cars present other risks. Cats will use them as shelter and sometimes nestle under or even in warm engines. Cats will also investigate any new car on their territory. When departing guests are loading the car, check that the cat is not in the vehicle before they go.

Store any garden or outdoor chemicals sealed in proper bottles and packets, and keep garden sheds shut. Cats will lick at spills, and can poison themselves very easily.

Outdoor cats meet other cats, risking infections, fights, and unwanted kittens. The best defence against all three is early neutering. Neutered cats are not interested in mating, and fight less in defence of territory. Be sure that your cat has the appropriate vaccinations (see pp 110–15), especially if you live in a densely populated urban area: the higher the number of cats, the greater the risks.

PROVIDING FOR AN OUTDOOR CAT

Cats trample plants and scratch up bare earth in flowerbeds as a toileting area. Push twiggy prunings between plants, or mulch with coarse gravel. Some plants, like *Coleus canina* or *Santolina*, are rumoured to be cat repellent, but their effectiveness varies from cat to cat.

SOCIAL DISEASES At higher densities in urban environments, socializing has its risks. Territorial disputes may be more frequent, but even friendly social contact can spread diseases such as feline leukaemia virus here.

The cat next door

By its very nature, an outdoor cat will venture beyond the confines of your own property. Very few people dislike cats so much that they will object to them strolling along the fence or sunning themselves on a shed roof, but plenty will be upset by your cat lurking under their bird feeder or burying faeces in their flowerbeds. In these circumstances, it is best to negotiate if your cat has been identified as the culprit. The law may be on your side, but common courtesy is not. In the interests of harmony it is often worth offering to supply a neighbour with cat-repellent crystals, pelleted lion dung, or a sonic deterrent.

Cats will scratch and might choose your favourite tree; put mesh around it until the cat has established a scratching place. Outdoor cats seldom eat plants, but some, such as monkshood (*Aconitum*), can poison through prolonged skin contact, so check your cat does not roll in them.

HUNTING

Cats will hunt; depending on where you live, this may upset a neighbour with a bird feeder, or even have an impact on wildlife under pressure. If you live near a protected site for any rare animals, particularly small mammals or ground-nesting birds, you may want to keep your cat in at night, or perhaps all the time. Bells on collars do not seem to hinder hunting cats, although special sonic devices have had some effect in trials. Scolding a cat that brings home prey will only confuse the cat, who is instinctively providing for its 'family'. It may not bring more prey home, but it is likely to continue hunting and simply consume its kills in private.

Cats can often co-exist quite peacefully with wildlife. Bird feeders, thoughtfully sited away from undergrowth and perhaps under a line or slender tree to provide a perch above, will help local bird populations more than a cat is likely to damage them. Even ground feeders can be protected in a cage.

CATS ALONE AND IN COMPANY

The traditional view of the feline lifestyle is that of the 'cat that walked by itself': an aloof and independent individual, needing no company and locked into an enduring conflict with the household dog. In fact, all cats need companionship of some kind. This is usually supplied by owners, but other pets can also fit the bill if introduced early in a cat's life.

SINGLE-CAT AND MULTI-CAT HOUSEHOLDS

The standard pattern of cat ownership is still the traditional one cat per household, which avoids a great deal of territorial and potential behaviour problems. An outdoor cat may loosely associate with other cats, and be glad to have an undisputed solo life indoors, where it can relax.

However, in most places the average number of cats in cat-owning households has been rising slightly, just as the number of pet cats as a whole has risen. Owners who will be away most of the day may have two cats to keep each other company. This can be a good idea, but needs care. Your home may have many rooms, but wherever one cat goes it will at least smell the other, so it is vital that they are highly compatible. Because cats are most open to experiences when they are young (*see* pp 50–51), by far the best companion is a littermate with whom

EARLY FRIENDSHIPS LAST This young cat is relaxed and comfortable around the dog – a non-aggressive companion breed – because it has been raised with canine company.

that cat is very familiar. Established cats often deeply resent the intrusion of a new cat, resulting in conflict rather than companionship. A kitten is more likely to be accepted by an adult cat, but as the kitten grows up the adult's behaviour towards it will become more robust. If your two chosen cats prove incompatible, you may have to become a single-cat household. Cats that are allowed outdoors may be able to maintain a truce, but incompatible indoor cats will be miserable.

CATS AND OTHER PETS

Contrary to folklore, cats can co-exist quite happily with dogs – as long as they are introduced to them early enough. A kitten that grows up with dogs around is far more likely to accept them, so if you plan to introduce a cat into your home, and you already have a dog, check the kitten's home first. Because dogs are more pliable and eager-to-please pack animals, it is usually easier to train a dog to accept a cat (*see* p 85), although terriers and other hunting dogs may not be able to resist the drive to chase any small, furry creature. Often, the cat comes to dominate the dog in a house, despite the size difference.

CLOSE COMPANIONS Raised with human contact, cats will seek it out all their lives. Indoor cats need it more than outdoor cats, and sharing a human bedroom, or even bed, may help to ensure peaceful sleep for both.

Multi-cat households

Studies of pet cats are rare, but one study of a household with fourteen indoor cats has been undertaken. The cats lived at about 50 times the density found in feral colonies. They managed this remarkably peacefully, but there were winners and losers: the most dominant male roamed all over the house, while the most reticent female spent most of her time confined to the top of the refrigerator. During the course of the study the dominant male died, and the living patterns of all the cats in the house changed, including the female on top of the fridge. Although she was rarely seen to interact with the dominant male, she ranged much more widely after his death, indicating that some subtle communication had been going on before.

Cats will find pet rodents, fish, and birds endlessly fascinating to watch, and quite satisfying to eat. Do not rely on a cage to keep your cat away from other pets: prising open pet cages is within the capabilities of many cats.

If you manage to introduce a kitten to other smaller pets, it may learn to accept them as companions rather than prey (*see* pp 50–51). But the effect seems to be limited and very specific, so a kitten raised alongside guinea pigs would still hunt hamsters, and relying on this trick could lead to some family trauma.

INCOMPATIBILITY ISSUES While this situation may provide entertainment for the cat, it makes the life of the other pet much more stressful.

FAMILY FEELING If you want two cats, littermates are the best option. They will already have an established relationship by the time they arrive in your home, and you avoid having an established pet and a newcomer.

TWO'S COMPANY A dog and a cat can be an ideal combination in a home. Cats naturally dominate dogs, often with fewer conflicts than between two cats, and harmonious companionship is good for both animals.

CHOOSING YOUR KIND OF CAT

For much of the domestic cat's history, the choice of what kind you had was limited for most people to the kitten on offer from a friend or neighbour, or the cat that turned up at the door and moved in. Although cats were bought and sold, little if any deliberate breeding occurred. But owners have always cared about both the appearance and the character of their cats, and increasingly choose according to those preferences.

THE BASIC CAT The most common type of cat in random-bred populations is a shorthaired brown tabby, and the word 'tabby' was once used to mean any female cat. This look is common because it results from three dominant genes, masking any oddities.

HUMAN PREFERENCES
Today, there is a wide choice of cats, from exotic breeds to the random-bred 'moggie', but humans influenced cat breeding centuries before pedigrees. The predominance of different tabby patterns (*see* pp 162–65) and the distribution of the van pattern (*see* pp 168–69) both point to human preferences playing a part in feline appearance as people chose which cats to look after or trade for and take home with them.

PEDIGREES AND MOGGIES
If you love a particular look, there may be only one breed that can provide it. Many of the distinctive features of pedigree breeds are imported or genetically recessive (*see* pp 152–53) and so rare among moggies, while others have been fixed by generations of painstaking selection.

To get a longhair, you will usually have to buy a pedigree, as they are uncommon in random-bred populations. They do, however, mean more work. If you want an easy-care cat, avoid those with full and fluffy coats.

A few breeds also have distinctive reputations: if you want a chatty cat that lives on your shoulder, choose an Oriental breed; if you prefer a self-contained individual, a traditional Western breed is more likely to fit the bill.

Pedigree breeds still make up less than half of all cats,

Shelter cats

Cats, both pedigree and moggie, come into shelters or rescue centres for many reasons. Some are strays. Some are ferals, whose kittens may be socialized and homed. Others have been handed in due to behavioural problems, but these sometimes turn out to be treatable health problems instead. And many are handed in simply because an owner is ageing, ill, starting a family, or for some other reason unable to cope. Rescue charities are often excellent 'matchmakers', expert at determining what kind of cat you need, even if you don't know yourself. Ask how many returns they get: if the percentage is low, trust their judgment.

PRESERVATION ORDER The Chartreux (*see* pp 196–97) was preserved by human intervention. A localized cluster of similar blue-coated cats was recorded in Britain, but died out.

VOCAL CHARACTERS Why Oriental cats are more lively and talkative than their Western cousins, nobody knows, but the reputation is deserved.

IMPORTED TRAITS The recessive longhaired trait from the Middle East, and pointed pattern from Thailand are mostly seen in controlled breeding.

even in the United States. Cats have been bred for a relatively short time and upbringing remains more important than genetics in behaviour, so unless you want a particular look, a well brought-up moggie makes as good a pet as a breed does. There is also some evidence that random-bred cats have fewer health problems than breeds.

ADULT OR KITTEN?

Although the most plastic period is before the 12 weeks at which most kittens go to new homes, they are still relatively open to learning for some time. Friendliness and inquisitiveness can be influenced for two years. Bear in mind, however, that you will have to do this by training and influencing, not to mention housetraining.

An adult is a known quantity. You may buy an adult from a breeder; in this case, be sure that it has been raised as a household cat. You may inherit one from someone unable to keep it; beware of taking on a 'problem' cat with high hopes. You may adopt from a shelter (*see* box). You may even be 'adopted' by a cat that simply walks into your home one day. If no one claims it, you may have acquired a cat in the oldest way.

CLOSE ENOUGH Looks 'fixed' in pedigree cats do escape into the wider population. You are unlikely to get a dead ringer for a Persian, but you can find doll-faced cats with fluffy coats.

MIXED SIGNALS Cats are naturally cautious but should not be shy or panicky. Although this kitten has backed away, its ears are still pricked; walk away from any kitten that has flattened, fearful ears.

CONFIDENT CHARACTER A lively, inquisitive kitten that explores everything around it is the one to choose. You will need to provide plenty of toys and distractions, but this is easier than dealing with a nervous introvert.

FROM A GOOD HOME

Wherever you get a kitten, the home and the mother are the best indicators of how it will turn out. If you meet a kitten in its home surroundings, you see its true character.

If you are taking the kitten of a friend's cat, you will know its background. But if you are buying from a breeder, be prepared to do some work. Is the breeder registered with an association? People outside the normal channels may be producing lovely cats humanely, but they may be avoiding welfare regulations, repeatedly breeding an overworked female, or using unhealthy lines to churn out poorly socialized kittens for money. Ask to see the kitten's registration papers, and talk to the breed association.

TO A GOOD HOME

Be prepared to answer a few questions yourself. Almost all breeders impose a spay/neuter agreement on a sale. If you are enthusiastic about taking it further, showing your neutered cat and working with an established breeder is the way to start breeding. Shelters will also have questions: they do not want to 'recycle' the same cat in a few months.

HEALTH AND CHARACTER

By the time kittens are ready to go to a new home, they are old enough to have had their first vaccinations. If your kitten is free from a friend, you need to arrange and pay for these, but if you are buying from a breeder, vaccinations should have been carried out and you should be given the records. Always ask for the vet's details.

Check over your chosen kitten for general good health. If you are buying a breed, check that the kittens have been screened for known problems. Hereditary defects can cost you a lot of money and a lot of heartache.

When you are choosing from a litter, look for positive behaviour, and choose the most curious, outgoing, and friendly kitten. Avoid the kitten shrinking into the corner: it may seem sweet, but personality problems become behaviour problems, and the most common behaviour problem in cats is indoor soiling.

Physical checks

1 Look for clear eyes, with no cloudiness, mucus, or inflammation. There should be no sign of the 'haw' or nictitating membrane.
2 Check that the ears are clean, free of parasites or inflammation, and smell acceptable. Check that the cat responds to sounds from an unseen source in a quiet place.
3 Look for a clean nose with no discharge. The mouth should be filled with clean, straight teeth, and the breath should be odourless except just after eating.
4 The coat should be clean, dry, soft, and tangle free. Stroke gently in all directions to check for any patchy areas, sores, or signs of parasites (*see* pp 110–111).

IN THE PINK In general a healthy kitten looks healthy, but it is always worth having a vet check for less visible problems. If you are buying a purebred, check out any breed issues and whether your kitten is screened.

MOVING A CAT

Cats are generally reluctant to leave a familiar place for the great unknown, but you may need to move your cat many times in its life. Most cats dislike travelling, although show cats can become quite blasé after a while. The first trip to consider is when a cat or kitten leaves its home and comes to yours, and it is worth taking some trouble to get things right from the start.

THE CARRIER ISN'T THE PROBLEM Having struggled with a reluctant ball of fur before visiting the vet, watch how willingly the cat returns to the carrier when it is time to go home; the problem is the destination, not the transport.

USING A CARRIER

A cardboard box or carrier is a false economy. This might contain a kitten, but not a cat ready to use its claws. With visits to the vet, possible emergency trips, and maybe visits to a cattery, it is worth investing in a robust, comfortable carrier (see box) and teaching your cat to like it.

1 If the cat explores the carrier before travelling, sleeps in it, and leaves its own body scent on the bedding, it will come to regard it as an unremarkable object. An older cat from a shelter, however, may already recognize and hate cat carriers.

2 Put a familiar cushion or blanket and some food treats in the carrier. A relaxed cat may be shut in before it thinks about getting out. For a less willing cat, you may need two people. Try wrapping the cat in a blanket; it can untangle itself once the carrier door is safely shut.

3 At the other end of the journey, make sure all the doors are closed, especially if bringing a cat into a new place, because it may bolt. When you let the cat out, don't fuss too much; give food treats and strokes.

4 Cats often hate carriers because they learn what is at the other end of a trip: usually a vet's surgery. Use your carrier for other purposes, or keep it out as the cat's refuge, rather than putting it away between trips.

TRAVELLING WITH A CAT

In a car, strap the carrier on a seat, ideally next to a person who can talk reassuringly. Even if cats do not seem to respond, it can help them to settle at the other end. Be prepared to change bedding on longer journeys: try disposable incontinence sheets in the bottom of the carrier.

If using public transport, check the regulations before you travel. Firms may refuse to carry pets, or refuse on the day if, for example, the weather is too hot or too cold. Ferry companies usually require cats to stay in the car. Airlines limit how many animals they allow in the cabin,

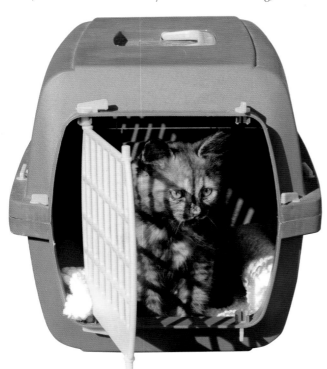

A REFUGE NOT A PRISON Try leaving the carrier on the floor in a quiet spot, with a blanket inside and the door open. The kitten may choose to sleep in it, or retreat to it as a place of safety. This will be a great help when you want to entice it into the carrier for a trip.

and increasingly only take animals in cargo. Always have your cat checked by a vet before flying, because stress may exacerbate any medical problems.

Pet passport schemes that avoid quarantine rely on microchip identification (*see* p 93) and vaccinations. All vaccinations must be up to date, and some must be done months before travelling, so start planning early. Think carefully before undertaking any travel involving quarantine. Find out whether you can choose the premises and how often you can visit. There are excellent providers, but also poor ones (*see* pp 98–99) that may provide for cats physically but give little or no human contact. This can irreparably damage the socialization of a young cat.

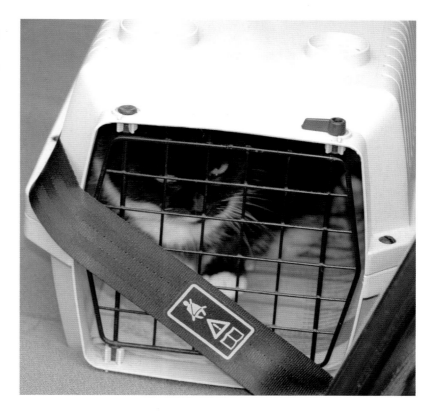

USING SEATBELTS Always secure the carrier properly in a car. When choosing which type of carrier to buy, check that it can be secured with a seatbelt: the best designs have moulded areas to hold the strap in place over the carrier, and cost no more.

Good carriers

Whatever the style or construction you choose, a carrier must provide clean, secure, and comfortable transportation. Always label your carrier clearly when you are travelling.
■ A wire basket is easy to clean, but it will need to have plenty of padding in the bottom.
■ A plastic box type may help a cat to feel secure; make sure that you buy one with plenty of ventilation.
■ Wicker is concealing, ventilated, and comfortable, but cleaning can be fiddly if a cat soils it.
■ Holdall style carriers can be folded for storage, but make sure they have a removable, washable lining.
■ Carriers for air travel need to be small enough to fit under the seat.
■ Cats travelling in cargo holds need special strong and leakproof carriers.
■ For longer journeys, food and water are needed; carriers with anti-spill bowls are available.

FOLDAWAY OPTION For those with limited space at home, these are ideal. The fabric is supported on a wire frame, which can be unclipped and folded flat when not in use, and set up for use in moments.

POPULAR CHOICE Plastic, box-type carriers are by far the most numerous on the market. Some of these have a top opening as well as a door: useful for inserting a reluctant cat.

SETTLING IN

Cats are stick-in-the-muds by nature. They dislike change, and because they are territorial animals they particularly dislike changes of surroundings. For the first few days in a new place they are likely to be nervous and upset, and their behaviour may be quite out of character. If the sweet, playful kitten you bought seems to have turned into a demon cat or a cowering wreck, then be patient.

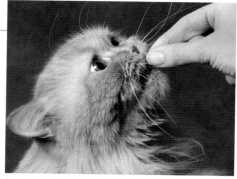

A LITTLE OF WHAT THEY FANCY It's worth planning treats into the diet to allow for rewards, comfort, and encouragement, especially in a new home.

PREPARING FOR YOUR NEW CAT

Get the home ready before you collect your cat. Put the bowls where you intend to feed it and have any other accessories, like litter tray and scratching post, in place.

TIDY AWAY HAZARDS A ball of wool is a traditional cat toy, but an unsupervised cat can suck it down like a piece of spaghetti.

Try to use the same litter as was used in the cat's previous home, and possibly even bring a small scoop of soiled litter to 'prime' it. Walk around the house doing a 'health and safety check', looking for places where the cat might get into trouble. Check that cables are under control, loop up blind cords that could be played with, and perhaps move vulnerable ornaments or house plants.

ON ARRIVAL

Let your new arrival come out of the carrier in its own time (*see* p 83). It is likely to explore methodically: surfaces will be sniffed for traces of other animals, and corners checked for hidden dangers or delights.

• From the start, discourage cats from leaping up onto surfaces where you would rather they wouldn't (*see* pp 96–97). Firmness at the outset is kinder than being soft at first and then toughening up your attitude later.

• Similarly, don't let cats explore places where you don't want them to go. Keep out-of-bounds rooms shut until they have settled into 'their' territory.

• If your cat will go outdoors, introduce it to the fresh air in short outings. Walk it around the garden, perhaps on a lead, with treats to entice it back if it strays too far.

HANDLING AND PLAYING

Frequent handling and playing when your cat arrives are vital to bonding. Kittens will still need to sleep a lot, with short bursts of play. Handle them gently, never squeezing, and do not lift them by the scruff of their necks.

Start a routine by playing with your cat morning and evening. Cats are most active naturally at these times; reinforce this and draw their overnight activity into the evening play.

PLACE OF SAFETY Your cat will seek out its comfort zone. It may be the carrier it came in, or the space under your desk; make sure it isn't the shelf where you keep your best sweaters.

Residents and newcomers

The rule with introducing a new cat to other pets is to take it slowly. The tactics used by zoos to acclimatize animals to each other's presence work equally well in the home.

■ Keep the new arrival and other pets, be they cats or dogs, in separate rooms at first. They should be provided with separate sleeping and feeding places.

■ Give each of them something with the other's smell on it.

■ Allow them to see each other but not make contact, perhaps through a toddler's stair gate across a door or with the two animals both held. Reward both of them for enduring the presence of the other.

■ Gradually allow more supervised meetings, always with rewards, so that each animal comes to associate the presence of the other with their favourite foods. Eventually they should settle down.

PLAY TIME You need to adjust your routines and lifestyle to your cat. Make sure that you plan enough time to fulfil your good intentions of playing and cuddling; put other things on hold for a bit.

KITTEN AND YOUNG CAT CARE

In the first few weeks of life, kitten care is almost exclusively the preserve of the mother cat. She is the kittens' sole source of food, and her actions in grooming, cleaning, and moving her offspring are an essential part of their development. Human intervention at this stage is limited to weighing, stroking, and checking for health. As the kittens mature and move away from their mother, a smooth transition is needed.

WHEN IS THE RIGHT TIME?
Cats are best taken to a new home at twelve weeks, and never younger than ten weeks. Vital socialization can be damaged if a cat leaves home at a younger age, leading to a range of behavioural problems, including compulsive suckling on cloth, fearfulness, and housetraining problems.

If an older kitten seems to have forgotten its housetraining when it arrives, don't panic. Because cats instinctively cover their waste, a tray of litter in a house of non-diggable floors should quickly re-establish training. If necessary, confine a kitten to areas without carpets at first.

CARING FOR A YOUNG CAT
Kittens can be fed virtually on demand while they are still growing fast. This growth is fuelled by plenty of nutritious food, ideally a special kitten food. Give four or

CATS RAISE CATS BEST These kittens will learn more about acceptable behaviour, such as limiting clawing and biting, if they stay in the litter until twelve weeks. Mothers and siblings are far better teachers than humans.

five meals a day, of just a few teaspoons at first, reducing to three larger meals at about six months, and switching to adult food and feeding levels (see pp 88–89) at about a year. Make any changes in diet very gradually: sudden changes can cause stomach upsets.

Groom a young cat regularly (see pp 90–91): it is useful for bonding and socialization. You should also be brushing your cat's teeth as the adult teeth appear between four and six months, and by six months you can begin to give cooked meat on the bone to help dental health (see pp 88–89).

HEALTH CARE
First vaccinations for young cats are given at eight weeks, with booster four weeks later. Kittens should not be allowed out, or to make contact with other cats, for ten days after these are completed. Get worm and flea treatments from your vet to be sure of the correct type and dose. Kittens can be treated for roundworms at four to six weeks old,

CAT THAT GOT THE CREAM Kittens fed milk will often prefer it when older, but those raised without it tend to choose water in adulthood. Some cats are lactose-intolerant and milk gives them diarrhoea.

VACCINATIONS The vaccinations given may vary depending on where you live and whether your cat is indoor or outdoor (*see* pp 110–15).

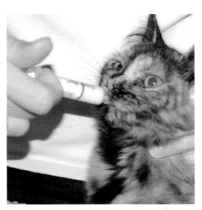

WORMING Different preparations are suitable for kittens and adult cats; very few are licensed for the youngest kittens.

FLEA TREATMENTS The spot-on treatments are suitable for use from about eight weeks, and are a simple, effective solution.

and then every two to three weeks until they are twelve weeks old. From then on, they should be treated for both roundworms and tapeworms every two to six months.

NEUTERING

The other important consideration with a young cat is to have it neutered before it reaches sexual maturity. If you have bought a pedigree, this may be a term of your purchase contract.

- Cats can be neutered from four to five months of age; females mature younger than males.
- General anaesthesia is used, but the cat can usually return home the same day.
- Cats generally need no special care after surgery, merely to take things easy for a few days.
- Females will have stitches that need checking and removal some days after spaying.
- Males need no further medical care after neutering.

REAL SEX KITTENS Cats can mate while they still look like kittens themselves, and some breeds are more precocious than others.

FEEDING YOUR CAT

The first rule of feeding a cat is not to let the cat choose the food, any more than you would let a small child choose every meal, because cats are just as prone as small children to make bad choices (*see* p 65). Present some variety, but beware of too much novelty or sudden change, which can cause cats to overeat or become picky.

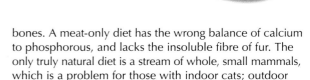

PROS AND CONS Dry food can be left for longer, useful if you are away all day, but wet food is closer to a natural diet.

DOING IT YOURSELF

Some owners advocate feeding a raw diet or cooking fresh food. While this seems closer to what a cat would eat in the wild, the picture is far from simple. A hunting cat consumes all of its prey, including fur, viscera, and

FAVOURITE FOODS
Cats tend to eat more of a new food, tailing off as the novelty wears off; don't be bullied into constant changes.

bones. A meat-only diet has the wrong balance of calcium to phosphorous, and lacks the insoluble fibre of fur. The only truly natural diet is a stream of whole, small mammals, which is a problem for those with indoor cats; outdoor cats will find some for themselves.

Food poisoning is a danger with raw food; cats in the wild do suffer from it and can die. If you insist on giving raw meat, you must be as happy about its source as if you were buying it for yourself, and some risk will still remain.

Taurine, an important protein to the feline diet, is impaired by cooking. Processed cat foods are now supplemented with taurine; a home-cooked diet could prove deficient in it, so you may have to provide supplements.

CHOOSING COMMERCIAL CAT FOOD

In recent years, dry food has become increasingly popular with owners, although possibly less so with cats because their sense of smell is a strong part of their appetite. Wet food is more digestible than dry food, and provides enough water for cats, who naturally drink little (*see* p 65); water that is drunk rather than ingested in food also tends to go into the cat's bowel rather than its urinary system. Dry food is convenient, but so are single-portion wet food pouches, so a good proportion of wet food in the diet is sensible.

Cat foods made to a fixed recipe are usually more expensive; those made to a fixed nutritional formula cost less, because they will use the cheapest ingredients available at any time to provide the same nutrition. It pays to read the packaging: ingredients are listed in descending order, and number one on the list should be meat, which is muscle, and meat by-products or derivatives, which include the animal parts we avoid but cats naturally eat. Cats have short intestines, and so they find vegetable

Self-cleaning teeth?

It is sometimes said that dry food can help to keep a cat's teeth clean, replicating the scraping action of bones. But cats can swallow the chunks more or less whole, and dry food tends to shatter, limiting the scraping. Do not rely on this to keep teeth clean. You can help to keep teeth clean by giving some meat on the bone, such as cooked chicken necks or oxtails. Start when the cat is young, but after its adult teeth have come through in the first six months of life. If your cat does not eat meat on the bone, clean its teeth regularly (*see* p 91).

BEWILDERING CHOICE When you go to buy your cat food make sure you have plenty of time and really read the small print on the back of the packaging, ignoring the marketing images on the front.

Percentages of protein, fat, fibre, and moisture should be listed. It is important to know the nutritional content on a 'dry matter' basis, without the moisture: if the moisture is 80%, the dry matter will be 20%. Divide the level of each nutrient by the dry matter figure, then multiply by 100 to give the percentage. On this dry-matter basis, a cat food should contain at least 26% protein and 9% fat.

OWNER'S RESPONSIBILITY
Some cats can naturally limit their intake or burn it off because they are so active. Others cannot, and need you to control their diet.

protein less digestible than meat. Cereals and vegetables provide fibre, but should feature lower on the list; here wet foods score over dry foods, many of which contain high levels of cereals.

NUTRITIONAL CONTENT

Energy is measured in kilocalories (kcal), and cats need about 40–65 kcal per kilogram of body weight (18–30 kcal per pound of body weight), depending on how active they are. Energy is often not listed on foods, but a standard can contains 150–200 kcal, making about one can a day suitable for a moderately active cat; big or busy outdoor cats can need a little more. Neutered cats of both sexes need about 25–30 per cent less than intact cats. Pregnant cats need twice as much, and lactating mothers' energy needs are so high that they ought to have free access to food at all times.

GROOMING A CAT

The natural cat is self-cleaning: it will pull out dead hair and skin cells with its barbed tongue, scratch off worn claw sheaths, and scrape its teeth clean shearing the meat from the bones of its prey. The domestic cat, however, is not a natural cat. It may have longer hair, it eats a prepared diet, and it lives in homes where scratch marks are not appreciated.

BATHING BEAUTY This is usually a trial for all concerned, but necessary if the coat is contaminated. Trim the claws and comb the coat first, use only a cat shampoo, and keep the water shallow.

GROOMING MITT A rubber brush is very good at removing dead hair without scraping your cat's skin. A mitt with bristles on the palm makes grooming a natural stroking action.

TEASING TANGLES Long hair is most likely to become tangled at the joints, where it is rubbed by the legs moving, and around the neck, where it is most luxuriant. These areas may need almost daily attention.

GROOMING ALL OVER

A cat with even moderately long hair may struggle to keep its coat in order, and suffer from hairballs (see p 44) through swallowing more hair than it was designed to cope with. Daily grooming is essential for longer-haired breeds, but even shorthaired cats can benefit (see box).

1 Use a wide-toothed comb to remove any snarls around the legs, ruff, and behind the ears. Divide the hair into sections and work on one at a time.

2 As you work on each section, part the hair down to the skin. Check for any tiny black specks; these are flea droppings and if you find them, treat the cat and its environment (see pp 110–11).

3 Use a brush on the tail and brush the hair away from the bony part, not along it. Many cats find brushing along the tail very uncomfortable.

4 In some flat-faced breeds, tears and mucous can stain or become encrusted on the eyes and nose. Wipe whenever necessary with cotton wool and warm water or antiseptic eye wash.

5 Check ears for excessive wax, particularly common in indoor cats. Remove with a proprietary softener on cotton wool; never use earbuds in the ear canal. Dark, gritty wax may mean mites, and in this case you should take your cat to the vet.

6 Gently massage the gums and teeth with a soft, small-headed toothbrush and pet toothpaste, paying particular attention to the back of the mouth. It may help to use food rather than toothpaste at first, or start with a cotton bud.

CLIPPING CLAWS

An outdoor cat needs sharp claws for marking, climbing, and defence, but the claws of an indoor cat can be clipped. This is not declawing, in which the whole claw is removed (*see* p 103): clipping means snipping off the sharp, dead tip of the claw with a guillotine-style clipper, like trimming your nails.

1 Begin when your cat is relaxed, perhaps after a meal. If it tends to wriggle, have a helper holding the cat so that you can concentrate on the paw. Talk soothingly.

2 Press gently on the top of the paw behind the toes. This will extend the claws, which are naturally retracted when relaxed. The dead part of the claw is white to brown, but the living, pink quick within it should be visible; avoid cutting into this.

3 Put the clipper over the dead tip of the claw and squeeze firmly, cutting straight across. It is better to cut off too little than too much.

4 Always give a food reward, even if your cat did not behave impeccably. The more it associates clipping with food treats, the better it will behave next time.

GENTLY DOES IT If you are at all nervous about clipping claws, ask for a lesson from your vet's practice or a professional groomer. With practice, you and your cat will both get used to it.

Why groom a shorthaired cat?

There are practical and psychological reasons to groom cats, beyond getting snarls out of hair.
■ Grooming is a chance to spot the signs of flea infestations.
■ Even a shorthaired cat may suffer from hairballs in heavy moult: brushing out dead hair is the simplest way to avoid these.
■ If anyone in the house is allergic to cats, it is a good idea to wipe the cat daily with a damp cloth. The most common allergen is a protein present in skin, hair, and saliva.
■ Grooming is an excellent way of bonding with your cat. Daily brushing, like stroking, is good for both of you.

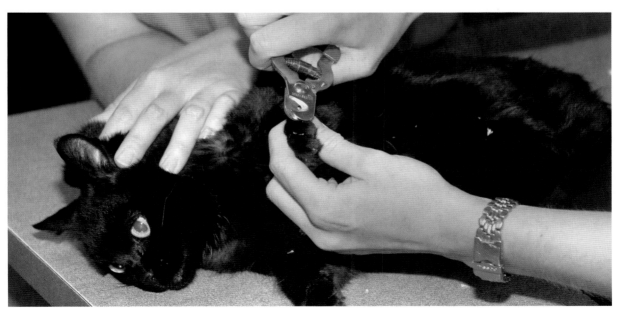

ACCESSORIES

Some people have a minimalist approach to their cats, while others delight in shopping for new toys, and include their pets on their Christmas list. Beyond the necessary basics, there is almost no limit to what you can buy. However, some things are likely to appeal to you more than they do to your cat: don't feel hurt if your carefully chosen toy purchases are spurned in favour of a discarded sock.

THE BEST CHINA Ceramic bowls are ideal because they do not retain odours and are heavy enough to stay put.

BOWLS AND TRAYS

While cats don't care about looks, bowl design is important. Plastic can retain smells of stale food or detergent, especially once scratched, which will put a cat off even the finest food. Ceramic bowls are better.

Shape is important because cats' sensitive whiskers are irritated if pressed against the edge of a deep bowl. Look for wide, shallow bowls, or use a plate for food.

A litter tray is essential for indoor cats, and can be useful for outdoor cats. A cat trained to use a tray may continue to use it if it is moved outside. Later, if the litter tray is removed and some used litter mixed into open ground, the cat will prefer that area for elimination, as long as solids are regularly removed. This can prevent conflicts with neighbours.

BASIC ECONOMICS To avoid using a lot of litter by changing it all very frequently, have a slotted scoop to remove clumps on a daily basis.

The tray must be large and deep to avoid scattered litter. Cats prefer privacy, so may like a covered litter tray. Owners may like deodorizing or even fragranced litter, but cats often find it repellent. Use the litter preferred by your cat, even if it would not be your first choice.

SCRATCHING POSTS

Every indoor cat needs a large, stable scratching post. A cat scratching a tree stands on its hind legs and stretches up, so the paw-to-paw length of your cat is the ideal post height; many fall short of this. If a post wobbles, your cat will instead use solid sofas and walls, so a wide base or a wall-fixed pad is essential. If your cat prefers to scratch horizontally, get a long floor pad.

Put the post in a prominent place; if the cat has begun to scratch somewhere, put the post there and cover the scratched surface with double-sided tape. Run your nails over the post to make a noise and get the cat interested, rub catnip on it, and give food treats after use.

WORK, REST, AND PLAY

Outdoor cats are usually happy to use cat flaps. Entice them through an open flap with food the first time. See-through flaps may help a nervous cat, and ones that can be locked allow you to keep your cat in, or others out, at certain times. If local cats coming in are a problem, flaps activated by a magnet in the collar are useful.

PAPER LITTER   CLAY LITTER   WOOD-BASED LITTER

Identification

Whether or not there is a legal requirement for a cat to wear identification, it is a sensible precaution. A roaming cat may be taken for a lost cat, unless it can be checked. Some owners do not like their outdoor cats to wear collars, fearing snags, but most collars incorporate an elastic section to minimize any risk, and cats are famously careful about where they poke their heads. An alternative is microchipping, in which a chip the size of a rice grain is inserted under the skin. The chip emits a unique code that can be read, usually by any make of reader. Microchips are also the basis of any pet passport schemes that avoid using quarantine.

TEMPTING TOYS Have toys the cat can chase alone, as well as some on sticks or strings that you operate.

In the absence of prey, indoor cats especially need toys, and will make their own if you do not provide them. From an early age, use chewable, lightweight toys, not your hand, to play with your cat: it will save trouble later. A small toy on a fishing rod can be flicked or trailed across the floor. Hollow toys can be filled with treats that cats have to work to get at, noisy toys excite interest, and those scented with catnip are the ultimate 'buzz' for susceptible cats. Cat gyms, with hanging or sprung toys on a climbable frame, are loved by some cats but regarded with disdain by others.

For snoozing after play, give your cat its own place. This might be just its personal cushion, a hammock hung from a radiator, or a covered bed. All will make it easier to keep a cat off forbidden beds or chairs.

COLOUR MATCHED Cats favour soft, fleecy beds, but many owners swear their real favourite is either where their hair shows up most, or the chair they match so you don't see them until you sit on them!

JUNGLE GYM The outdoor cat has a whole world of diverse natural experience just waiting outside the door each day. The indoor cat needs a similar level of stimulation if it is not to become frustrated.

TRAINING A CAT

It is a common assumption that a cat cannot be trained. Cats lack the pack mentality that makes dogs so biddable, but they can still learn. There are many troupes of performing cats across the world, and cats are used successfully in film and television, where their behaviour must be controllable and predictable.

THE RIGHT REWARDS
The key to successfully training a cat lies in the method of training used. Training towards desired behaviour must be frequent, regular, and always incorporate plenty of food rewards. Little and often is the best method, giving whatever treat your cat finds most irresistible.

POSITIVE TRAINING Training a cat towards desirable behaviour is pleasurable for both parties: cats are always pleased with food, and feeding a cat is very rewarding.

It is useful to have a cat that comes when it is called. From an early age, call your cat to meals by name and give a reward to start the meal when it comes. Next, call between meals and reward with a treat.

You can extend this approach to anything the cat needs to learn. Use a food treat to entice a cat through a cat door for the first time, or as a reward for using a scratching post rather than the sofa. Giving treats to the resident cat when a new cat is introduced also helps speed up acceptance of the stranger.

SUBTLE PUNISHMENTS
Cats will not stop doing things just because they are scolded, and are likely to resent whoever does the scolding. It is best to trick your cat into feeling the world, not you, is punishing it. To do this, you need to act at a distance.

You can chase your cat off kitchen work surfaces, tables, or windowsills and shout at it. But when you are not there, your cat will find these places perfectly peaceful. If you make the places unpleasant instead, it should not take long for the cautious cat to give them up.
• Put double-sided sticky tape on out-of-bounds surfaces, where it can be left in place until the cat gives up trying to access these areas.
• On kitchen surfaces, a squirt of washing-up liquid is unpleasant underfoot and distasteful to lick off, and is easily removed when you come home. Stop when you no longer find skid marks through the washing-up liquid.
• Use double-sided tape on furniture you want to protect from scratches.
• Spray forbidden places or items with smells that cats dislike. These include citrus and herbal smells, so citrus-

THE WAY TO A CAT'S HEART Food is a potent reward for any animal, but especially so for cats. This is why basing early training around mealtimes – such as calling your cat to be fed – is such a good way to start.

based furniture polishes and essential oils are useful. Avoid strong oils like cinnamon, which can melt plastic and burn skin, or tea tree oil, which is harmful to cats.

• Keep a loaded water pistol to hand and spray your cat, staying out of sight, when it misbehaves. Some owners of indoor cats discourage escapes by letting the cat out and having someone outside spray it immediately.

• Sonic deterrents, fixed or hand-held, emit a high-pitched noise cats find unpleasant, and can be used briefly to unsettle a misbehaving cat.

TRAINED TEMPLE CATS These monks found that when they were meditating, their cats would jump through their circled arms to get their attention. A little training, and the cats had all the attention they could wish.

Clicker training

Cats respond well to training in which the noise of a clicker is used alongside food rewards; eventually the food is phased out and the cat responds to just the click.

■ Click after the cat has done what you want, when you give the reward; the click is the reward, not the command.

■ Click once when giving each food reward: more clicks will blur the training, not reinforce it.

■ Avoid using commands until the cat knows that a certain action earns a reward and spontaneously does it for the reward.

■ Clicker training does not use punishments, so is a particularly suitable method for cats.

CAT-SITTERS AND CATTERIES

Given the choice, most cats would never leave home. An outdoor cat with a cat flap will patrol, hunt, and sleep without its owners as long as a neighbour fills its food and water bowls every day and provides some friendly chat and head rubbing. But without daily company and play, an indoor cat can feel abandoned and upset. If you do not have a house-sitter, it is best to arrange care outside the home if you are away.

COMFORTABLE LODGINGS Each enclosure should provide a vantage point for the cat to survey its new territory. The cats' records should always be available on the door.

AWAY FROM HOME

Your cat might need to leave home for reasons other than holidays: during house moves or building work, cats may be happier elsewhere during the disruption. Friends could look after an indoor cat, but an outdoor cat would either chafe under unaccustomed confinement or have to run the gauntlet of local cats. The alternative is to use a cattery.

Make sure your cat is carrying proper identification; catteries may ask you to remove a collar, so consider microchipping (*see* p 93). Ensure whoever is caring for your cat knows its personality, likes or dislikes, and eating and sleeping patterns. This will help them to care for it and spot any changes in behaviour that might indicate problems. They should feed the cat the same food as it usually has, to avoid stomach upsets.

Inform the cat-sitter or cattery of any health problems; catteries may refuse cats with infectious diseases. Write down the name and instructions for any medication clearly, and make sure there is enough to cover the time away.

USING CATTERIES

When you are sending your cat into such a different environment, there are a few extra considerations to take into account.

HOME ALONE Your cat may miss you while you are gone, but as long as a daily visitor or temporary sitter provides a similar routine and a daily dose of attention, then it will adjust.

Choosing a cattery

Always visit first and be nosy. A good cattery will be confident that they stand up to scrutiny at any time. Don't make a decision until you are happy.

■ Health and cleanliness are paramount. There must be a 65 cm (26 in) gap or a solid barrier between pens. Walls and floors should be sealed, smooth, and impervious, to allow thorough cleaning.

■ Pens should be large, with fresh air, natural light, and a solid roof if outdoors. There should be shelves for vantage points and an enclosed sleeping area with bedding, accessible whenever the cat wants. Each pen should carry information on the occupant.

■ There must be two levels of security: if a cat slips out through an open pen door, it should still be in a secure corridor.

■ You should have a real sense that the people running the place like cats. The cats should look content and well cared for, alert and interested.

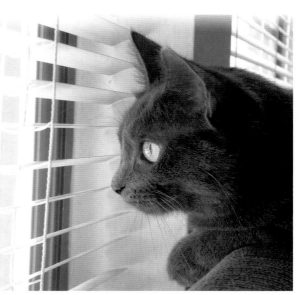

SOMETHING'S UP Cats are acutely aware of their environment: they notice bags being packed, more phone calls than usual, or any change in your behaviour. This is how they know when to vanish just before you go.

1 Ensure that all flea treatments and vaccines are up to date. Catteries may ask to see a vaccination record from your vet. Check if you need insurance, or if this is covered in the cattery charges or available as an extra. Also ask whether they have a practice vet or use the customers' vets; they should always have your vet's contact details.

2 Allow plenty of time for travel delays, dropping your cat in the day before you go, and collecting it the day after you return. Extending visits at short notice may not be possible in busy periods.

3 Ask about the cattery routine. It may not be the same as your routine at home, but a cat will adapt better to a new routine than it will to no routine at all. Think hard before putting an elderly cat in a cattery: they adapt less well to change.

4 Ask to take your cat to its pen to settle it in, rather than handing it over in an office. Take along something familiar, such as cleanish bedding (but still with your cat's own smell) and a few toys. Check whether you can leave your cat carrier; some catteries prefer you to take it away.

HOME COMFORTS Make a list of all the things you use with your cat day-to-day and check that you can leave the ones that your cat will appreciate at the cattery with it.

THE ELDERLY CAT

Cats are living longer than ever before, with better nutrition and veterinary care. At about ten years of age, a cat could be considered elderly, and its nutritional, medical, and behavioural considerations begin to diverge from those of a younger cat. In some cats these changes seem minimal, and many go on playing or hunting right up to the end, but in others they can be quite marked.

GROWING OLD GRACEFULLY Your older cat will generally slow down and appreciate the comforts of warm, soft places more. Many an ebullient young outdoor cat has aged into an indoor-only pensioner.

FEEDING

Smaller, more frequent meals suit a slower digestion, and a lower metabolic rate and activity levels may mean the older cat requires less food. You may have to control this, but diminished senses of taste and smell can also make food less appealing. Dental problems are common in older cats, and can reduce food intake, while conditions such as hyperthyroidism can increase appetite.

Owners can contribute to old cats becoming fussy eaters. Feeling that food is one of the few remaining pleasures, they offer tastier morsels to counter any drop in appetite. If a cat is truly in the last stages of illness, there is no harm in treating them, but otherwise, cats live longer and happier lives if fed wisely, not too well.

SIGNS OF ILLNESS One advantage of an indoor cat is that it is easy to monitor food and liquid intake and output. Excessive thirst may be missed in a cat that drinks from outside water sources.

PERSONAL HYGIENE

Only a small number of cats actually groom less often with age, and this is often linked to chronic illness. In others, decreased flexibility makes some areas difficult to reach; help your elderly cat by grooming with a soft brush, being gentle on joints and bony areas.

Most older cats soil the house at one time or another. Outdoor cats may become reluctant to relieve themselves outside due to the weather or intimidation by younger, feistier cats; try providing litter indoors instead. There may also be medical problems, so always consult a vet. Changes in faeces can indicate constipation or bowel disorders, while increased thirst or changes in urination can indicate kidney failure, diabetes, or hyperthyroidism.

MOBILITY, ACTIVITY, AND SLEEP

Almost all cats become less active with age. You may need to move food, litter, and scratching post closer together. Outdoor cats remain indoors more, but keep vaccinations and parasite treatments up to date. Older cats may not initiate play, but should still be played with gently for physical and mental stimulation, although. Most hunting cats become less successful and stop; in this case, start tooth brushing (*see* pp 90–91) .

Old cats sleep more, but their body clocks can get out of step and they may start calling at night. Activity and crying at night can also be a symptom of senility, hyperthyroidism, or other illness.

Old cats are often bony and look for soft beds. They regulate their body temperature less reliably and usually choose warm spots, like a sunny conservatory, or a heat-retaining beanbag. Older cats are more at risk of hypothermia, and an outdoor cat that habitually stayed out at night may need to come indoors instead.

MOOD CHANGES

Almost all cats become more affectionate towards their owners, and frequently more vocal, and routine becomes more important. Some cats appear to become senile, becoming lost in their own homes, yowling, and giving up on personal hygiene. Mental and physical activity may prevent or delay this, but nothing will reverse it.

They may become either more laid back or more cantankerous towards other cats. In general, those living with lively younger cats or kittens become more tetchy. When one of two cats in a household dies, the survivor generally searches and calls for a time, but can then seem more contented than before. Sleeping in the dead cat's favourite spot may not be a sign that they miss them, but a claim of the best seat. Wait to see how a lone cat settles before acquiring a new cat who may upset the balance.

Time to let go

At some time you are likely to have to consider euthanasia. Reasons for euthanizing your cat might include any of the following:
- A disabling injury or incurable disease with no hope of recovery.
- Pain or discomfort that cannot be controlled by medication.
- Senility or other behavioural changes that make a cat a danger to itself or others.
- A quality of life reduced by frailty or loss of senses to the point where life holds no outward pleasures.

GRUMPY OLD CATS Some cats suffer from senility problems. They may become bewildered, demanding, aggressive, fearful, or unpredictable.

BEHAVIOUR PROBLEMS

Some problems in cats occur because the cat has not been socialized properly as a kitten, or has suffered some trauma. But many more are the result of unrealistic expectations and a failure on the owner's part to understand that a cat is a cat, with its own unique and hard-wired needs and drives. Owners may think of their pets as small fur babies, but to treat them as babies can only invite trouble.

SPRAYING PROBLEMS

Territorial urine spraying is a natural behaviour. It cannot be stopped, but it can be redirected. The best way to prevent spraying is neutering, but if this is left until a cat is sexually mature, even neutered cats can and do spray. Early neutering is overwhelmingly the best defence.

Intact cats, male and female, will spray. Outdoor cats rarely spray in the house, but at the edges of their territory (*see* pp 38–39). An indoor cat can only spray indoors; the cat has no choice but to spray, so responsibility for ruined walls lies with the owner. Breeders often provide intact cats with special quarters to protect their homes. If you must have an indoor cat, provide an outdoor run. The cat is likely to spray more here because it is near the edge of the territory, and you may stop spraying indoors.

INDOORS AND OUT Outdoor runs that give a cat a larger and more interesting territory can alleviate or avoid many of the problems associated with an indoor-only lifestyle.

Scratching and declawing

Scratching is usually only a problem with indoor cats. It is most easily dealt with by providing an appropriate scratching surface (*see* pp 92–93). If the cat refuses to use a scratching post, change the design or position, and put physical and aromatic protection on the surface currently used. Clipping (*see* p 91) and adhesive 'soft tips' for claws are another. Declawing (*right*), although allowed in some countries, is not an answer. Declawing is an amputation: it is like cutting your fingertips off at the first knuckle. A declawed cat can no longer stretch and work its muscles while scratching, no longer scratch itself, defend itself, or even walk normally. Sore paws can cause fear and aggression, and can even lead a cat to stop digging in a litter tray and soil the floor.

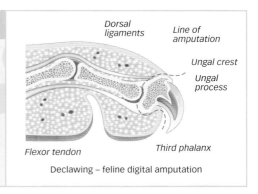

Dorsal ligaments
Line of amputation
Ungal crest
Ungal process
Flexor tendon
Third phalanx

Declawing – feline digital amputation

LETTING IT ALL OUT A well-socialized cat will have learned not to claw or bite hard in play, but instinctive hunting behaviour, including the kill, needs an outlet throughout a cat's life, through toys to 'kill'.

SOILING PROBLEMS

Soiling floors can indicate a medical problem. If medical causes are ruled out, the most likely problems are the tray or the litter. A tray that was big enough for a half-grown kitten may no longer be comfortable for a full-grown cat, which then 'forgets' its housetraining. The tray may be in the wrong place, perhaps too near the food bowls, or in a position that is too busy. The litter type could be wrong: dusty litter can make cats sneeze. Any change in litter can also cause problems; if you have to change brands, reward your cat every time it uses the litter. Scoop or fully change the litter daily; a wet layer will put your cat off.

AGGRESSION PROBLEMS

Aggression towards other cats in the home is a common problem. Neutered cats are less territorial, but your home must be big enough to allow two cats refuge from each other. Go through slow introduction processes.

Aggression towards humans is rare in a properly socialized kitten. More common is the tendency of cats to turn around during play or stroking and claw or bite the hand that strokes it, suddenly and without warning. This is thought to be a result of overstimulation. Never smack or shout at a cat that bites like this: simply say 'No' sharply, and withdraw. Use toys for play (*see* p 93) and limit stroking – some cats can only stand short periods.

CATS WILL BE CATS Some physical signs of aggression are normal in a cat's life: they have no verbal communication.

CAT FIGHTS

Fighting is natural. All cats, domesticated and wild, fight to win or defend hunting territories and mating opportunities, and females fight to defend their young, and use aggression to discipline them. Even kittens playfight as practice and to establish dominance hierarchies within the litter. But fights can lead to injury, transmission of diseases, and behaviour problems, so serious spats are best averted.

WILDCAT STRIKE With narrowed eyes, all teeth on display, ears pricked, and in all probability making an enormous racket, this is definitely a cat on the warpath

PLAY OR FIGHT?

Sometimes playing looks like fighting: playing cats will chase each other, grapple, roll, and cuff each other around the head. Flattened ears, fluffed fur, and an arched stance (see pp 34–35) mean more fight than play. Continual hissing, growling, or screaming indicates a serious scrap. Even these can be over in a short time and with few real blows exchanged, but if it escalates you need to intervene.

TYPES OF AGGRESSION

Most feline aggression is related to status and territory (see pp 38–39). Posturing and vocalizing escalate to an attack: sometimes the threatened cat turns away, and the problem has solved itself, but sometimes it stands its ground.

PLAY FIGHT With fur lying flat and claws only partly extended, these young cats are trying out their skills rather than settling a serious dispute. This kind of play can become a fight, but cats need to learn their boundaries.

Intact cats, or those only neutered after sexual maturity, may also show sexual dominance aggression, seizing a cat by the scruff of the neck and mounting it as if mating.

If you introduce a kitten to a household already 'owned' by an older cat, the resident may seem tolerant at first but later treat the younger cat more roughly: cats tolerate more wandering and cheekiness in kittens than in mature adults.

Displaced aggression happens when a cat suffers some indignity, and vents its anger on the most accessible target. For example, a cat might see another cat spraying outside, but because it is confined indoors it will turn and attack an indoor companion. Unless you spot the trigger, the attack looks unprovoked and inexplicable.

STOPPING FIGHTS

Never try to physically separate fighting cats. Sudden, loud distractions are effective, so shout or clap your hands. If your cats fight regularly, a shrill whistle or squirt of water may distract and discourage, but never directly punish them.

Once the cats are distracted, throw in a couple of toys: sometimes cats will redirect their energy into 'killing' these instead. If not, separate the protagonists until they calm down. This can take anything from minutes to days, and you may have to bring them back together gradually, as with a first introduction (see p 85).

REDUCING THE RISK OF FIGHTS

There is no perfect number of cats or infallible recipe for harmony. There are some things you can do, however, to give the best chances.

PERSONAL SPACE Some cats, especially littermates, will curl up together to snooze. Others may prefer to keep their distance. Your cats, not you, will make this decision.

• To minimize territorial and dominance problems, get kittens from the same litter at the same time. They will be familiar with each other, and already have some pecking order established.
• Aggression is vastly reduced in cats neutered before sexual maturity. In an outdoor cat, neutering reduces fights with strange cats and the transmission of diseases, and in an indoor cat it makes for a more peaceful home.
• Even one unneutered cat among other neutered ones can upset the behaviour of all.
• If access to food bowls or litter is a cause of conflict, provide two. Feeding cats in opposite corners of the room where they cannot see each other should defuse jealousy.
• Make sure your home has plenty of desirable sitting spots. If there is one 'best' seat, such as the only chair in a sunny window, cats will vie for it.
• Make sure your cats have interesting lives. If they have plenty of toys to attack and exercise with, they are less likely to carry play with each other too far.

Using medication

If all else fails, can medication help? Vets can prescribe mood-altering drugs to reduce either aggression or anxiety in cats. These are not a permanent solution, and should be used alongside a behaviour-modification strategy, ideally worked out by a specialist vet or a behaviourist recommended by your vet. Although the drugs given are also used in humans, never be tempted to 'scale down' the dosage and medicate your cat yourself: animals respond to drugs differently. Some, but far from all, owners find that the scent of catnip or of Feliway, a synthetic version of cats' facial scents, help to calm the atmosphere.

THE FAMILY THAT PLAYS TOGETHER Kittens learn each other's ways from the first day out of the womb. Littermates have worked out all their issues by the time you get them.

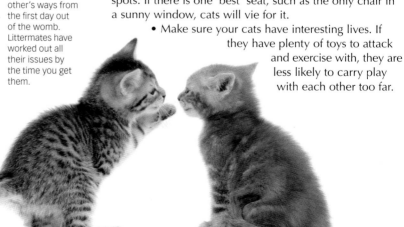

EMERGENCY CONDITIONS

Roaming, investigating strange substances, and taking prey all expose the curious cat to the dangers of falls, shocks, burns, or poisoning. You may need to act to prevent or minimize damage before you reach a vet. Although immediate care is valuable, do not spend too long trying to deal with the situation yourself: once you have done the basics, the most important thing is to get your cat to a surgery and a much greater level of care.

TOO HOT TO HANDLE Cats love the sun, but on really hot days will seek out shade. A cat in control of its location is unlikely to get heatstroke, but monitor confined cats.

HEAT EXHAUSTION

Although they love to lie in the sun, cats are vulnerable to overheating, especially if accidentally shut in a sunny conservatory or car. Warning signs of heatstroke or heat exhaustion are laboured breathing, lethargy or unconsciousness, and possibly vomiting. Remove the

Shock

This is a clinical state that can be caused by bleeding, burns, gastric problems, poisons, and some medical conditions. The signs are pale or white gums, a pulse of over 250 beats per minute, and breathing at over 40 breaths per minute. Treating shock takes highest priority.

Lay your cat on its side, with its head extended and its hindquarters raised: this sends blood to the brain. Use pressure to stop bleeding, and give artificial respiration or heart massage if needed (see p 109). Keep the cat warm and get to a vet urgently.

cat to a cool place and wet it all over with cool water. Do not try to give it anything to drink if it is unconscious. Look out for shock, and take the cat to a vet.

ELECTRIC SHOCK

This is mostly a danger within the home, where cats may play with and chew electrical cables. Sharp feline teeth are able to penetrate electrical insulation, and if they do the results are usually fatal.

If you coat vulnerable cables with foul-tasting liquids (*see* pp 96–97), your cat should soon leave them alone. But if you find your cat apparently unconscious, having chewed cables, switch off the supply before you do anything else. Treat for shock and contact the vet.

DIARRHOEA AND VOMITING

Vomiting or diarrhoea can both dehydrate a cat, so you should always monitor the situation. Dry, tacky gums indicate dehydration. With vomiting, withhold food but give water or ice cubes every hour. After six hours without vomiting, try food every hour in small amounts. If vomiting persists for more than 24 hours, or if there are other symptoms such as those of poisoning, see a vet.

For diarrhoea, withhold food for 12 to 24 hours. Liquid diarrhoea or conditions persisting beyond 48 hours should be treated by a vet; be prepared to take faecal samples in sealed containers.

POISONS

Cats are particularly vulnerable to poisoning. One reason for this is their habit of licking themselves clean, which means that they will ingest substances if their coats are contaminated. If your cat has unidentified substances on its coat, clean them off with mild detergent and rinse thoroughly. Poisoning symptoms can be subtle, and include lethargy, drooling, staggering, spasms or tremors, vomiting, racing or slow heart, and abnormal breathing. Inducing vomiting can be dangerous with certain toxins; you should call a vet for advice immediately.

• Plants might seem no danger to carnivorous animals, but indoor cats in particular may nibble on the greenery. Lilies and other plants in the lily family, such as hyacinths and amaryllis, are particularly dangerous. Dumb cane (*Dieffenbachia*) and philodendron can cause the throat to swell and close; poinsettias and other euphorbias also have irritant sap. You can find lists of dangerous garden plants relevant to your locality on the web.

• Household chemicals obviously include many toxins and should all be kept sealed and secure. Car antifreeze is a common poison. Cats picking up any spills on their paws are in great danger, as very small amounts are lethal.

PREVENTION IS BEST A few drops of citronella or other herbal oil (not tea tree) mixed into a carrier oil and smeared on electrical cables, could prevent your cat forming a dangerous habit. Cats soon learn.

• Garden chemicals designed to kill pests such as insects or slugs are usually also toxic to mammals. Used correctly, they are highly unlikely to cause injury or death to pets, and recorded poisonings are extremely low, but spillages or heavy overuse are obviously riskier.

• Pest poisons, particularly those used against rats, pose a real danger. Even if the bait is inaccessible, a slowly dying rodent is easy prey that may be caught and consumed by a cat.

• Medications, whether they are prescribed or over-the-counter, have a recommended dosage. Exceeding this, for example using more flea medication 'for good measure', can result in toxic effects. Giving human or canine medicines to cats is also highly dangerous.

KEEP FLUID LEVELS HIGH With both diarrhoea and vomiting a cat can become dehydrated. Offer plenty of water, and talk to a vet if it is refused.

BASIC FIRST AID

Cats are generally too cautious to get themselves into trouble in high places, tight spots, or over-reaching jumps. They usually suffer little more than the odd sprain, cut, or minor wound; these can often be dealt with at home with no further worry. But if the worst should happen, be prepared. Keep calm, confine your cat, and move it carefully. If you are in any doubt about the seriousness of the injury, take the cat to the vet.

ASSESSING THE SITUATION

When faced with a hurt or distressed cat, the first thing is to assess what has happened and what needs to be done.
• Is the cat in danger where it is? If so, the first priority is to move it to safety without further injury, well supported and flat.
• Will you be in danger if you move the cat – is it in a precarious place? If possible call someone to help you.
• Is the cat secure? Hurt cats may try to hide, so close off any escape routes and cover the cat gently with something soft, like a towel.
• What is the cat's condition? Feel gently all over for tender spots or swellings. Check vital signs and remember invisible internal injuries are common.

Treating wounds

Wounds in cats can be hard to assess. Cats do not bleed profusely from surface wounds: they clot quickly and you may not even notice some minor wounds. Always have anything that hints of possible greater trauma checked by a vet, because internal bleeding can be dangerous. Fight wounds may be small and not bleed much, but they are often deep and infected, and may require antibiotics.

BURNS Flush burns, whether from heat or from chemicals, with plenty of clean, cold water and then treat as for minor or more serious wounds. Watch for signs of shock (*see* p 106).

MINOR WOUNDS Dab clean with water or 3 per cent hydrogen peroxide. Do not try to clean more serious wounds; use direct pressure to control bleeding and get to a vet.

Vital signs

Become familiar with these. Your vet can show you how to take the temperature. Note down anything abnormal.
■ Press the chest on either side behind the forelegs or press into the groin to take the pulse. It should be 100–160 beats per minute, or up to 260 in kittens.
■ Cats take from 20 breaths a minute when relaxed to 100 when agitated.
■ Normal body temperature is 38.0–39.2 °C (100.5–102.5 °F).
■ The gums should be pink: pale or bluish gums are danger signs.

THE VANISHING CAT If your cat disappears for any unusual length of time, or you find it lurking in some odd, out-of-the-way spot, check it over. Cats will often instinctively hide when hurt.

Road accidents

Traffic is a major danger for cats, because it moves faster than they do. Studies show that young, bold cats, from seven months to two years of age, are most at risk. Deaths are also higher for cats that spend time outside after dark, so keeping cats indoors overnight is valuable. Any cat that appears to have been involved in a road traffic accident should be taken to a vet, even if they appear unhurt; they may have internal injuries and go into shock hours later.

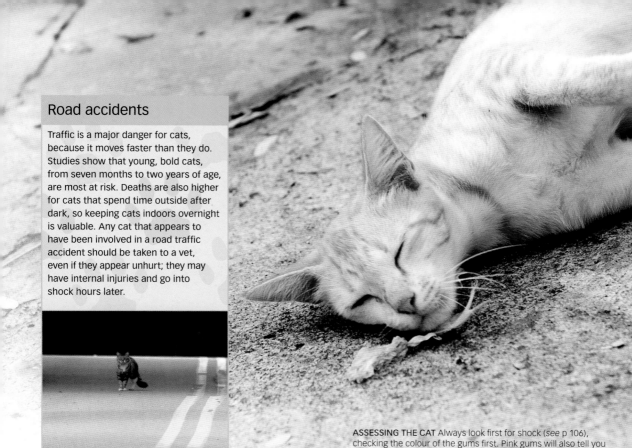

ASSESSING THE CAT Always look first for shock (*see* p 106), checking the colour of the gums first. Pink gums will also tell you that the cat is breathing. If not, also feel for the heartbeat.

Cardiopulmonary resuscitation

❶ To clear the airway, remove any visible obstruction with fingers, pliers, or tweezers. If it is stuck, or nothing is visible, put your hands on either side of the ribcage and press quickly and firmly, or put the cat on its side and strike the ribcage firmly with your palm three or four times.

❷ A pulse but no breathing means artificial respiration is needed. Lay the cat on its side, clear the airway, and pull the tongue forwards. Put your hand around the closed muzzle and blow gently into it until you see the chest expand. Let it deflate. Repeat at twenty to thirty breaths a minute.

❸ No pulse means the cat also needs heart massage. Place fingers and thumb behind the elbows, either side of the sternum. Press firmly at a rate of just under two compressions a second, administering one breath for every six compressions. Pause every two minutes, and stop after thirty minutes or if the heart starts beating.

PARASITES

Parasites are the main everyday problem for cats. The threats vary according to where you live, with some greater than others. Every animal carries flora and fauna inside and outside. Many of these are beneficial, like the bacteria in the gut that digest food, or the normal skin fauna, but can become harmful if their natural balance is disturbed. Others are detrimental and irritating, and routine treatments are used to protect against them.

ROUNDWORMS AND TAPEWORMS

Worms are picked up from prey such as rodents or birds, fleas, or even from the ground. They live in the intestines, and either eggs or worm segments are shed in the faeces and transmitted via grooming. If picked up by humans, some can travel through the body and settle in the eye. Worm infestations are not always easy to identify, unless they are quite heavy; the symptoms can range from a pot-bellied appearance to vomiting, diarrhoea, dehydration, and weight loss.

Roundworms look like spaghetti, and the most common species, *Toxocara cati*, can infect humans. The segments of tapeworms resemble grains of rice. *Taenia taeniaeformis* is picked up from infected prey and does not infect humans; the more common *Diplidium caninum* is also spread through fleas that carry their eggs, and can infect humans. The same worming treatments are used for both.

Worming treatments for your cat must be carried out on a regular basis to prevent reinfestation; flea treatment is also vital. Indoor cats are less susceptible to infestations; outdoor cats that hunt are most vulnerable. Over-the-counter treatments are effective but are not suitable for kittens: talk to your vet about treatments for these.

REGULAR TREATMENTS It is recommended that outdoor cats should be wormed every two months. Indoor cats need worming less often, perhaps only every six months, but should still be treated.

DIRECT AND INDIRECT EFFECTS Parasites can cause symptoms from diarrhoea or constipation to hair loss or anaemia. They also weaken a cat, making it more susceptible to viral or bacterial infections or diseases.

MICROSCOPIC PARASITES

These parasites are less common, and need to be confirmed by laboratory tests and treated with prescription medicines. Dark or bloody diarrhoea is a symptom of hookworms and wireworms, while coughing can indicate lungworms, and asthma-like symptoms may mean heartworms.

Toxoplasma gondii lives in the cells lining the intestines of mammals, and in cysts in muscle tissue. Infection is from prey or raw or undercooked meat. Symptoms are fever, vomiting, diarrhoea, or pneumonia, but may not appear unless the infestation is severe. Eggs in the faeces can be transmitted to humans. The dangers of cat litter to pregnant women in particular are well known. Wearing gloves to change cat litter is always advisable, but banishing a healthy cat from a clean home during pregnancy is not usually necessary; handling raw meat and eating undercooked meat are also dangers.

Giardia is picked up from water, even tap water in some places. Cats can carry it for years without symptoms; the most common symptom shown is diarrhoea. Infections

TICKS Lurking in long grass, these bite into the skin, swell up with ingested blood, and then drop off.

FLEAS These will survive all year round in a heated house, and pass on tapeworms.

are rare, but spread in multi-cat environments, where scrupulous cleanliness and regular litter changes are vital. Giardia also affects humans, but whether it is passed from cats is not certain.

EXTERNAL PARASITES

Fleas are the most common external parasite of cats, causing not only itching, but allergic reactions or skin infections. Signs are scratching or black flea droppings in the coat. Highly effective treatments are available as spot-on liquids applied monthly to the nape of the neck. These spread across the skin and kill fleas or prevent reproduction. Traditional flea collars can cause reactions in some cats. Prevention is far easier than cure, because cure means treating not only the cat but its environment: vacuuming and discarding the vacuum cleaner bag immediately, then applying special insecticides and insect growth regulators.

Ear mites (*Otodectes cynotis*) are very common on young cats. They are usually found in the ears, but also on the face, neck, feet, and rump, and can survive off their host for several weeks. They do not pierce the skin or suck blood, but are irritating, causing scratching, head-shaking, sores, infections, and a discharge resembling coffee grounds. The treatment is a solution and mite-killing drugs for the ears, and anti-flea treatments on the body.

Walking dandruff (*Cheyletiella blakei*) tends to be a parasite of young cats. It burrows into the skin and fills with colourless fluid. Symptoms are scratching, dandruff, hair loss, lesions like millet seeds, and red bumps on the head, neck, and back. Both the cat and the home need to be treated. The mites do not reproduce on humans, but the bites cause itchy pustules.

Ticks, which can carry microscopic parasites and the bacterial infection Lyme's disease, are a seasonal problem

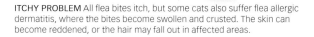

ITCHY PROBLEM All flea bites itch, but some cats also suffer flea allergic dermatitis, where the bites become swollen and crusted. The skin can become reddened, or the hair may fall out in affected areas.

in some places. Some of the spot-on treatments provide protection against these, but if your cat is bitten kill the tick with a proprietary product specifically for cats and then remove it with tweezers on the base, where the mouth parts are, never on the body. If your cat seems lethargic, testing for Lyme's disease may be advisable.

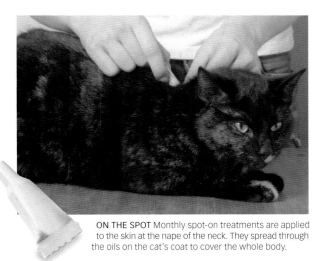

ON THE SPOT Monthly spot-on treatments are applied to the skin at the nape of the neck. They spread through the oils on the cat's coat to cover the whole body.

INFECTIOUS DISEASES AND VACCINATIONS

Cats by nature live largely solitary lives, coming together for mating and brief skirmishes over territory. We have led them to live in smaller territories, with increased contact, and now see many infectious diseases passed between them. These are of most concern in catteries and rescue centres, where rigorous care over separation is needed to prevent their spread, but also to anyone with a free-ranging cat, especially where feline populations are dense.

FELINE INFECTIOUS PERITONITIS (FIP)

This is a mutation of feline enteric coronavirus. Many cats carry the coronavirus, which is spread through ingestion or inhalation from saliva or faeces, but FIP develops only in a few. Very old or very young cats, or those with compromised immune systems, are the most vulnerable. FIP infects white blood cells, causing a massive inflammatory response. Symptoms include diarrhoea, jaundice, loss of appetite and weight, or fever. FIP is incurable and usually fatal. Treatment is aimed at keeping the cat comfortable. A vaccine that seems to give some protection has been licensed in the United States and some other countries.

FELINE LEUKAEMIA VIRUS (FELV)

Feline leukaemia virus (FeLV) is not a cancer, like human leukaemia, but a virus that suppresses a cat's immune

NO VISITORS Keep kittens away from older cats beyond their immediate family, because they will not have any immunity to infections or diseases they carry. FIP in particular affects kittens.

system. It is transmitted by sharing a feeding dish, grooming, or from a mother to her kittens. More cats carry antibodies to the virus than carry the infection, so have successfully fought it off. Those that do not, carry it for life; infected cats may die within months or live for years without symptoms.

Nearly a third of infected cats die as a result of the infection, usually from forms of leukaemia, lymphoma, or anaemia. Vaccines give good but not complete protection. Diagnosed cats should be separated from uninfected cats. Any general signs of poor health, discharges, gingivitis, or painful or swollen areas are a cause to visit the vet. There is no cure for FeLV: treatment is for the secondary problems.

FELINE IMMUNODEFICIENCY VIRUS (FIV)

Commonly known as feline AIDS, this virus is usually transmitted by deep bite wounds in fights. It attacks the feline immune system, exhausting immune cells. Infected cats often have fever and enlarged lymph nodes within a month or two of infection; these symptoms then disappear and cats are latent carriers of the virus. They may have persistent diarrhoea, fever, general loss of condition, signs of chronic infections, cancers, and blood disorders.

A vaccine, which does not give total protection, is available in some countries, like the United States. There is no cure, but with good care, a FIV-positive cat can live a near-normal lifespan with no signs of sickness for years.

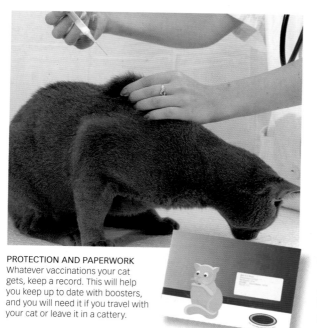

PROTECTION AND PAPERWORK Whatever vaccinations your cat gets, keep a record. This will help you keep up to date with boosters, and you will need it if you travel with your cat or leave it in a cattery.

CAT FLU

Cat flu is caused by either feline calicivirus (FCV) or, more seriously, feline herpesvirus (FHV). It is spread by grooming, sharing bowls, or by sneezing. This is a major symptom, as are runny eyes and nose, and fever. Swollen lymph nodes are common, and mouth ulcers may cause drooling. After a week or two, most cats recover, although kittens may be left with permanent wheezy breathing and discharge and need antibiotics all their lives. FCV can cause chronic gingivitis or persistent limping, with a high temperature; FHV can cause ulceration of the cornea that leads to the loss of the eye if untreated.

Always take a cat with flu symptoms to the vet. Antibiotics to control secondary infection may be needed. Cats that lose their appetite need aromatic food to tempt them. Keep the cat in a steamy bathroom for an hour to help breathing, and clean runny eyes. Vaccination for FHV is effective; there are many strains of FCV, so vaccine protection is less complete. FHV-infected cats remain carriers; FCV-infected cats may or may not continue to shed the virus.

CONTACT NOT NECESSARY Some diseases are most easily spread by fight wounds, and others by social contac, but some can be airborne or carried on hands or clothing.

NON-INFECTIOUS CONDITIONS

Not all feline problems are caused by infectious diseases; some conditions are inherited, or caused by environmental factors such as how much and what type of food a cat eats, its level of exercise, and so on. As better diets, vaccinations, and medications increase the lifespan of the household cat, new health problems emerge. Wear and tear causes organs to fail or brings to light inherited problems that were not obvious in youth.

AT RISK Some inherited problems are associated with particular breeds: Abyssinians (*left*) and Persians (*right*) are two of quite a list with known weaknesses.

URINARY TRACT PROBLEMS

Cats suffer a range of urinary tract problems. Problems with many contributory factors, such as diet, stress, and hormones, are often referred to as feline lower urinary tract disorder (FLUTD). Greatly increased thirst is a symptom, as are blood in the urine, and frequent or obviously uncomfortable urination. If urination stops, the kidneys cannot function, and death may result in under two days, so do not delay. Plenty of water is vital.

At the other extreme, older cats may become incontinent. Sometimes this is treatable, depending on the cause; in the meantime, ensure you keep the cat clean, because acidic urine will burn the skin.

KIDNEY PROBLEMS

If kidneys fail, toxins left in the blood make the cat ill. Chronic kidney disease is progressive, incurable,

THE WEAKEST LINK Cats are particularly prone to kidney and urinary tract problems in old age. Males, females, pedigree breeds, and moggies are all affected.

TEMPTING BREW If an elderly or sick cat seems disinclined to drink, try flavouring the water with meat stock to tempt the appetite.

and fatal. The kidneys fail to filter toxins, while allowing protein to leak out. Symptoms include loss of appetite and weight, increased urination, and bad breath, but cats may lose two thirds of their kidney function before showing symptoms. Treatment is aimed at reducing pain and keeping minerals in balance through special diets and supplements.

DIABETES

Diabetes is more common in older cats, and seems to be becoming more common. Symptoms include unusually high thirst and urination, dehydration, lethargy, and weight loss in spite of an increased appetite. In type 1 diabetes, the pancreas produces too little insulin, so the body cannot take up sugar from the blood. Insulin injections are often needed, although some cats can take pills instead. In type 2 diabetes, the body's cells have stopped responding to insulin. Insulin is not needed, but a low-calorie, high-fibre diet must be followed.

CIRCULATORY CONDITIONS

The most common form of heart disease is cardiomyopathy, in which the heart muscle enlarges, straining the heart and increasing the pulse rate. It puts a strain on other organs and may cause cold, bluish extremities; fluid also leaks from the lungs into the chest cavity, causing breathing problems. The cat may become lethargic or unconscious. Hypertrophic cardiomyopathy is found at higher levels in some breeds, such as the Maine Coon (see pp 262–67) American Shorthair (see pp 200–203), and Ragdoll (see pp 280–85). Medications have varying degrees of success.

A PROBLEM FOR PETS AND PEOPLE Diabetes is a growing problem in both human and feline populations. The reasons are similar in both cases: a sedentary lifestyle contributing to excess weight.

HEALTHY EATING The right diet makes an enormous contribution to the well-being of your pet, helping to ensure a reasonable weight, sound heart, and functioning kidneys.

Thromboembolisms or blood clots can occur at any age; saddle thrombus, a clot in the aorta to the hind legs, is more common in older cats. Surgery or clot-busting drugs are needed, but many treated cats keep the use of the legs.

CANCER

Cats are not highly susceptible to cancer, although the chances increase with age or in cats infected with FeLV. An early diagnosis is important, but symptoms are vague, so lumps general impressions of unwellness should merit a visit to the vet. Chemotherapy can give short-term remission, and where amputation is necessary, cats usually adapt well. Unspayed females are at greater risk of mammary tumours, but these can be successfully removed if spotted early. For incurable cancers, euthanasia is recommended.

MONITORING AND MAINTAINING HEALTH

Just as you have a family doctor for your own or your family's health, you will need a relationship with your chosen vet for your cat's health. Maintaining your cat's health may involve nothing more than booster vaccinations and parasite treatments until the very end of its life. But a little extra care is worthwhile: early diagnosis and treatment can make all the difference to illnesses.

ANNUAL SERVICE Your cat should be given a thorough check up at the same time as vaccination boosters. This makes changes easier to spot.

MONITORING HEALTH

Cats are very good at pretending that nothing is wrong, even when they are seriously ill. As well as veterinary check ups at the same time as booster vaccinations (*see* pp 112–13), watch for subtle shifts at home. Check weight, eyes, ears, mouth, and skin condition. If you have more than one cat, you may find that a healthy cat treats one that becomes sick differently.

VISITING YOUR VET

Tell the surgery as much as you can about the problem. They may ask you to bring in samples. For urine, try placing a clean tray of litter inside a plastic bag, vacuuming out the air, and sealing the bag: feeling the familiar litter underfoot, the cat will urinate on the plastic, allowing collection of a sample. Ideally, your cat will be used to its carrier (*see* pp 82–83) and can be kept calm at the vet's. If it needs to stay there, leave a familiar blanket and toys, and arrange for it to have its usual food if possible.

HOME NURSING

Cats do not like a lot of fuss when ill. They prefer peace and simple home comforts to recuperate in their own time.
• Provide a warm, comfortable bed in your cat's favourite spot or in a more secluded place.
• Follow your vet's instructions on diet, and give small, frequent meals, warmed to body temperature. If your cat is not drinking, you may need to give water in the same way you administer medicine.
• Confine outdoor cats indoors until completely well again to avoid exposing them to infections, stresses, and other complications.
• Always finish any course of medication, even if your cat appears better. Low levels of infection can remain even when the original symptoms have disappeared.

DO THEY KNOW SOMETHING YOU DON'T? Pay attention to changes in the relationships between your pets: often a cat will notice that another cat in the household is ill before any symptoms show.

GIVING MEDICATIONS

Speed, confidence, and firmness are key to success: cats are seldom fooled by medications hidden in food. If your cat is not co-operative, you may need to enlist help, or wrap it in a blanket and hold it between your knees. If you are worried about all those teeth, use a syringe-like pill dispenser.

1 Grasp the head gently in one hand from above, with forefinger and thumb either side of the muzzle. Tilt the head up slightly; this relaxes the lower jaw.

2 If the mouth opens, put the pill in with your other hand. If not, hold the pill between thumb and forefinger and gently pull the chin down with the middle finger.

3 Hold the mouth shut and wait for the cat to swallow, perhaps stroking the throat. Check the cat does not spit the pill out on release.

HOLD FAST Holding the head firmly from the back and tilting it up makes it hard for a cat to escape or bite you. Give a food treat after to make the job easier next time.

DON'T OVERLOAD Although giving liquid medicines may at first seem like the easier option, there is a risk of choking a cat. Ask for a demonstration at your vet's if you feel unsure.

GIVING LIQUIDS

Liquid medicines are given with a spoon if your cat is willing, or a syringe if it is not. The procedure is much the same as for giving pills, but the head should not be tilted back when you put the liquid in, or the cat may choke. If using a syringe, squirt the liquid gradually into the back of the cheek to trickle into the mouth.

Some thicker liquids or gels can be smeared on the paws; the cat will naturally lick them off. This is an ideal way to administer hairball remedies.

SUPERVISED TREATMENT Keep a free-ranging cat indoors until it has completed a course of medicine and is fully fit. One excursion can mean missed medicine and ineffective treatment.

When to see the vet

Some problems require immediate attention, because they may indicate life-threatening problems like blood clots (see p 115). Others are more general signs of long-term problems, and watching your cat at home for a little longer may help you to give your vet a fuller picture.

Call the vet immediately if your cat shows:
- Breathing difficulties
- Bluish or cold extremities
- Persistent vomiting or diarrhoea
- Staggering or loss of balance
- Extreme lethargy
- Seizures or paralysis
- Difficulties urinating

Investigate and book an appointment for:
- Excessive scratching or licking
- Head shaking
- Coughing or gagging
- Changes in appetite and thirst
- Increased urination
- Increase or loss of weight
- Dull, harsh, or unkempt coat
- Behaviour changes

CATS IN CULTURE

From gods in ancient Egypt to demons in medieval Europe, from everyday mousers to pampered pets, the cat has occupied a range of niches in human society over the millennia since it was first domesticated. Art, literature, and everyday artefacts tell us a great deal about these different roles in the past as well as the present. Perhaps the greatest shift in the role of the cat has come in the 20th century, when it overtook the dog as the most popular pet in many places, and came to occupy a more central role in human affections.

CATS FOR COLLECTORS From the thousands of mummified cats found in ancient Egyptian burial sites, to the arrays of figurines produced for the ornamental market today, the cat has almost always been in strong demand.

THE SPREAD OF THE CAT

If agricultural mouser is the oldest feline profession, ship's cat is surely the second oldest. From Egypt across the Mediterranean to Greece and onwards through Europe, or eastwards to India and beyond, ships took cats to the farthest reaches of the Old World. Later, the descendants of those cats crossed the oceans to reach Australia and the Americas, always working their passage protecting the ship's stores.

PERMANENT FIXTURE Powered by sail, oars, steam, or internal combustion engine, almost every ship that has sailed for over a thousand years has had at least one cat as part of the crew.

LEAVING EGYPT

Some classical sources claim that Egyptians would not sell cats to foreigners, and would buy back any they found abroad and bring them home. This must be taken with a pinch of salt: towards the end of its great dynasties, Egypt was not powerful enough to impose an export ban. Images from before 1000BC show cats aboard Egyptian seagoing ships, and around this time the domestic cat turns up in texts from the Near East. Finds of carvings and bones, however, imply the cat was there much earlier, from around 1700BC, about the time when cats were introduced to Greece.

TRAVELLING CLOTHES As the cat spread, new coat mutations appeared and became concentrated in different places. Solid-coloured and black-and-white cats are first recorded in Greek writings.

GREEK CATS

The earliest Minoan frescoes on Crete show cats in hunting scenes very similar to those of ancient Egyptian art. Nothing suggests that the cat had a religious role at this time, although it was later associated with the goddess Artemis, who was said to transform herself into a cat.

From around 800 to 500BC, after the 'dark ages', the Greek word for cat appears: *ailouros*, meaning 'moving tail'. Also at this time there is the first mention of black-and-white coats, so the cat's appearance had changed significantly from that of its wild ancestors.

In literature from this time, such as Aesop's fables, the cat is a farmyard mouser; the cats of Greece had left their exalted status on the sands of Egypt. Aesop's cats seem familiar to us: they are crafty, opportunistic, and supremely self-centred. The Greek cat seems lived alongside humans, but not as a close companion.

Greece became something of a distribution centre for cats. Settlers sailed to the Balkans, Italy, France, and Spain, taking cats with them; Phoenician traders may also have brought the cat to western Europe.

THE CAT AND THE ROMAN EMPIRE

Cats appear on artefacts from Italy from about 400BC, often under chairs just as in Egyptian art. By the time of the Roman empire, cats appeared in frescoes and floor mosaics, painted on pottery, and carved on funeral memorials. Some depictions suggest that the cat was regarded as a lucky animal, and its image was used to protect a person or place.

Across Europe, finds of cat bones are associated with military sites. The Roman army depended on good supplies, and so needed guardians for those supplies; the cat seems to have worked its way across Europe. But bones from domesticated cats and kittens dating to 250BC, found at a site in Dorset, seem to show that the cat arrived in Britain before the Roman conquest.

Trade with the east was by sea to India and overland to China; by either route, the cats went where the trade went, and they are mentioned in a Hindu poem from India dating to the second century BC. The Roman empire carried on trade with the east, and the cat reached China sometime before the fifth century AD, either overland by the Silk Road, or on one of the many ships that left from Red Sea ports every year.

NEW WORLDS

At the start of the 17th century, colonists sailed to America with their cats, and a whole new continent opened up. A high proportion of cats with extra toes (polydactyl – *see* pp 358–59) among ships' cats has left

True colours

Coat colours today still hint at where cats originally came from. Solid colours are most common on the coast of modern Morocco and in central Britain, suggesting that cats were brought north by Carthaginian traders. The distribution of red and tortoiseshell coats, such as the example below, a later mutation, is different, with the highest concentrations spreading eastwards from Turkey, but there is also a curious concentration in the Faroe Islands, Scotland, and Iceland. This suggests the Vikings brought them there through trade around 1000AD. The ticked tabby pattern common in Asian cats shows the cats that went east were largely north African stock.

a lasting influence on the cats of New England, where this trait is unusually common. This phenomenon is known as the 'founder effect'. When a large population grows from a small initial group – the founder population – the traits in that founder group are obviously multiplied and remain strongly influential in their descendants. A characteristic, such as long hair, extra toes, or a particular coat colour, might be rare in the wider population but is found at a higher concentration in the new population. Mapping the frequency of these traits is a powerful tool for discovering how and even when populations shifted around the world.

It is not clear just when the cat arrived in Australia. Possible early arrivals might have come from occasional contact with Indonesia, or from shipwrecks and landfalls made by early navigators and Dutch shipwrecks, but cats were certainly brought here when Europeans started to settle in the 1780s. Give or take some smaller islands, by the 19th century the cat had padded its way to every inhabited part of the globe.

SACRED CATS

Distinctions between the physical and the spiritual realms, or between humans and animals, were blurred in ancient religions. An Egyptian pharaoh could be simultaneously human and divine, as could the animals associated with the gods and goddesses, such as cats, bulls, and birds. It would be stretching a point to say that these animals were themselves worshipped, but they were treated with reverence. However, it should be remembered that accounts of how the Egyptians treated cats come mainly from outsiders, and like all travellers' tales, they may be exaggerated.

THE RISE OF THE CAT

Cats first appeared on sacred knives and amulets, probably for their ability to kill snakes. Texts called the sun god Ra the 'Great Tomcat', and cats resembling servals were depicted slaying his enemy, the serpent Apophis. Cat-headed figures later appeared as guardians of the gates to the underworld.

Several goddesses, such as the warlike Sekhmet, had lionesses' heads; others, like Hathor, who influenced sexual energy and fertility, had a cat's head; cats under women's chairs in paintings may be a symbol of fertility. The cat-headed Bast, or Bastet, was a protective and maternal goddess. The prominence of her city of Per-Bast, or Bubastis, rose after 945BC as the home of the ruling family; this was a prime time for cats.

STRANGE PRACTICES

The Greek historian Diodorus Siculus wrote that 'whoever kills a cat in Egypt is condemned to death … An unfortunate Roman, who had accidentally killed a cat, could not be saved, either by King Ptolemy of Egypt or by the fear which Rome inspired.' In *Strategems of War*, Macedonian writer Polyaenus claimed that the Persian king Cambyses won the battle of Pelusium in 525BC by arming his soldiers with cats, which the Egyptians would not harm. Perhaps strangest is the account from Herodotus's *Histories*: 'Moreover when a fire occurs, the cats seem to be divinely possessed; for while the Egyptians stand at intervals and look after the cats, not taking any care to

DOOR STAFF The vast sphynx at Giza is world famous, but it is far from unique in its function. Smaller sphynxes were carved in their thousands to flank the doors of burial chambers, guarding the transition from life to death.

OLD GODS NEVER DIE Renewed interest in pagan religions in the 20th century has led to deities like Bastet finding their way back into ritual invocations. Amulets and artworks depicting her are again popular.

extinguish the fire, the cats slipping through or leaping over the men, jump into the fire.' These are secondhand accounts, however, and may be ancient urban myths.

Herodotus also wrote that when a cat died the household went into mourning and took the mummified body to Bubastis. Not all were taken to the sacred city; there are several cat cemeteries near temples. Many of the mummies are of young cats whose necks had been broken, and the grisly conclusion is that cats born around temples were culled to control their numbers and provide offerings for pilgrims at major festivals. Inscriptions show a faith that the cats would become stars in the sky with the gods.

THE SPREAD OF THE CAT CULT

In ancient religions, lions had been associated with earth-mothers and licentious goddesses, like Babylonian Ishtar. Gradually the cat supplanted the lion, and passed into European religions as the animals themselves spread; but as they moved further from their Egyptian roots, the cats were demoted from living representations of goddesses to symbolic companions. Bast was equated with the Greek goddess of the hunt, Artemis; her Roman counterpart, Diana, had a chariot drawn by cats, as did the Norse fertility goddess Freya. The Roman goddess of love, Venus, was also often depicted with a cat.

In Asia, cats were not deities, but were regarded as valuable creatures worthy of respect in the Hindu and Parsee religions, although Buddhism originally looked down on them because a cat was said not to have wept at the funeral of the Buddha, but engaged in hunting rats instead. Cats were, however, always welcome in temples as quiet companions that protected scrolls from mice, and so they acquired a sort of second-hand spirituality. A cat that died would be buried at the temple, and cats were depicted in amulets and statuettes. Across the east there are traditions of luck and rituals associated with different kinds of cats (see pp 128–29); Thailand in particular has traditions surrounding the Siamese (see pp 220–23) and the Korat (see pp 236–39), which appealed to Westerners who imported Oriental breeds.

THE END OF ANIMAL DEITIES

The older religions were supplanted in many places by Christianity and Islam, with a single god and a clear divide between physical and spiritual, humans and animals.

In Islam, there is a tale that a cat saved Prophet Mohammed from a snake bite, another that the markings of the tabby cat were left by the stroking of his hand, and another that he cut off the sleeve of his robe rather than disturb his cat, Muezza, who had fallen asleep in it.

Islam's respect may have contributed to its persecution by European Christians (see pp 126–27), which coincided with the time of the Crusades; there was no systematic persecution of the cat in the Orthodox Christianity practised farther east.

FELINE GLOBALIZATION Cats as symbolic guardians are found around the world, from this cat at a Shinto shrine in Japan to the lions that flank the doors of the New York public library.

TEMPLE CATS The Siamese (*see* pp 220–23) and Birman (*see* pp 276–79) both carry striking patterns and tales of favoured religious status. If today's temples are a guide, a cat of any coat was a welcome worker and companion.

CAT MYTH AND SUPERSTITION

Exalted as sacred, and persecuted as demons, cats have also been subject to any number of superstitions, good and bad, over the centuries. They have had more than their fair share of religious persecution, as well as a wide variety of powers attributed to them, ranging from weather prediction to healing.

EARLY CHRISTIANITY
The ancient folklore of Christianity abounds with positive tales of cats. In one legend, cats were created from the sneeze of a lion on the Ark, when Noah needed a way to keep down the mice; and a cat killed hordes of mice sent

UNLUCKY FOR SOME Solid-coloured cats are less common than tabbies, and a black coat is a good nocturnal disguise; to its enemies, the much-maligned black cat was unnatural and up to no good under cover of night.

HISTORICAL REFERENCE When medieval and Renaissance artists used cats in religious scenes, they were often making a point: Dürer's cat at Eve's feet is a malevolent force. Modern artists play with such references.

by the devil to distract St Francis of Assisi from his prayers. The mouse was often the symbol of the devil in these tales.

PERSECUTION AND REHABILITATION
Despite its usefulness, the cat came to be associated with heresy. The situation was at its worst in the Middle Ages, when there was violent persecution of anyone stepping out of religious line. The cat, an everyday companion but associated with old pagan religions, became a witch's familiar, a demon sent by the devil to help them.

In 1233, Pope Gregory IX decreed the cat diabolical in a Papal bull. As the representatives of the devil, cats were if anything more vulnerable to persecution than their owners; almost certainly, many more were killed. The town of Metz, in France, had a festival during Lent in which cats were publicly burned; this seems to have been most popular in years of bad luck, such as the 1344 outbreak of the disease St Vitus' dance, caused by ergot poisoning. Famously, Ieper or Ypres in Belgium had a tradition of throwing cats from a belfry into the town square at the end of the annual fair.

Belief in the malevolent power of witches faded from the start of the 18th century, until cats were completely rehabilitated. Today in Ypres, stuffed cats are thrown as part of the Kattenstoet festival every three years, complete with performers in feline costume, giant effigies, and a mock witch-burning.

GOOD LUCK AND BAD LUCK

In Russia and Scandinavian countries, putting a cat in a cradle either brought fertility or protection. Sneezing cats might predict colds in the family, future wealth, or simply good luck. A tortoiseshell cat was a bad omen in some places; in others it could see into the future.

In North America, a black cat is bad luck; in Britain it brings good luck. In Germany, which way the cat crosses your path determines the nature of the luck, while in France, finding one white hair on a black cat and plucking it out brings a happy marriage.

WEATHER WATCHING

In Europe, cats repeatedly washing their ears meant rain was coming. Cats clawing at the curtains meant high winds, while those licking their fur the wrong way foretold hail.

In southeast Asia, taking a cat in a basket to every house in a village and sprinkling it with water at each stop petitions the god of weather, Indra, to send rain. In Thailand, the Korat (see pp 236–39) is particularly favoured for this rite.

FURRY FORECAST It has been speculated that cats' ears are sensitive to changes in air pressure before a change in the weather. Sadly, no study has substantiated this as a basis for cats' supposed forecasting abilities.

MANEKI NEKO Modern reproductions of this cat may even have a battery-powered arm that waves back and forth to welcome you and your money.

PROSPERITY

Across Asia, the beckoning cat is a symbol of good luck in business. In Japan it is called Maneki Neko, literally 'beckoning cat'. In Thailand the goddess of prosperity, Nang Kwak, holds her hand up in a similar gesture and sometimes has a cat's tail.

Cats have also been associated with the harvest. This superstition has a dark side, as cats were buried in newly sown fields to ensure a good crop, or slaughtered at harvest. In China, black cats on a farm may portend famine, but in parts of eastern Europe they foretell plenty.

Mummified cats have been found within the fabric old buildings across Britain. One theory is that good mousers were buried after a lifetime's service, to continue their work.

TRUTH OR MYTH? It can be hard to separate Oriental fact from Western fancy in the history of some breeds. Western cat lovers felt that the pointed pattern must mark a cat out as special; whether this was true at home is not always clear.

CATS IN LITERATURE AND ART

From *Puss in Boots*, whose audacity wins his master a title, lands, and the hand of a princess, to Dr Seuss's *The Cat in the Hat*, who causes ever-greater chaos but restores order in the nick of time, cats have long been a favourite literary subject. And although originally mainly valued for their symbolic meaning in art, more recently the grace, poise, and mischievous behaviour of cats has proved a rich source of inspiration to artists.

THE FELINE PERSPECTIVE

Many children's books tell tales from an animal's point of view. The longest-lived example is Judith Kerr's Mog, a black and white cat who lived through decades with the Thomas family and eventually died in *Goodbye Mog*.

A slightly older readership can turn to SF Said's *Varjak Paw* books, tales with a touch of Jedi mysticism and sly undertones about the wilder nature of cute pets. The name seems to be a pun on Paul Varjak, from *Breakfast at Tiffany's* (*see* pp 134–35). Varjak is a misfit in his highly bred, indoor-cat family, who ends up saving the day.

SMUG AND SARCASTIC CATS

Lewis Carroll's Cheshire cat, which fades out of sight leaving nothing but a grin, has a tricky way of answering

THE CAT IN THE HAT The perfect rainy day companion, Seuss's cat is a modern take on 'trickster' folk tales, bringing a little chaos to remind people that there is life beyond the routine.

questions and a general air of self-satisfaction that seem to sum up the feline being.

The cat is often a wry commentator on human folly. Perhaps the most perfect example is the Saki story *Tobermory*, in which a cat with the power of speech wrecks a country party by revealing the guests' private opinions of each other – he comes, inevitably, to a messy end. More circumspect and successful is Lloyd Alexander's Dream-of-Jade. Full of wry wisdom, she runs rings around the Emperor of China's advisers and ends up writing the laws. And *The Rabbi's Cat*, portrayed in comic-book form by Joann Sfar, gains the power of speech and argues the finer points of theology with its owner.

WITCHES' CATS

The literary legacy of Christian persecution is the figure of the witch's cat. Rudyard Kipling's Cat that Walked by Himself is in fact a witch's cat; all the other animals are drawn into serving humans with the aid of magic woven over a fire by the woman, but the cat comes on his own terms and makes himself useful because he chooses too. Most famous among modern witches' cats must be Hermione's cat Crookshanks in the *Harry Potter* books, a huge red tabby with a squashed face and bow legs, who can spot a villain hiding out as a rat. He is based on a real cat that JK Rowling encountered before writing the books.

PUSS IN BOOTS He may appear now as a cute pet, but the original tale tells of a wily old survivor equipped with cunning, nerves of steel, and a killer instinct.

CATS IN ART

The earliest cats in art appear under women's chairs in Egyptian paintings, associated with all things feminine. In European medieval and Renaissance art, some artists included the cat in scenes of the Madonna. Baroccio painted the famous *Madonna del Gatto* and included a slumbering cat in his *Annunciation*.

A less sacred and more sensual use was made of the cat's association with femininity by Japanese artists. The 18th-century Utamaro was one of many who included cats in his many prints of courtesans. His work influenced the 19th-century Impressionists. Most notable was Edouard Manet's *Olympia*, shocking at the time for its portrayal of a bold and composed nude staring out of the canvas, which includes a small black cat at her feet.

SHAKING OFF SYMBOLISM

Much European art until the 18th century was concerned with religious and historical themes and heavily symbolic. Cats are mostly included to symbolize treachery or danger. However, in the 18th century, cats started to appear as a component of a contented domestic scene. American folk art often portrays the cat as a simple domestic companion.

An influential Oriental cat artist was Utagawa Kuniyoshi. He made endless ink drawings of his own cats, completed a famous triptych of 100 cats, and dressed them in kimonos

FACTORY-STYLE ART The original 'Pope of Pop' artist Andy Warhol kept his lively sketches of cats for private publication, but his trademark style of silk-screening has inspired many others seeking fifteen minutes of fame.

in cartoons. In the 20th century, cats proved a very saleable genre. Andy Warhol printed sketches of his cats privately for friends in the 1950s, but they have since become highly popular. Some artists have specialized in cats, with British painter Martin Leman among the first commercial successes.

MYSTERIOUS MEANING Nobody knows who the four people here are, or why they are smiling or laughing. The artist, Niccolo Frangipane, was a 16th-century Venetian painter chiefly of religious scenes.

CATS ON SCREEN

Although cats don't make the reliable, easily trained, obedient performers that are needed for Lassie-style fame, they have played their part onscreen for the whole history of cinema and television – although sometimes they have been drawn, to make life easier. Cats have padded through storylines as support characters and stars, become celebrities in their own right, and given us some of the entertainment world's most iconic images.

THE GENUINE ARTICLE

Real cats on screen are usually the accessories of female characters, and perhaps the most famous is Cat, the ginger tom in *Breakfast at Tiffany's*, who plays spectator to the burgeoning romance of Holly Golightly and her neighbour Paul Varjak. Famously thrown out of Holly's life and then reclaimed in the rain scene at the end of the film, Cat was in fact played by about nine cats in the course of filming. Another ginger tom sidekick is Jones, the Nostromo spaceship's cat and the only character other than Sigourney Weaver's Ripley to make it out alive in *Alien* – a very different female role, but the association with cats seems unshakeable.

Perhaps in a nod to witchy tradition, the two witches in the *Buffy the Vampire Slayer* series, Willow and Tara, adopt a kitten, Miss Kitty Fantastico. Although the kitten only appeared in a few episodes, she achieved cult status and even commemoration in the online community *The Kitten, The Witches and the Bad Wardrobe*.

But one cat is forever associated with a man: Blofeld's Persian from the James Bond film series. Initially, the villain's face was never seen, just a close-up of his hand stroking the pampered feline. This became so famous that the scene has been referred to and parodied down the years, most directly in the *Austin Powers* films, where the supervillain Dr Evil keeps a hairless Sphynx cat.

CAT PEOPLE

The old adage says, 'Never work with animals or children'. One way of including cats without using real cats has been the recurring theme of 'cat people'. The thriller of that title, from 1942, concerned a curse that turned people into black panthers, but the domestic cat has had its share of metamorphoses.

The most famous of these is of course Catwoman, one of the most enduring females from the superhero world – certainly the only one an actress can play without denting her credibility. Her first screen appearance was in the 1960s television series, when Eartha Kitt helped to fix her in the public mind. Later, in the 1990s, Michelle Pfeiffer brought a darker version to the big screen in *Batman Returns*. Halle Berry's less successful *Catwoman* had the outfit, but not the lines.

On television, science fiction series have had fun with the idea of genetically altered cats, like the far future spaceship's cat in *Red Dwarf*, who has evolved

LUCKY EMBLEM In the late 1920s, a US Navy bomber squadron adopted Felix the Cat carrying a bomb as their insignia. After they were disbanded, a fighter squadron took the same 'Tomcatters' insignia.

into human form but kept distinctly feline traits, and the human-feline hybrids of New New York in recent *Doctor Who* storylines.

IF CATS COULD TALK

Movie-makers have also often turned to animated cats. The cartoon cat Felix was the first animated character of the silent era to achieve real star status. While his star waned with the coming of sound, cats animated in cartoons or as computer-generated special effects have never looked back, although the picture is not often

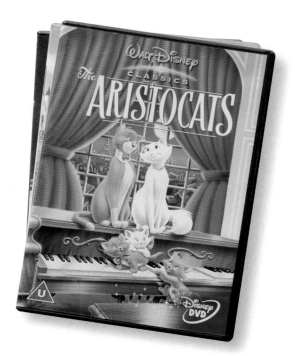

DISNEY RULES Both the setting and the colours of the leading tom and queen were first used in the 1960s musical cartoon *Gay Purr-ee*, but *The Aristocats* has achieved wider fame.

AWARD WINNER The main cat playing Cat in *Breakfast at Tiffany's* was Orangey. Hepburn was nominated for an Oscar for her role in the ever-popular film: Orangey won the animal version, a Patsy.

favourable. Disney's portrayal of Siamese cats in *The Lady and the Tramp* is seen as libellous by cat fans, and the cosy tale of Duchess and her romance with O'Malley the alley cat in *The Aristocats* barely made up for it. Top Cat and his band of slackers taught alley-cat morality, and the endless conflicts of Tom and Jerry filled the lives of thousands of children with suburban violence, something parodied in extreme form by *Itchy and Scratchy*, the cartoon-within-a-cartoon in *The Simpsons*.

An often overlooked animated feline film is *Gay Purr-ee*, from 1962. In turn-of-the-century Provence, Mewsette runs away to the glamour of Paris. Here the unscrupulous Meowrice grooms her to be a mail-order bride for a rich American cat. It features jazzy numbers, artistic pastiches of Monet, Gauguin, Toulouse-Lautrec, and Picasso, the voice of Judy Garland, and exceedingly tortured puns.

More recently, computers have given real cats voice and expression on screen. Notable examples are the family cat who wants to be rid of Stuart Little, and the evil feline masterminds in *Cats and Dogs* – so perhaps the cat hasn't come so very far. But the most catlike cat of recent years is a new interpretation of an old role. Puss in Boots, as portrayed in the *Shrek* films, is suave, sleek, and sophisticated – apart from a tendency to hairballs.

INCREDIBLE JOURNEY The original tale of lost pets finding their family starred a Bull Terrier and a Siamese cat. By the time of 1990s film *Homeward Bound* and its sequel, both had been replaced with cuddlier types for modern viewers.

COLLECTABLE CATS

For some people, just owning a cat is not enough. Dedicated feline enthusiasts may decorate their homes, themselves, their cars, and even their mobile phones with feline imagery of all kinds. Whatever your taste and budget, there is a world of collectables and ephemera available to suit. Not all of it is new, either: cats have been popular for a long time, and there are vintage and antique items to seek out as well.

FELINE FACE Masks for carnivals or balls are made to be elegant and desirable, and cats have always been a popular theme.

CARTOON CATS

Although cats were exalted in ancient Egypt, cartoons of cats herding geese, waiting on rats, or defending fortresses against armies of mice also appear in satirical papyrus scrolls and on scraps of stone or pottery.

In the late 19th century cats began appearing in European cartoons and comic strips. Theophile Steinlen

RETRO COLLECTION Cats can appear in the oddest places, from fireworks to everyday household objects. Items like this decorated tin box often be found for quite reasonable prices, and have their own naive charm.

drew naturalistic cats in his *Sans Paroles* cartoon sequences, while British artist Louis Wain, now highly collectable, depicted his human-like cats fully dressed or engaged in activities like golf.

The surreal *Krazy Kat*, which ran from 1913 to 1944, was one of the most influential cartoons ever. Centred on Krazy Kat's unrequited love for Ignatz the mouse (who throws bricks in return), it has been praised by intellectuals and art critics, and cited as an influence by many later cartoonists.

FELICITATIONS Picture postcards have been collected since they first appeared in the 1890s. Cats feature on good luck, Halloween, Christmas, and greetings cards.

ADVERTISING CATS

Cats have been used to advertise products for centuries, from gin to matches. The secret of this popularity is in the colour of the cat: almost all are black, and in the days before inexpensive colour printing, the need for a strong black and white image made a stylized cat an attractive choice for many.

ORNAMENTAL CATS

For those with the odd shelf to fill, there are figurines to collect. Distinctive and popular breeds, such as the Siamese (*see* pp 220–23), are reproduced in their thousands in china. For those with a more international view, there are Maneki Nekos (*see* p 127) to collect. Of course, there are fluffy stuffed cats aplenty on the market. The classic German toy company Steiff has been making cats of various styles for decades, both as children's toys and increasingly for collectors. Today, there are even taxidermists who will preserve passed-on pets for owners who just can't say goodbye.

Top cats

When one thinks of cartoon cats that have achieved fame and wealth, one of the first to spring to mind is of course Jim Davis's Garfield. Challenging him, however, is Sanrio's Hello Kitty, a white cartoon cat with a signature bow by her ear, created for children in the 1970s. She is now a fashionable brand for adults, with pop stars, models, and celebrities wearing her merchandise.

FANCY FIGURINES Whether you favour the naturalistic, the stylized, the prettified, or the kitsch, there is a wealth of figurines for cat collectors.

BREEDS AND SHOWS

Although the cat fancy is not much more than a century old, it would be wrong to think that we did not influence feline appearance before this. We may not have controlled cats' breeding choices, but we decided which cats were cherished and which surplus kittens were disposed of, and we took cats to new climates; all this fostered solid-coloured coats, a new range of patterns, and the longhaired gene. The earliest 'breeds' were simply recognitions of local variations that had evolved as a result of these choices; only in the 20th century did the fancy become creative, with an explosion of new breeds.

HYBRID PIONEER A new departure in breeding, the Bengal was the first recognized breed with an ancestry beyond the African wildcat.

THE START OF THE CAT FANCY

As working animals, dogs had been bred and shown for centuries before cats got in on the act. And when they did, at the end of the 19th century, it was a beauty pageant from the start. The only way to classify cats for showing was to go by their looks and their history. All the early breeds were geographical and historical 'types', and even today the differences between many cat breeds are principally aesthetic.

EARLY CAT SHOWS IN BRITAIN

Cat shows of a sort have been going on at country fairs for centuries. The earliest recorded took place at St Giles Fair in Winchester in 1598. This was more like a working dogs show, with prizes in categories like 'best ratter'.

The first official cat show in the modern sense was held at Crystal Palace in London in July 1871. The cats appearing at this show were not working mousers, but the elite pets of the leisured classes – although there was a class for 'cats owned by working men'. The event was

WINNERS TAKE ALL The scale and aim of cat shows has changed greatly since they began. The first show aimed to make cats valued and improve their welfare, but prizes captured the exhibitors' imagination more.

organized by writer and artist Harrison Weir, who sat as a judge and wrote all the breed standards. Queen Victoria purchased two blue Persians at the show, giving a royal seal of approval both to cats and cat shows. Weir went on to found the National Cat Club (NCC), which is the oldest surviving club today.

By the turn of the century breeding and showing was well established in Britain, with classes for native breeds like the British Shorthair and Manx, and exotic imports like the Siamese and Abyssinian. In 1910, the Governing Council of the Cat Fancy was founded, and became the largest association in Britain.

THE AMERICAN STORY

The start in the United States was slightly later than in the United Kingdom. Informal cat shows had also existed there for a long time before the first 'official' show, which had 176 entries and was held at Madison Square Garden in New York in May 1895, organized by Mr James T Hyde. The Best Cat crown was claimed by a Maine Coon.

After several clubs made false starts, the American Cat Association (ACA) was formed in 1904, making it the oldest American registry surviving today. But the cat fancy in North America had a quarrelsome start. A splinter group from the ACA formed the Cat Fanciers' Association (CFA) in 1906, and this registry has come to dominate. Yet another splinter in 1919 led to the formation of the Cat Fanciers' Federation (CFF), which still survives.

A feminine business

Although the first two cat shows were organized by men, the cat fancy was from the start overwhelmingly female, a situation that still persists to some extent today. Early lists of breeders and exhibitors are full of married women, drawn from the social classes that had the time and money to pursue this new hobby. And money was needed: even in 1900, the most valuable cat in the United States was Napoleon the Great, whose owner turned down an offer of $4,000.

EARLY BREEDING AIMS

The number of cat breeds recognized was relatively small at first, and the breeds were types that already existed. All the breeders were doing was preserving known types and breeding them to each other. Of course in doing so they aimed to perpetuate or 'fix' the best characteristics and breed out perceived flaws, like the squints, kinked tails, and white toes of the Siamese. That the breeds changed over the years is obvious, but the changes were gradual and did not seem to be making something new, merely perfecting something old.

Later in the 20th century came a surge in numbers both of new breeds and of new registries. The two are not unconnected, because those with the desire to create something new came into conflict with those who merely wished to preserve the old, and schisms were inevitable.

SIAMESE SQUINT Early Siamese (see pp 220–23) arrived with crossed eyes and a host of tales to explain them. The trait was even included in the early breed standard.

PADDY PAWS The Maine Coon (see pp 262–67) was the first 'show' breed in the United States, with local competitions in New England from the 1860s before the first Madison Square show.

REGISTRIES WORLDWIDE TODAY

The world of cat breeding and showing changed a great deal in the course of the 20th century. Understanding of the genetic codes that underpinned different characteristics brought a new scientific approach to breeding, and increased international travel brought examples of new types and breeds from around the world. New ideas and literally new blood came into cat breeding, and inevitably there were disagreements and splits.

SEEDS OF DISCORD

Many of the older registries (*see* pp 140–41) are still slow to accept change. Many more recently formed organizations, on the other hand, are eager to accept the new. From the start there have been differences of opinion and rival registries, and with new grounds for argument, fault lines developed into schisms. New 'man-made' breeds were not the only source of argument; changing the looks of older breeds was another. Traditionalists felt, for example, that it was better to keep cats as they had looked for the history of the fancy than to encompass every colour. Others asked why they should not have every breed in every colour?

ONE COLOUR, TWO BREEDS
In most associations, this is a red-point Siamese. But in CFA standards, this 'newer' colour remains a Colorpoint Shorthair.

INTERNATIONAL SPLIT Sometimes one breed can develop two different ways internationally, as with the UK and US versions of the Cornish Rex (*see* pp 310–17).

THE BIRTH OF TICA

In CFA, breeders are members of clubs, which in turn are members of CFA. Some members, who wanted to control their association directly, formed The American Cat Fanciers' Association (ACFA), but in 1979 this split, and The International Cat Association (TICA) was formed. It was instantly popular, and came to be the second biggest association in North America, with affiliates internationally.

TICA is a 'genetic' registry: they class cats by genotype and show them by looks, or phenotype. TICA has also always been open to innovation, and has many newer breeds on its books; once a breed has achieved full recognition here, it is easier to win it elsewhere.

EUROPE AND BEYOND

The Fédération Internationale Féline (FIFé), founded in 1949, is based in Europe, but has members in 36 countries. Like TICA, it is a direct membership organization and a genetic registry, but it has a strong bias against breeds with traits that might harm the cats' welfare.

The World Cat Federation (WCF), founded in 1988 in Brazil, now has clubs in several countries, with a extremely strong showing in the Russian Federation and eastern Europe, with a particular interest in emerging local breeds.

COMMONWEALTH COUNTRIES

The Canadian Cat Association was formed in 1960. Canadian breeders also exhibit in TICA and CFA shows. The Australian Cat Federation (ACF) was formed in 1972, and has strong links with FIFé. Since 1980, Australia has also had the Co-ordinating Cat Council of Australia (CCC of A). The New Zealand Cat Fancy (NZCF) is a liberal registry, encouraging 'do-it-yourself' creativity; Catz Inc is even more adventurous, recognizing breeds like the polydactyl Clippercat (*see* p 358). The South African cat is broadly represented by the Southern Africa Cat Council (SACC), which recognizes many rexed breeds as well as the Scottish Fold and Munchkin (*see* pp 354–57).

INTERNATIONAL CO-OPERATION

The nearest thing the cat-showing world has to the United Nations is the World Cat Congress (WCC), founded in

BREED IN EXILE
Although the Scottish Fold (*see* pp 346–49) derives from a Scottish farm cat, it is mainly recognized by associations in North America.

2001. It has several major national organizations as members: FIFé, CFA, TICA, WCF, ACF, NZCF, CCC of A, GCCF, and SACC. The aim is for showing categories, standards, and names to be less confused internationally. These organizations often compete for members: the move to co-operation is a novel development.

PUBLIC SPECTACLE From the start, cat shows have not been just for the exhibitors. The very first one-day show in London was soon followed by a three-day show due to public demand, and the popularity keeps growing.

PREPARING A CAT FOR A SHOW

Showing is not as simple as turning up with a cat in a carrier and having it judged: both physical and psychological preparation of the cat are important as well. Long before the show, advance training is in order. Closer to the time, there are some special beauty treatments undertaken for a show, in addition to the usual good grooming you would give a cat day-to-day.

BORN TO IT There are kitten classes at shows, which allow young cats to get used to wearing their ribbons and take hustle and bustle in their stride.

LONG-TERM PREPARATIONS

A cat needs to be completely calm when handled by strangers at a show, because any fearful or aggressive behaviour results in disqualification. It should be used to standing on a table and having its mouth and ears examined: make this a regular part of grooming. A cat that is unused to wearing a collar may fret at wearing its identifying tag on a ribbon around its neck, so getting used to this is a must. Your cat will also need to travel to the show in a carrier and stay in pens at the show for hours, so get it used to being calm in a confined space.

Before any show, a cat must be thoroughly checked for general health. If the show has 'vetting in', an unwell cat will be turned away, but it is not worth showing a cat in anything less than perfect condition anyway.

SHOW GROOMING

Although a cat may keep its coat perfectly clean and tidy, and good health is the best guarantee of a good gloss, a little extra help may achieve the best result. Long coats benefit from powdering, with talcum powder or Fuller's earth, while a bran bath brings out the sheen on short coats.

Bran bath for short coats

❶ Heat about 180 g (6 oz) of bran in the oven to a little warmer than hand temperature. It is rubbed into the coat against the direction of growth to ensure that it gets down to the roots.

❷ Leave the bran in the coat for as long as the cat will tolerate it – at least a few minutes. Then brush it out – any brush will do, although a wire 'slicker' is most effective. All traces of the bran must be removed from the coat before the show.

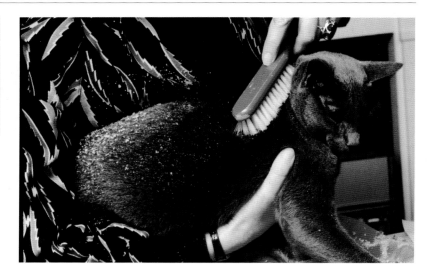

THE DAY BEFORE PREPARATION

The day before a show, the claws must be clipped, and the ears, eyes, nose, and anal regions made spotlessly clean. White paws may also need a last minute wash.

All in all, it should be clear why show cats need not only early practice but a rock-solid temperament: this may even be exerting a selective pressure on pedigree characters (*see* p 79).

Bathing your cat

If the cat is dirty, a wet bath (using a shampoo known to be safe for cats) may be necessary; this should be done at least a week before the show, because it can make the hair temporarily lifeless, especially on longhaired cats. The coat must be combed before bathing, as the water will make any tangles worse, and continuously combed as it is dried with warm air, to avoid new tangles; these cannot be cut out, because a clipped coat means no showing. Shorthaired cats can often get away without a bath, but with 'spot cleaning' of any troublesome areas.

Powder bath for long coats

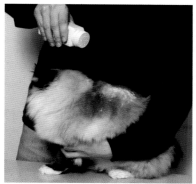

❶ After careful grooming to remove any debris and tangles, the coat is brushed the wrong way and saturated with the powder down to the roots. With a particularly long coat, like a Persian, this stage alone can take hours.

❷ Once it has had a chance to absorb excess oil, the powder is brushed out. It is vital that every trace of powder be removed, because any powder visible in the coat during judging can mean disqualification.

PICTURE PERFECT Daily wiping of the face and regular care of ears is vital for top show cats, sometimes together with special preparations.

SHOWING A CAT

For the spectator, a cat show can be an entertaining experience with unrivalled shopping opportunities for accessories; for exhibitors, it means hard work and nail-biting tension. The organization of shows varies from one association to another, with not only different rules about which cats can be shown, but different arrangements for how they are shown, vetting in, and the way prizes are awarded.

CAN YOU ENTER?

Some registries only allow cats registered with them to be shown; others operate an 'open door' policy of showing cats registered with other recognized registries, although cats will need to be registered with them to claim titles or progress to greater success. Household pets are usually welcome at shows, judged in their own separate class, but check what constitutes a household pet for that registry.

GETTING THE PAPERWORK RIGHT

All associations need entry paperwork submitted well in advance. Within the registries there are different categories, and there are different types of show in each association's calendar. How cats progress through different levels of award also varies from one association

MOMENT OF TRUTH Judges are experienced breeders themselves, usually with many years' experience. There are qualifications within each association, and some are recognized across associations.

LESS IS MORE These pens are adorned with nothing more than the prizes won by the cat in the course of this show. This is less colourful than a ring show, but easier to run in many ways.

to another. Terminology can be confusing: for example, the term 'novice' means in FIFé a cat seeking recognition in a breed but unable to prove its background, but in CFA a cat not yet registered, regardless of pedigree.

THE JUDGING

Some associations, such as TICA, CFA, and FIFé, have 'ring' shows, where the cats are kept in pens outside the show area until their class is called. Because the cats are removed to a separate hall for judging, these pens are allowed to be highly decorated. Owners use linings, curtains, rosettes from previous wins, whatever takes their fancy, making ring shows more spectacular. In other associations, including GCCF, the cats are kept in one pen, in which they are judged. To rule out any subtle influence on the judges' opinions, the owners are excluded during judging and these cages are all identical. The exception to this rule is the Supreme Show, which is a ring show.

TOP CAT Only the cats that come top in ordinary shows can be entered into higher levels of competition such as Supreme shows and Cat of the Year awards.

BREEDING

Cats are famously fertile, and most queens are instinctively excellent mothers. Nonetheless, breeding cats, be they pedigree or moggie, should not be undertaken lightly for either fun or profit. While it is true that domestic cats have bred freely for centuries, the consequence of this freedom has almost always been a surplus of kittens, which were often disposed of in ways that we generally find unacceptable today.

DECIDING TO BREED

Some regard calls for pet neutering from breeders of pedigree cats as aimed at protecting a profitable market. The truth is that good, responsible breeders are unlikely to make much profit, once registration, showing fees, stud fees, veterinary bills, and other costs are taken into account. Animal welfare charities also call for neutering, and their only interest is to reduce the numbers of unwanted cats, often young, in overcrowded shelters. Breeding without known homes for the kittens is irresponsible. The old idea that a female cat should have one litter before being spayed, for physical or psychological well-being, is now discounted, and vets safely neuter cats before they reach sexual maturity, which has many advantages (*see* p 33).

FICKLE FASHION All kittens are adorable, but when a new breed or a new look captures the public eye, even pedigree kittens are subject to the laws of the free market and vagaries of popularity.

MATCHMAKING Cats do not make matches for life, and pedigree cats do not even choose their own mates. Photographs may be exchanged, the breeders will meet and see each other's cats.

PREPARING TO BREED

For pedigree breeders, the work starts not with a queen in heat, but with paperwork, photographs, shows, and genetic charts. Because the owner of a top show cat will not want their name on the pedigrees of less successful cats, a lot of time and work in showing is needed before a match. Of course, this puts breeders who feel that there is something wrong with the breed standards at a disadvantage; for example, breeders who disliked many modern standards set up the Traditional Cat Association (see p 154). Reputable breeders will try to continue working with other like-minded breeders within a structure of some sort, rather than striking out on their own with a tiny number of cats and no second opinion on their practices.

Once a cat is established and ready to mate, there are bloodlines to be checked for undesirable inbreeding, possible health problems, and desired traits such as colour, followed by a range of current health checks and blood tests. Only when all these boxes are ticked does the physical work begin.

GETTING DOWN TO BUSINESS

Although feline courtship is not prolonged, and familiarity is not always necessary for a successful mating, some courtship is helpful. At the very least, swapping items with the two cats' scents on them can help to break the ice. Once together, the male may follow and physically court the female. The queen dictates the timing of mating, and no intervention will speed it up or slow it down.

The queen will roll and purr, and if stroked along her back may lower her body to the ground and raise her rump, flicking her tail to one side, a display position called lordosis. At first the male simply sniffs, and if he moves too fast may be physically attacked: an experienced male watches the female carefully for signs of increasing readiness, and takes his time.

When she is ready, the queen crouches in lordosis, and the male mounts her, ejaculates almost immediately, and withdraws, all within about thirty seconds. The pain of the barbed penis withdrawing (see p 46) provokes the female to howl and turn on him. It is important that there is somewhere for the male to escape to, like a chair or shelf, at this point; mating cats should not be confined in a small space.

Both cats keep their distance as they groom themselves, calming and cooling down. The pain does not dissuade the queen, who will initiate mating again quite soon, perhaps within twenty minutes. This can continue for hours or days, and breeders usually put the cats together several times over two or three days. During this time the queen must be kept away from all males to be sure of the parentage; left to her own devices, she may mate with another and produce a mixed litter (see p 47).

BLATANT ADVERTISING Most queens in heat roll, squirm, and rub up against everyone, leaving their intentions in no doubt. But there is always the occasional demure one, who comes home pregnant with no warning.

PREGNANCY AND KITTENING

A feline pregnancy lasts about two months; at the start a queen is tranquil and placid, but she will become restless as the birth approaches. Cats usually cope well with pregnancy and birth, rarely requiring any outside assistance. Good nutrition and care during pregnancy, a warm, secure birthing spot, and an attentive eye in case of trouble, are usually all that is needed.

BULKING UP A pregnant queen usually looks fairly normal until almost halfway through the pregnancy. After this, the kittens' increasing size will make her visibly bulkier, and she will slow down in her activity.

THE PROGRESS OF PREGNANCY
The first sign of pregnancy comes at around 14 to 21 days, when the nipples become firmer and 'pink up' and the belly usually begins to swell visibly. By about 30 days, a vet or an experienced breeder may count the kittens by careful feeling, but the bones are still soft. After 45 days the bones will show on an x-ray, but there is always some level of risk associated with radiation, and many

vets recommend against it. Avoid medications during pregnancy, and never vaccinate a pregnant queen, or any other cats in the house that may 'shed' vaccine.

In the early stages of pregnancy a cat should be active, to keep fit for the birth. Quality of diet is more important at first than quantity; deficiencies can contribute to loss of kittens or birth defects. Commercial foods carry recommendations for adjusting feeding, perhaps giving highly nutritious kitten food. Most foetal growth happens after day 24, and demand for food usually increases steadily before dropping off just before delivery. Feeding more frequently, up to four times a day, is the best way to meet the mother's needs.

PREPARING FOR THE BIRTH
Put together a birthing kit; in most cases, these items need not be used, but be prepared.
• A notepad to record how long deliveries are taking, because this is the first alert for any possible problems, and scales to check the kittens' weights.
• Disposable gloves, antibacterial handwash, and clean facecloths in case you need to move or rub the kittens.
• Clean, blunt-tipped, sharp scissors, thread, and an antiseptic suitable for cats in case you have to cut and tie off the umbilical cords.
• A carrier, in case a trip to the vet is necessary.

CARE DURING AND AFTER BIRTH
Birth usually progresses smoothly (*see* pp 48–49). Some cats prefer to be alone, others like the comfort of a familiar

Birthing place

Although the queen's favourite spot to lie may be her owner's bed or a sunny seat, she is unlikely to give birth here. She needs to feel secure, often with walls on all sides, so will usually pick a more secluded location. As soon as she starts scouting out her 'nest', provide a box with layers of bedding, perhaps already used by her. Place it somewhere warm and secluded, or where she seems to be looking, but do not be offended if she does not use it; just be grateful if she does not choose somewhere too inaccessible.

VITAL TOUCH You can and should handle kittens from birth for good socialization. A domesticated cat will not reject handled kittens, because she is used to your smell and lives in your home.

voice: all do best when given peace and quiet. A sign of trouble is the mother pushing heavily for over 45 minutes without a kitten emerging, although a break of more than a few hours during delivery is not unusual. There is some evidence that pedigree breeds have less trouble-free deliveries than moggies, with more stillbirths and some breeds having difficulties in as many as 22 per cent of births. New breeders are usually advised to work with an experienced breeder as a mentor until they become used to dealing with problems.

Each kitten should be given a quick visual check and weighed. Once all have been born and are nursing, remove any uneaten placentas and soiled bedding. It is natural for mothers to move their kittens after birth, so have a fresh bedding box similar to the birthing box ready – but don't be surprised if she has ideas of her own.

The most important care to give the new family is to make sure that the mother is well fed, because she fuels all the kittens' growth (see p 49) through her milk. Weigh the kittens daily; this is the best way to monitor progress and spot problems early. The handling also socializes the kittens, and the mother cat will not reject the kittens.

SIMPLE CHECK
Weigh kittens immediately after birth, before putting them to suckle, to give a good baseline to judge their development. Weigh them daily after this.

BREED STANDARDS

By and large, breed standards are all about aesthetics. Dogs have been bred to hunt, herd, retrieve, or guard, horses to race, pull, or carry, even cattle to provide milk or meat; these practical requirements have affected what the different breeds look like. All anyone has ever required of a pedigree cat is that it should be beautiful, so the breeds are largely 'art for art's sake', created for no other purpose than to adorn the world.

THE RULES OF BEAUTY

Some requirements of breed standards are common across all breeds and almost all associations. The common traits that will lead to a cat being disqualified are undescended testicles in male cats, an abnormal number of toes, kinked tails, and crossed eyes. Other disqualifications are more idiosyncratic: CFA usually disallows white lockets or buttons.

Breed standards set out the maximum points that can be awarded for each area of the cat's appearance, which will be added up to give the total score out of 100. The allocation of points is not the same for all breeds, because different traits are more or less important in each. The traits that are required in the breed are described under specific headings of head, eyes, ears, body, legs, colour, and so on. The descriptions can be quite lyrical, although they tend to be less open to interpretation nowadays.

HEALTH ISSUES

Breed standards emphasize health and general conformity. General requirements, such as cleanness of eyes, ears, and nose, should mean that only a healthy cat can win prizes and influence the future of the breed. Other requirements, such as a normal number of toes and a kink-free tail, aim to breed out any physical deformities lurking in the genes. Breeds with traits that may inherently harm the cat's welfare, such as the Manx (see pp 332–37), which in its completely tailless show form is prone to several serious congenital defects, remain contentious.

GOLD STANDARD Most breed standards allow more colours today, like the 'golden' shades.

DISTINCTIVE FEATURE With its characteristic ticked pattern and rich colour, the Abyssinian coat carries a high number of points in the standards of all major registries.

NEW TRENDS IN CAT BREEDING

To understand why there is such a wide variety of breeds and breed associations, and why they inspire such passion, one needs to look at why breeders put in so much time, effort, and money to have cats from a particular bloodline win a particular beauty contest. Where did this variety come from, and perhaps more importantly, where is it going?

PRESERVING THE OLD

There are those who complain that historic breeds have moved away from the natural original. In some cases, this has resulted in new breed clubs and even registries, such as the Traditional Cat Association (TCA). Mainstream breeders say that the modern, supermodel look of Siamese (*see* pp 220–23) is a 'refinement' of the original; those who disagree with this interpretation breed TCA Traditional Siamese and 'Old-style Siamese' in the United Kingdom.

OLD AND NEW The Siberian (*see* pp 274–75) is said to be an old breed, naturally developed in Russia's cold eastern expanses; it is new in the west, however, emerging only after the Iron Curtain fell away.

NEW BREEDS

At the start of the cat fancy, there were very few breeds, all of them existing types. Today, even the most conservative registries recognize over thirty breeds, the more liberal over fifty, many of them man-made.

FACT OR FICTION? Disagreement still continues between aficionados who see the Birman (*see* pp 276–79) as an eastern temple cat and ancient breed, and cynics who suspect it is a French fancy first concocted in the 1920s.

Some of these are foreign imports, long known in a distant land but new elsewhere. Other breeds exist purely because somebody found them beautiful. The creator of the Burmilla was simply enchanted with the offspring of an accidental cross, and perpetuated them. Once the genetics behind feline traits were understood, people didn't just dream of their perfect cat: they set out to create it.

RUNNING WILD

One trend of recent years has been the rise of the 'wild cat', for those who really want a tiger on the hearth. The first hint of things to come was the spotted Ocicat (*see* pp 250–51) and the briefly popular California Spangled (*see* pp 252–53). The next step was not to imitate wild cats, but create real hybrids. The first and most widely accepted was the Bengal (*see* pp 362–67), but others followed (*see* pp 368–69). Hybrids remain contentious: some hold that they are beautiful and tractable, others that they are unpredictable, often abandoned, and unhealthy.

THE DOG IN DISGUISE

The other, strangely contrasting trend of recent years has been the 'lap cat'. The classic of this type is the Ragdoll (*see* pp 280–85), a breed whose unique selling point was the claim that it flopped placidly like a ragdoll when picked up. Much of the mystique was hype, but the breed's instant appeal showed that as the cat overtook the dog in popularity, what many people wanted was a dog-like cat. This has led to a change in how existing cat breeds are described. While once the aloof, regal image of the cat was iconic, breeders these days emphasize cuddliness and dependence.

CONTROVERSIAL CAT Few breeds have a beginning as eccentric or dogged with wild claims as that of the Ragdoll, but it has turned out to be a healthy, popular breed.

X FACTOR The Bengal (*see* pp 362–67) is an interspecies hybrid, but most kittens born today are several generations away from an original cross. Breeding policies with regard to outcrosses vary internationally, with outcrosses generally diminishing worldwide.

CAT COLOURS

Genetically, colours are black- or red-based, but other early divisions still influence breed standards. The typically 'Western' colours of black, blue, red, cream, tortie, and blue tortie were the first colours recognized. Imported Oriental cats brought the 'Eastern' shades of chocolate, lilac, cinnamon, fawn, and caramel. These were not allowed in traditional Western breeds for a long time, while Oriental breeds were not recognized in red shades, although these existed in the East.

WHAT MAKES SOLID COLOURS?

Cats' coats, and our skins, are both coloured by melanin. This is made up of eumelanin (black and brown), and phaeomelanin (red and yellow). Coat colours are produced by genes modifying these two; as well as the major genes described here, groups of 'polygenes' influence the warmth of any colour, known as rufousing.

Solid colour or melanism is caused by a recessive version of the tabby or agouti gene. One copy of the dominant form (*A*–) makes a cat tabby (*see* pp 162–65), but two copies of the recessive form (*aa*) make it solid. Because two copies of the recessive form are needed, melanism is uncommon; add to this the

EASTERN SHADES Lilac is the chocolate mutation of the black gene modified by the dilute gene, and is regarded as an 'Oriental' colour.

camouflage disadvantage, and it is obvious why black cats are rare in the wild.

EUMELANISTIC COLOURS

The browning gene affects eumelanin and has three forms that give black (*B*–), chocolate (*bb*), and cinnamon (*b'b'*). It can be modified by the dense pigment gene, which gives dense colour in its dominant form (*D*–); the recessive form (*dd*), 'dilutes' black to blue, chocolate to lilac, and cinnamon to fawn.

There is thought to be a dilute modifier gene, which in its dominant form (*D^m*–) turns blue, lilac, and fawn to caramel or taupe, leaving them unaffected in its recessive form (*d^m d^m*). Some dispute this, even suggesting that some form of the inhibitor gene (*see* pp 160–61) may be responsible.

PAINTED BLACK The solid black or self coat was one of the first mutations to occur after the cat was domesticated, being recorded in ancient Greece.

SPICE TRADE Cinnamon was recognized after the other eumelanistic shades, and confirmed as a mutation of the black gene in 2004.

Solid coat colours

Dense colour	Dilute colour	Modified colour
Black *B– D–*	Blue *B– dd d^{m}d^m*	Caramel *B– dd D^m–*
Chocolate *bb D–*	Lilac *bb dd d^{m}d^m*	Caramel *bb dd D^m–*
Cinnamon *b^{l}b^l D–*	Fawn *b^{l}b^l dd d^{m}d^m*	Taupe *b^{l}b^l dd D^m–*
Red *O– D–*	Cream *O– dd d^{m}d^m*	Apricot *O– dd D^m–*
Tortoiseshell *B– D– Oo*	Blue tortie *B– dd Oo d^{m}d^m*	Caramel tortie *B– dd D^m– Oo*
Chocolate tortie *bb D– Oo*	Lilac tortie *bb dd Oo d^{m}d^m*	Taupe tortie *bb dd D^m– Oo*
Cinnamon tortie *b^{l}b^l D– Oo*	Fawn tortie *b^{l}b^l dd Oo d^{m}d^m*	Brown tortie *b^{l}b^l dd D^m– Oo*

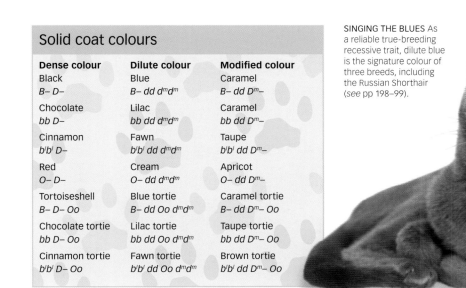

SINGING THE BLUES As a reliable true-breeding recessive trait, dilute blue is the signature colour of three breeds, including the Russian Shorthair (*see* pp 198–99).

PHAEOMELANISTIC COLOURS

The orange gene in its recessive form (*o*) lets eumelanistic colours through. In its dominant form (*O*), it gives phaeomelanistic red; the dense and dilute modifier genes that affect eumelanistic colours also act on this gene, producing cream and apricot. *O* also suppresses the *aa* trait, letting tabby markings show. This gene is sex-linked, because it is located on the X chromosome. Males have only one X chromosome, so are either *O* or *o*. Because females have two X chromosomes, they can have red shades (*OO*), eumelanistic shades (*oo*), or tortoiseshell (*Oo*), a mix of red and black. Depending on the browning and dilution genes carried, there are different colours and shades of tortie. Male torties are rare, and often sterile, because they have genetic or cellular abnormalities.

the eumelanistic shades. Black or blue cats fade over time to become amber or a pale tan, except on their paw pads and along the spine. These shades were thought at first to be chocolate and cinnamon from an accidental cross, but test breeding and microscopic examination of hairs has disproved this. These new 'x colours' have been called 'fox' but 'amber' has gained more approval. The proposed name for the gene is *B^m*.

A NEW MODIFIER?

The Norwegian Forest Cat seems to have a new mutation that changes

MIXED MESSAGES In tortoiseshell cats, the mix of red and black areas is naturally random, although breed standards call for specific colour distributions.

STRIPED, BLOTCHED, AND SPOTTED TABBIES

The stripes of the tabby pattern are made up of crisply defined areas of solid hairs set against areas of banded or striped hairs. All cats are tabbies in their genes. They may have other genetic traits that cover up or suppress their pattern, but every cat carries a tabby pattern, a reminder of its wild past hidden beneath the modern sophistication of different coat colours and shadings.

WHAT MAKES A TABBY

When a banded hair starts to grow, it is dark. At a predetermined point, pigment production slows, producing a lighter band, then increases again, producing a darker band. The lighter banding, called agouti, can be seen in both eumelanistic black shades and phaeomelanistic reds (*see* pp 158–59). The colour of the coat is that of the darker bands, so a 'brown' tabby is genetically a black;

MACKEREL STRIPES The word tabby appears around 1638, describing a fabric from Baghdad. By 1695, it was used for tabby cats, whose markings resembled the fabric.

TRUE COLOURS Sometimes 'ghost' tabby markings can be seen on a plain cat. If these are strong, it may be hard to say what is a self with ghost markings and what is a weakly defined tabby.

and although the agouti band on a brown tabby is yellowish, is is not the yellow of phaeomelanin, but 'shredded' eumelanin pigment.

Conflicting theories propose that all tabby patterns are different forms of one gene, called T, or that they are controlled by at least two genes, M^c and T: both notations are given here.

HIDDEN TABBIES

The main gene that controls whether a cat looks tabby or not is the agouti gene or allele. The dominant form ($A–$) shows the tabby pattern, but the recessive (aa) gives solid coats (*see* pp 158–159). It works on black-based colours, but the gene for sex-linked orange lets the tabby patterns shine through. The other main suppressor of tabby patterns, the inhibitor gene, gives smoke and shaded colours (*see* pp 164–65). In some combinations, this restricts colour to the tip of the hair, so no pattern is seen at all.

The various albino and white spotting patterns that give pointed (*see* pp 166–67) and white (*see* pp 168–69) cats also mask tabby over most or all of the coat.

STRIPES, BLOTCHES, AND SPOTS

The basic tabby pattern of the African wildcat is striped. This is called mackerel in the domestic cat, and is caused by the dominant T or M^c gene. This was the coat that the cat wore for the first few thousand years of its domestic life, and is still the most common tabby pattern.

Much later a new pattern appeared: the blotched or classic tabby. In this, the plain and agouti areas produce a swirling pattern, usually with a central blotch or 'bullseye' on the flank. This is a recessive mutation of the striped tabby gene, written t^b or m^c. Because it is recessive, cats need two copies of it to show the blotched tabby pattern, and it remains less frequent in moggies. It is most common in Britain, spreading through France and western Europe.

The lines of both patterns may be broken up into spots, probably by a separate gene, the spotted tabby modifier. Its dominant form (S^p-) gives a spotted coat; its recessive

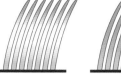

TABBY HAIR TYPES The lighter areas of the tabby coat have banded hairs (*left*); this is called 'agouti' after a small South American rodent. The darker markings are made of solid coloured hairs (*right*).

form ($s^p s^p$) lets unbroken pattern show. African wildcat markings are variable, and this may be an ancient pattern. Breeders of some spotted cats argue that there must be other spotting genes, because the spot shapes and patterns are so varied, but no concrete conclusions have yet been reached.

Tabby patterns

Pattern	Agouti	Tabby type	Modifier
Mackerel tabby	A–	$T-$ or M^c-	$s^p s^p$
Classic tabby	A–	$t^b t^b$ or $m^c m^c$	$s^p s^p$
Spotted tabby (over mackerel)	A–	$T-$ or M^c-	S^p-
Spotted tabby (over classic)	A–	$t^b t^b$ or $m^c m^c$	S^p-

CHANGING SPOTS The spotted pattern is the hallmark of the Ocicat (*see* pp 250–51) and the Egyptian Mau (*see* pp 248–49). We may have selected against this wild-looking coat in the early history of the domestic cat.

BRITISH EXPORT The blotched or classic tabby has swirling lines and a central blotch on the flank, sometimes called oyster markings. Mapping the occurrence of this mutation suggests that it arose in mainland Britain.

TICKED TABBIES AND OTHER TABBY MUTATIONS

Although tabby cats are the 'default' original pattern for the cat, there have been plenty of mutations down the millennia. One of the more intriguing is the ticked pattern, while there are other variations in the colours and patterns of tabbies, with endless suggestions of new genetic mechanisms to control them. Add into this the possibility of new genes from wild cat hybrids, and the name 'tabby' covers a very wide range of patterns.

THE NON-TABBY TABBY
At first glance, the ticked tabby doesn't look like what most people would call a tabby at all. There are no alternating bands or swirls of light and dark, as seen in the other tabby patterns (see pp 160–61); darker markings are restricted to facial lines and barring on the legs and tail, while the body has no solid-coloured hairs at all: every hair is banded with lighter agouti and darker areas.

CAT IN HARE'S CLOTHING The ticked tabby pattern resembles the finely stippled coat of a rabbit or a hare, although the colour is much warmer.

In free-breeding agouti cats, some ghostly markings of solid-coloured hair may be found, but in pedigree cats of the pattern – especially the Abyssinian (see pp 240–45), after which this tabby pattern is sometimes also named – breeders have worked to eliminate these and minimize markings on the face, legs, and tail.

This pattern seems to have occurred in cats that were traded to the Middle and Far East, rather than into Europe, because it is fairly widespread in Oriental cats but was not known in Europe until the coming of the Abyssinian.

TICKED TABBY GENETICS
There are currently two conflicting theories about tabby genetics: according to one, the patterns are three forms of the same gene, called T, while according to the other they are controlled by two different genes, T^a for the ticked tabby and M^c or m^c for the others (see pp 160–61). Whichever theory is followed, T^a will always be shown if it is carried. If it is another form of the same gene as the other tabby patterns, it is called dominant, and if it is a different gene it is said to be epistatic, but whatever the terms, the effect is the same: if just one copy of the ticked gene is present (T^a–), it masks all other patterns. The cat will be ticked, but may carry other tabby patterns hidden beneath it.

Whether one or two copies of the gene are carried makes a difference: cats with two copies of the T^a gene ($T^a T^a$, called homozygous) are thought to have less barring than cats with only one copy.

GRIZZLE AND GLITTER
The 'grizzled' pattern is seen in the Chausie (see p 369), perhaps due to some inheritance from the jungle cat. The legs and face are fully coloured, but hairs on the body have pale, greyish agouti bands, apparently with silver tips. Whether this is a new tabby mutation

or the result of other genes acting on a standard domestic cat pattern is not yet known.

Bengal (*see* pp 362–67) breeders aim for cats with plenty of 'glitter' in their coat: this may be apparent on the tips (mica) or the whole shaft (satin), and under the microscope appears as particles of mica in the tips or air pockets within the hair shaft. It is not exclusive to Bengals, and is thought to have come from the domestic side of the original cross, but this is the only breed that has pursued the trait. The trait seems to affect only tabbies, not the solid-coloured Bengals that are sometimes born.

OTHER TABBY MODIFICATIONS

Breeders see so much variation in tabby patterns that they have suggested many hypothetical modifier genes affecting the patterns of a tabby cat. *Confusion* gives

ELUSIVE TRAIT The rich patterning of the Bengal coat is readily apparent; the 'glitter' is acknowledged to be virtually impossible to capture on film. This is one breed that really must be seen at a show to be fully appreciated.

adjacent hairs different numbers and widths of colour bands, and together with *Erase* is suggested as a mechanism that removes the residual markings on limbs. *Chaos* (a word that does spring to mind after thinking about tabby patterns for a while) intermixes dark and light areas, disrupting the normal striped pattern. In the ticked tabby this might also help eliminate barring, but it is also suggested that it might be responsible for marbled tabbies, in which the tabby markings are paler in the centre or 'hollow', such as the Sokoke (*see* p 255) and Bengal breeds.

WALK ON THE WILD SIDE These hollow tabby markings are characteristic of the Bengal's wild forebears. They are not unknown in domestic cats, but have been heavily selected against in pedigree breeds.

SMOKE, SHADED, AND TIPPED COLOURS

These modified coats include the shades known as silver and gold: precious, eye-catching, sought after, and in feline coats, frustratingly complex and poorly understood. Although the main gene that causes whiteness in the hair shaft is fairly sure, the factors that make the difference between a silver cat with or without tabby markings are not. Combinations and modifiers are suggested and argued over, with no absolute consensus.

THE INHIBITOR GENE

For a long time, it has been commonly understood that the inhibitor gene is responsible for smokes, silver tabbies, and shaded or tipped coats. In its dominant form (*I*–), it causes hairs to be coloured at the tip, and white at the base or all the way up the shaft. But either the gene is very variable in its expression, or it does not act alone but is modified by other genes, sets of related genes (polygenes), or even non-genetic factors that affect just how much of the hair is white or coloured.

SMOKE COLOURS

The smoke coat is a solid colour with a shimmering white undercoat; in a longhaired cat this may only be seen when the cat moves, but in shorthairs it is usually much more apparent. Smokes are always solid colours (*see* pp 158–59), meaning they have the recessive non-agouti (*aa*) pair or allele. Combined with the dominant inhibitor gene (*I*–), this gives a solid coat with a white undercoat.

Some breeders think that there may be a separate genetic combination responsible for smokes; smoke Egyptian Maus show some spotting, so may not be genetically solid, but this could also be caused by incomplete expression of the non-agouti allele letting through 'ghost' tabby markings, and the effect being exacerbated by the white undercoat.

SOLID SILVER Silver-shaded cats may be allowed green eyes in breeds where the standard usually calls for copper.

SMOKE WITHOUT FIRE A silver undercoat beneath a solid self top coat can be a dramatic effect in cats with long or rexed coats.

SILVER TABBIES, SHADED, AND TIPPED COLOURS

Silver tabbies have a clear tabby pattern, but the lighter areas are a clear silver-white, instead of the usual warmer shade. Shaded and tipped (often called chinchilla) cats both have a substantial silver undercoat with a soft overlay of their colour in shaded cats, or a sparkling sprinkle of colour on the very tips in a tipped cat; (in the red shades these are called cameo and shell cameo). But both of these types, the patterned and the plain, are genetically some form of tabby pattern (*see* pp 160–63), combined with the dominant inhibitor (*I*–) allele. It is thought that a 'wide band' gene (W^b) holds the key to the difference between these coats: without this, cats would be silver tabbies, but with it they would be shaded or tipped, possibly depending on whether they carry one or two copies, although plenty of argument still goes on about the existence of other genes. Another theory is that there are two genes, one removing colour near the base of the hair, the other further up the shaft.

STERLING QUALITIES The exact genetic combination that makes up the silver tabby is still a matter of some dispute, but the results are handsome.

GOLDENS

The golden series of colours is relatively new and not well understood. It is thought that two copies of the recessive form of the inhibitor (*ii*) give a golden coat. This would make the golden versions of the coats in the table (*left*) the same as the silver versions, but with *ii* rather than *I*– in every case. Another theory is that the W^b gene, in the absence of the *I*– gene, may be responsible for the shading.

Silver Persians sometimes turn golden in adulthood, and silvers of all kinds can suffer 'tarnishing'. The gene or genes responsible is not yet known.

Smoke, shaded, and tipped coats

Coat	Main genes	Modifiers
Smoke	*aa I*– ??	Some hold that the smokes are in fact *ii*
Silver tabby	*A*– *I*– $w^b w^b$	Plus the relevant tabby pattern
Shaded	*A*– *I*– $W^b w^b$	Plus the relevant tabby pattern
Tipped (Chinchilla)	*A*– *I*– $W^b W^b$	Plus the relevant tabby pattern

TOUCHED AT THE TIPS This coat is also known as chinchilla, because it resembles that of the chinchilla, a rabbit-sized rodent from the Andes.

POINTED PATTERNS

In the earliest days of the cat fancy, the pointed pattern was so extraordinary in the eyes of the public that the cats carrying it were described as 'an unnatural nightmare of a cat', but it captured the imagination of breeders. Today, the pattern is far more widespread in pedigree breeds, and even surfaces in the free-breeding feline population, as a result of accidents and escapes, but it still holds exotic allure.

UNKNOWN ORIGIN

Exactly where and when the pointing mutation arose remains a mystery. It is believed to have happened at least 500 years ago, somewhere in Asia, and pointed patterns were recorded in the Thai *Tamra Maew* or *Cat Book Poems* dating to before the 1760s.

TABBY POINTS Although first seen in the West in self-coloured cats, the pointing gene is found mixed with every coat colour and pattern in its native land. Less dramatic than seal points, they are still striking.

CLASSIC COLOUR For most people, this seal point is still the 'real' Siamese. The colour is genetically black, degraded to a very deep brown on the points and faded out to fawn or even cream over the body.

The earliest, and for some time the only, pointed cat in the west was the Siamese (*see* pp 220–23). But the pattern has been exported to many other breeds, starting with the Birman (*see* pp 276–79) and the Himalayan or Colourpoint Persian (*see* p 258), and today many breeds are accepted in pointed patterns, especially the newer ones.

POINTED CATS ARE ALBINO

Pointing is a form of partial, heat-sensitive albinism, controlled by several mutations of the same gene, called C. The dominant form (C) allows fully expressed solid colour (*see* pp 158–59), tabby pattern (*see* pp 162–63), or silvering (*see* pp 164–65). Its recessive alleles cause colourpoint or Siamese pointing (c^s), sepia or Burmese pointing (c^b), and complete albinism with blue or pink eyes (c^a or c). Pointed forms are dominant over these other albino forms. The combinations possible (shown in the chart opposite) make it clear why complete albinism is so rare: every other form of the gene must be absent for a true albino to show through.

HOW POINTING WORKS

This gene controls the first step in the production of pigment, causing it to be heat-sensitive; pigment is only produced in the skin over cooler areas. This gives the characteristic darker 'pointing' on the coolest parts of the body: the extremities of the legs and tail, and the face, which is cooled by air in the sinus cavities of the skull.

The colourpoint form reduces pigmentation most dramatically, giving bright blue eyes and a light beige coat with highly contrasting dark 'points'. The sepia form causes a lesser reduction in pigment production, resulting in green eyes and a dark coat with much more subtle points.

Sepia and colourpoint are 'co-dominant', meaning neither form will mask the other if a cat carries one copy of each. Instead, the cat will show the mink or Tonkinese (*see* pp 218–19) pattern, which has a softly coloured body with points less subtle than a Burmese, less striking than a Siamese, and turquoise or aquamarine eyes.

Pointing will overlay all other possible patterns, so the extremities may be solid, tabby, or even silvered.

Pointed patterns

Coat colour	Possible genetic combinations
Fully coloured	CC, Cc^s, Cc^b, Cc^a, or Cc
Colourpointed	c^sc^s, c^sc^a, or c^sc
Mink	c^sc^b
Sepia	c^bc^b, c^bc^a, or c^bc
Blue-eyed albino	c^ac^a or c^ac
Red-eyed albino	cc

Temperature changes

Pointed kittens are pale or white at birth, going on to develop darker points over the first few months of life, and continuing to grow darker as they age. Adult cats living in warmer climates also tend to have paler bodies and smaller coloured areas than those living in cooler regions. But the most dramatic effects are seen if a pointed cat is injured and has to wear a bandage, especially during the moulting season: new hair that grows under the bandage will be lighter because of the increased warmth.

SOFTENED EFFECT Modifying polygenes, a cooler climate, and other shades, such as this chocolate point, can give a much softer, subtler shading than the classic seal point coat.

WHITE AND BI-COLOURED CATS

Like snow covering a landscape, white in cats hides other colours beneath it. The other genes for colour and pattern are still present in the cat: their effects are completely hidden beneath the white, but will appear in any offspring. Sparkling white cats are undeniably eye-catching, but like a white suit the coat shows up any dirt, tear staining or other marks. An unkempt, ill-groomed white cat is a miserable sight.

CALICO CAT This tortie-and-white cat shows some 'ghost' tabby markings (see pp 160–61) on the red areas, but none on the black. If it were tabby all over the coloured areas, it would be a 'patched' or tortie tabby and white.

HOW THE WHITE COAT IS CREATED

A white cat can be the result of three different genetic traits acting on melanocytes, the cells that make the pigment melanin (see pp 158–59). Firstly, it may be albino. Albinism disables melanocytes, resulting in an albino with a white coat and pink or blue-grey eyes.

The other two whites are an all-over white gene and a white spotting gene. Both produce white in the same way, which differs from the albino mutation: they block the movement of the melanocytes in the embryo to the skin. This overrides all other genes for pigmentation to produce a white coat.

SOLID AND SPOTTED WHITE

All-over white caused by the dominant white gene *W* is often referred to as dominant white or epistatic white. The number of melanocytes is reduced, but often there are some present, and kittens may show a smudge of colour.

Bi-colours or white spotted cats are created by the dominant spotting gene *S*: a cat that carries two copies of this has more white than a cat with only one. When white covers most of the body, the coat is still a coloured coat overlaid with very large 'spots' of white. It is possible that a cat could be rendered solid white by the spotting gene.

SPOTTED PATTERNS

Spotting usually follows a regular pattern. Cats with the least spotting have it on the breast and belly, and as the amount increases it progresses over the neck, chin, and front legs, then over the flanks and onto the head, as in the van pattern (see pp 292–93). The tail is often left coloured.

SPOT OF BOTHER Lockets or bibs of white are commonly seen on otherwise solidly coloured random-bred moggies. Some breed standards disallow them, while others accept them as part of a 'natural' look.

It is likely that there are several modifying genes interacting with the spotting gene, but none have any effect that has been isolated enough for certainty. A separate gene has been suggested for 'lockets', the small white spots on the throat, breast, or belly. A 'gloving' gene or variant of the spotting gene (S^b) is also suggested as a cause of mittens.

WHITE CATS AND DEAFNESS

The blocking of melanocyte migration also affects the eyes and ears. Reduced melanocytes mean many white cats have blue eyes. The restriction may be uneven, resulting in odd-eyed whites. In bi-colour cats, an eye within a white patch may be blue.

Melanocytes in the inner ear (see pp 60–61) are vital for passing sound to the brain. The white or spotting gene can cause deafness on one or both sides by blocking movement of melanocytes to the ears. The majority of blue-eyed white cats – but not all – are deaf.

CALICO CATS

Spotting has an odd effect on the tortoiseshell (see p 159) pattern. In solid torties, the colours are usually quite evenly and finely mingled, giving a mottled effect. Add the white spotting gene, however, and the coloured pattern breaks up into larger,

distinct patches. Somehow, the effect that the spotting gene has on melanocyte migration in the embryo also affects the migration of the different tortoiseshell colours. In North America, the resulting pattern is often called 'calico', after the cotton cloth printed with bright patterns.

White and bi-colour patterns

Level of white	Genetic background
All over	W–, SS, or albino
Van pattern	SS
Low to medium	Ss
Locket	Ss or possibly an unnamed gene
Mittens	Ss or possibly S^b
None	ss

PURE WHITE The presence or absence of head markings on white kittens does not seem linked to future hearing, but may indicate whether the cat carries one or two copies of the white gene.

PIED BEAUTY In the early days of the cat fancy, bi-colours were often snubbed as 'mismarked' cats; today there is broader appreciation of dramatic contrasts such as this cat's striking eyeliner. This level of white is called harlequin in FIFé.

EYE COLOURS

The colours of cats' eyes are extraordinary. Nothing like this range exists in the wild, or indeed in any other domestic animal. Dogs look up at us with big brown eyes, but a cat may look at a king with eyes of any shade from palest blue to softest green, or even deep, startling copper. The fanciful owner can even find a cat with eyes to match their own. But just what makes this rainbow of colours, and why are there so many?

WHAT MAKES UP EYE COLOUR?

The first factor influencing eye colour is the pigment in the iris (*see* pp 58–59). This is melanin, and gives shades from yellow through copper to brown or black. The other factor is the tissues over the iris. These are clear, because the cat needs to see through them, but just as glass has a tint when looked at edge-on, this layer refracts light and influences the colour, effectively giving a blue 'tint'.

These factors are not related, but vary separately. Together, they give a range of shades: pale golden eyes come from light melanin and little tint, copper eyes from dark melanin and little tint, while pale green is the result of pale melanin and a deep tint, and deep green eyes of deep melanin and deep tint.

Neither factor is controlled by just one gene. Eye colour is 'polygenetic', which provides an infinite variety of subtle shades. Regardless of what breed standards call for, coat colour and eye colour are not genetically related: blues can have copper eyes in the Burmese (*see* pp 210–17), and green in the Korat (*see* pp 236–39).

WHAT ABOUT BLUE EYES?

All kittens are born with blue eyes, and begin to develop their adult colour after a few weeks. The exceptions are blue eyes found in pointed (*see* pp 166–67) or white (*see* pp 168–69) cats. In these cats, the iris is a pale pink because it has little or no melanin, and the eye colour is determined by the refraction of light alone. The eyes are pale blue in most Western cats, but deep blue in Siamese (*see* pp 220–23). There are also some Orientals (*see* pp 224–29) that have fully coloured bodies but eyes tantalizingly close to blue. Just how this trait is produced and passed on could prove interesting.

WILD EYES Just as the default coat of the cat is a brown tabby, the default eye colour is hazel. This sits roughly in the middle of the spectrum of colours seen in breeds.

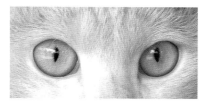

PALE GOLD With no blue and the palest yellow iris, this colour is common in moggies and found in some breeds that emphasize a natural look, such as the Norwegian Forest (*see* pp 268–73).

MID GOLD This deeper, more striking tint is preferred in many breeds, for example in the Bombay (*see* pp 234–35), an American breed that was created to resemble a black panther.

DEEP COPPER This is the classic eye colour associated with most colours of Persian (*see* pp 258–61). It shows up well against the coats of blue breeds, such as the Chartreux (*see* pp 196–97).

PALE GREEN This blend of pale gold and a light blue tint is a classic shade with a black coat in moggies. It is essential for breeds such as the Korat (*see* pp 236–39).

MID GREEN This deeper shade is created by a strong blue tint, and so it is associated slightly more with Eastern cats than European types. It is found in the Oriental breeds.

DEEP GREEN This shade looks particularly striking with silver coats, and is often aspired to in silver tabbies. In shaded and tipped silver coats, an even bluer shade is sometimes called for.

PALE BLUE This china blue is generally associated with white or bi-colour cats, but pale shades are also found in some pointed cats if they have not been bred selectively for a deep blue.

MID BLUE Deeper blues are found mainly in pointed cats. In related breeds, a very pale underlying iris may occasionally give a shade that is almost blue in a non-pointed cat.

DEEP BLUE This is the epitome of the Siamese (*see* pp 220–23), and now exported into other breeds. Although the early cats had quite light eyes, breeders now reliably get deep blues.

HUMAN INFLUENCE

African wildcat eyes are hazel-gold, with only a faint hint of green. Even in domestic cats, the most common eye colours are in the middle of the possible ranges: gold to a golden-green. These are produced by moderate amounts of melanin and a moderate blue tint. The deeper tones produced by more melanin are less commonly seen, and these are the colours that pedigree breeders pursue.

Breeders have also pursued deep blue eyes in Siamese; the eyes of the breed today are darker than those seen in the ordinary pointed cats of Thailand, which can have eyes as light as a white cat. This deeper cast extends to the other Oriental breeds, whose green eyes tend to be deeper and bluer than the green eyes of Western breeds. When the Siamese has been crossed with other breeds to introduce the colourpoint pattern, the intensity has usually been diminished.

DIFFERENT GENE, SAME COLOUR People sometimes assume that the blue eyes of pointed cats are by their nature always darker than those of white cats. This is not so; some pointed cats have simply been bred for darker eyes.

BUILD AND SHAPE

Shape or 'type' is a major part of what defines a breed, and can account for one-fifth to over one-third of the points in a show. A pointed pattern or a particular colour might be the most obvious identifying characteristic of a breed, but it is far from the whole story. The length and thickness of the legs, and the relative sturdiness or slenderness of the body, are essential to the overall picture – and prizes on the show bench.

COBBY CATS

At the chunky end of the range are what might be called the 'cold-climate cats', with a sturdy, heat-conserving build. The standards for these breeds are full of words like massive, well-muscled, broad, sturdy, and thick, and a good example is the Persian (*see* pp 258–61) or the Exotic (*see* pp 184–87). The ideal is a short, wide body with a deep chest, carried relatively low on short, thick legs that end in large, round paws. Even the tail is relatively short and thick. The massiveness of the body should be the result of heavy boning and muscle – there is no breed standard that calls for a fat cat!

A slightly less massive build is classed as semi-cobby. Exactly where 'cobby' shades into 'semi-cobby' is tricky to define, and varies with the association or country. For example, the British standard for the British Shorthair (*see* pp 188–93)

COBBY CAT The Exotic has no long coat to hide any possible deficiencies in build and make it look rounder than it is.

COBBY OR SEMI-COBBY The British Shorthair is described both ways. Its build is strong, but should never be portly or thuggish.

refers to it as cobby, but the Cat Fanciers' Association (CFA) standard omits the word, and The International Cat Association (TICA) calls it semi-cobby.

HAPPY MEDIUM CATS

Breeds of medium body conformation sit, as the name implies, somewhere in the middle of the range. Their bodies are neither short and broad nor long and slender, but more or less approximate the natural type of the African wildcat, a well-proportioned rectangle. Their boning is neither heavy nor fine, their legs slender but not model-thin, and while they are not short, as in the cobby breeds, they should not look markedly long in relation to the body. The overall look might best be described as athletic. This is the look aspired to by several breeds that aim to recreate or preserve a historical type. One example is the Abyssinian (*see* pp 240–45), which is described as 'medium' in its CFA breed standard – although in the United Kingdom the Governing Council of the Cat Fancy (GCCF) classes it as foreign.

SEMI-FOREIGN AND FOREIGN

These builds are associated with breeds from the Orient, although some of the modern breeds created in the West will have this build; through accident or design, they may well start out with Oriental blood in their make-up.

The semi-foreign body is not particularly long, but lithe and slender. The legs are graceful and should look elegantly long in relation to the

MEDIUM The standard for the Bengal (*see* pp 362–67) says it must not resemble a domestic cat, but its moderate, strong body build is pure, natural cat.

FOREIGN The Oriental Shorthair is typical of the look expected in Far Eastern breeds. The emphasis here is on a delicate structure rarely, if ever, seen in free-breeding cats, even in Southeast Asia.

SEMI-FOREIGN The Russian Shorthairs are of a lean but muscular type, with legs that are longer in relation to the body than in more European types, but still strong and sturdy-looking.

body. Breeds of semi-foreign type include the Russian (*see* pp 198–99), the Tonkinese (*see* pp 218–19), or the Egyptian Mau (*see* pp 248–49).

Foreign cats are altogether more svelte. These are 'warm-climate' looks, with everything geared to maximum surface area for the size, allowing a cat to keep cool. The word 'long' can be applied to just about everything. The body is long and tubular, the legs long and slender, the tail long and thin. This is the look of the Siamese (*see* pp 220–23) and Balinese (*see* pp 300–301), and the Oriental Shorthair (*see* pp 224–29) and Longhair (*see* pp 302–303).

THE CHANGING FORM OF CATS

There is no perfect shape for a cat; fashions, and so breed standards, do vary from place to place and from one era to another. Because cat owners have a strong tendency to believe that the shape of their beloved pet is really, truly the perfect shape for a cat, some of the traits that have become established breeds can be quite surprising when looked at objectively – and some of the traits that haven't are even more so.

CHANGING LOOKS

Some words mean slightly different things in different breed standards, and the standards for some breeds vary from place to place. The Burmese (*see* pp 210–15), Persian (*see* pp 258–61), and Cornish Rex (*see* pp 310–17) all differ from one side of the Atlantic to the other. In addition, cat types do not stand still over time. By and large, there has been a drift away from the middle ground towards the more striking, dramatic ends of the spectrum. Persians have become cobbier, and the supermodel-type Oriental breeds are far removed from the average cat.

MODERN LOOKS The Siamese (*see* pp 220–23) was always lighter in build than burly European breeds. Today it is a lean, some would say skinny, breed.

ORIGINAL OR IMPOSTOR? Breeders of more substantial Siamese cats claim they are holding true to the type of a century ago, while their detractors say these cats are simply poor examples of Siamese.

Broadly speaking, standards tend to be more exaggerated in North America than they are in Europe, with the cobby cats being more massive and the foreign cats more etiolated. The phrase 'ultra-type' is sometimes used of the more exaggerated examples of both, and while the breeders of ultra-type cats are proud of their achievements, others are less delighted.

The size of the cat is one thing that does not seem to have changed very much. The Maine Coon (*see* pp 262–67) is still about the top of the range, and although there was speculation about miniature cats when the Singapura (*see* pp 246–47) appeared, cats living a cushy pet's life have unsurprisingly proved larger than the underfed originals from the streets. Persians have been miniaturized, with 'toy' and 'teacup' versions on the market, but no other breed seems keen to import or copy the trait.

PECULIARITIES OF TYPE

Most breed standards call in some words or other for a cat that appears harmonious in all its parts. But this is not the case for all breeds: some are identified by their very oddity, and mutations that would have died out in nature have often been seen as the basis for new breeds.

The oldest of these breeds in the West is the Manx (*see* pp 332–37), with its short or absent tail, resulting from a gene with some damaging side-effects. Its Oriental counterpart is the healthy Japanese Bobtail

KINKY CAT Cats with short, kinked tails are relatively common across Asia, and new short-tailed breeds have turned up to keep the Manx and Japanese Bobtail company.

(*see* pp 340–41), which has been immortalized in Japanese art for centuries. Recently, other bobtailed breeds have appeared in North America, together with some with fanciful suggestions as to their origins.

Perhaps strangest among the modern breeds is the peculiarly dwarfed Munchkin (*see* pp 354–57). Few breeds have caused so much controversy, even within the one major association, TICA, that has recognized it. The short legs are seen as an endearing feature by those who love the breed, but a dangerous deformity by the rest of the world, and this situation is unlikely to change. Just where acceptable 'type' shades into 'deformity' is a thorny issue.

DWARF CATS Although unpopular with registries, the Munchkin has a cute name and a host of nicknames, such as Rughugger, and a band of fans who create curly coated and other versions.

HEAD FORM

Just as feline build varies from svelte to sturdy (*see* pp 174–75), so the shape of the head and set of its features vary from one breed to another. Because breed standards call for a harmonious overall look, the head will match the body: breeds with rounded, broad bodies will have rounded, broad heads. But there is more to it, with eye shapes and the exact placement of the ears also coming into play.

FOREIGN HEAD This distinctively triangular face with large, flaring ears is typical of the Oriental Shorthair and all related breeds. The profile is no less distinctive, having a long, smooth line with only a slight dip at the eyes.

COBBY HEADS

This is the look of many old Western breeds, like the American Shorthair (*see* pp 200–203). To complement their broad bodies, cobby breeds have broad, rounded heads with full cheeks and wide muzzles. The profile usually shows a 'break' or change of angle between the eyes, leading down into a short, broad nose and muzzle with a strong chin.

The eyes are generally large, with a shape ranging from round to a broad oval, level, and widely spaced. In general, the ears are short, broad at the base, and rounded at the tips. The exact placement and angle at which they are carried varies from breed to breed, but they tend to be fairly upright at the corners of the head.

MEDIUM HEADS

This is, as ever, a hard thing to define. Even the Bengal (*see* pp 362–67), which has a head tending to neither extreme, has standards that say it should be 'as distinct from the domestic cat as possible'. Although Oriental in origin, the Korat (*see* pp 236–39) has a head described as 'heart shaped'. Breeds with faces described as 'modified wedges' with curves fall into this category, and the forehead flows into the nose in a continuous curve rather than with a stop or break. The eyes are round to oval, but may be set at more of a slant than in cobby faces, and the ears tend to be larger than on cobby heads, but still broad rather than long, and rounded over the tips.

COBBY HEAD Broad, strong, and rounded in every part, this is the classic cobby head. Due to the large muzzle and full whisker pads, cats with this face type often look as if they are smiling.

SEMI-FOREIGN AND FOREIGN

Less modified 'modified wedges' shift into the foreign category, where the look is more angular; some call the less dramatic examples 'semi-foreign'. The whole head is longer and narrower, and the planes range from shallow curves to near flat. The profile tends to be straighter, sometimes with only the slightest change in direction leading into a muzzle that is no longer rounded, but tapering. The eyes are distinctly oval and set on a slant, and inevitably closer together, while the ears are large, long, and pointed at the tips. They usually flare out from the corners of the head. This is the look of breeds from the Russian (*see* pp 198–99) to the Siamese (*see* pp 220–23).

INDIVIDUAL LOOKS

Within these broad outlines there is room for quite a variety of looks. As an example, one can look at the faces of three of the 'natural' farm and forest type breeds we have today: the Maine Coon (*see* pp 262–67), the Norwegian Forest (*see* pp 268–73), and the Siberian (*see* pp 274–75).

All three of these are large, sturdy, longhaired breeds drawn from populations adapted to cold climates. All three have suitably large and handsome heads. So what

WILD WAYS The emphasis on triangles in the structure of the Norwegian Forest's face gives it a slightly wild look. It is still easy to imagine these cats living by their sharp wits in farm barns through a Scandinavian winter.

MEDIUM HEAD The expression of the Bengal is intense and singular, but the broad, medium wedge with gentle curves and slightly rounded chin holds back from extremes to give a good example of a moderate type.

differentiates them from one another? This was one question that breeders of the Siberian had to answer when seeking recognition for their breed. The face of the Maine Coon, as described in the breed standards, is noticeably about right angles. The muzzle must have squareness, the chin should give the impression of a 90° angle in profile, and so on. In contrast, the face of the Norwegian Forest is described as an equilateral triangle with, for example, less pronounced whisker pads. And when the standard for the Siberian was written, the words full, rounded, and curvature were brought to the fore.

CHANGES IN HEAD TYPES

Just as body type varies from place to place and over time, so does head type. Two breeders from different countries may have different ideas of the same breed, and highly praised winners from early shows would win nothing at shows today. In some cases, these changes have been dramatic enough to engender 'new old' breeds.

THE BURMESE HEAD

For decades, the Burmese looked the same in all fancies, but in the 1970s everything changed in the United States. A new look, with a strikingly rounded, domed head (*see* pp 210–11), swept the showbench, as did a cat by the name of Good Fortune Fortunatus. He soon appeared in the pedigrees of many American Burmese, but he carried a lethal genetic deformity known as the Burmese head fault or craniofacial defect. The breed took a different course in other places (*see* pp 212–15), and consequently American bloodlines are often banned to avoid importing the lethal gene.

EUROPEAN BURMESE This is the look still favoured in Europe and Commonwealth countries. It was accepted as a separate breed by CFA in the late 1990s.

ULTRA-TYPE HEADS

Health concerns about head shapes are part of the often heated controversy over so-called ultra-types. At one extreme is the Persian (*see* pp 258–61), which originally had a longer, more recognizably feline nose. Gradually, it became shorter: the result is impaired breathing and blocked tear ducts. Some breeders – and it seems pet buyers – have turned away from this look. At the other extreme is the Siamese, with a narrow head and slanted eyes. Detractors complain that the 'haw', usually hidden in the inner corner of the eye, is increasing visible.

It is sobering that these two breeds have the highest recorded incidences of birth problems, attributed to their extreme heads. This may suggest that these are not functionally sensible designs.

PERSIAN NOSE Red Persians were the source of the 'Peke-face', no longer seen but echoed in the general type. The GCCF standard calls for the nose leather to be below the bottom of the eyes.

JUNGLE LOOKS In keeping with its wild looks, the breed standard for the Bengal (*see* pp 362–67) calls for a head that is slightly on the small side relative to the body.

SHORTHAIR BREEDS

Adapted to a hot climate, the African wildcat (*see* p 27) has a close-lying, short coat, and the cat that spread across Europe and to the Orient had this coat. Even today, the vast majority of ordinary moggies still wear it, so the shorthair breeds have to work that bit harder to stand out from the crowd: their type must be distinctive and consistent, their painstaking breeding clear for all to see. Many are distinguished by a particular coat colour or pattern, from the cloudy blue of the Korat (*see* pp 236–39) to the spots of the Ocicat (*see* pp 250–51).

ABYSSINIAN COAT This ticked tabby pattern was unknown in European cats when the Abyssinian was introduced, so it immediately set the breed apart.

EXOTIC

ORIGIN United States (1960s)

SYNONYM None

WEIGHT 3.5–7 kg (8–15 lb)

BUILD 🐱

TEMPERAMENT 🐱

COAT CARE 🧤

COLOURS All colours in self, tortie, bi-colour, smoke, shaded, and tipped; classic, striped, and spotted tabby patterns; pointed pattern

The Exotic is a teddy bear of a cat, with a soft, plush coat; a soft, slightly squeaky voice; and round, bright eyes in the middle of a round, foreshortened face. It is essentially a shorthaired Persian (*see* pp 258–61), with the same gentle, quiet personality but without the chore of daily brushing to keep it looking good.

BLACK SELF   BLUE SELF   BROWN CLASSIC TABBY   RED STRIPED TABBY   SILVER SHADED   LILAC POINT

BREED ORIGINS

The breeders who started the Exotic actually had something else in mind when they made the first crosses of Persians to American Shorthairs (*see* pp 200–203) in the 1950s. The aim was to introduce the silver coat and green eyes of the shaded or tipped chinchilla Persians into the American Shorthair; similar crosses to revive the British Shorthair (*see* pp 188–93) were also recorded in the United Kingdom at the same time. The result was a handsome cat with the coat they wanted but a face and body that were far from the American Shorthair look.

The illicit crossbreeding caused problems within the American Shorthair breed as Persian looks seemed to creep in, and to resolve the issue it was suggested in the 1960s that these crosses should be developed as a breed in themselves, and the name Exotic was coined.

Several other breeds were used in the development of the Exotic, including the Burmese (*see* pp 210–11) and even the Russian (*see* pp 198–99); nothing of conspicuously Oriental type was used, because the long-term aim was to bring the face and body conformation of the Exotic into line with that of the Persian.

BREED DEVELOPMENT

The Exotic's breed standard originally differed from that of the Persian – for example, there was no requirement for a nose break, to allow for the American Shorthair ancestry – and some Persian breeders feared that interbreeding of Exotics and Persians would produce Persians with inferior coats or longer faces. This made it hard for Exotic breeders to work with show-winning Persian bloodlines. As the breed progressed in the 1970s, however, the standard was amended to bring it closer to that of the Persian, and resistance began to diminish.

The breed standards for the Exotic now match those for the Persian in

RED All red and cream cats show tabby markings, and one effect of the short coat of the Exotic is that markings show up more clearly than in a longhair.

Exotic popularity

Over the decades, the Exotic has been steadily creeping up in popularity. It has almost made it into the top ten most popular breeds in the United Kingdom, where it seems to be holding steady while the Persian declines, and it is the most popular shorthair breed and third most popular breed overall in the United States.

BROWN CLASSIC TABBY The blotched or classic tabby pattern shows well in a Persian coat. The Exotic's short coat shows off stripes and spots just as well, but the classic remains a classic.

TORTOISESHELL Blacks, reds, and the tortoiseshells that result from crossing these remain among the most popular colours for the Exotic breed.

all but coat length: they call for a rounded cat with stocky legs, and a large, round head with a sweet expression. The breed has been fully recognized by every major registry, and is even included in the longhair or Persian divisions, despite its short hair. Exotics sometimes produce long-haired kittens; in some registries these are automatically pets, without a show category, while in others they are treated as Persians.

CREAM POINT While the pointed colours in the Persian breed were at first kept separate in the Himalayan, they were accepted in the Exotic under the breed name from the start.

OWNING AN EXOTIC

Is the Exotic just a low-maintenance Persian? Although short enough not to matt or tangle, the coat is thicker and more 'plush' than that of many other shorthair breeds. A little extra grooming once or twice a week will keep it glossy and soft. The face may need more frequent attention, due to some inherent problems of the 'pansy-like' shortened look.

When it comes to behaviour, there may still be some differences. Owners often say that the Exotic is a more active and outgoing cat than its longhaired cousin, being willing to play for hours and hunt for the toys after they have been put away. This might not be a difference in breeding, of course: it may simply be a happy result of not being burdened by a heavy and insulating coat all year.

In their basic character, however, Exotics are much the same as Persians. They are easy-going, self-contained, and quiet cats, affectionate without being noisily demanding – their quiet voices are hardly used at all. Add this

BLACK SELF Black has been a popular colour for the Exotic since its earliest days, and remains so today. Black selfs feature prominently in lists of show winners.

accommodating personality to an easy-care coat, and it is not hard to see why the breed's popularity has swelled over the years.

HEALTH CONCERNS

The Exotic suffers from the same health concerns as the Persian. They have a similarly high incidence of the inherited disorder polycystic kidney disease (PKD). This causes cysts in the kidneys, which are present from birth, but enlarge and fill with fluid in adulthood, usually when cats are between three and ten years of age. The first signs are lack of or increased thirst and urination, decreased appetite, and weight loss, ending in kidney

RED TABBY AND WHITE Bi-colours were looked down on for some time during the 20th century; today they are more popular. Standards vary as to how much white is desirable and what its distribution should be.

failure. The rate at which the disease progresses is not uniform, and cats may die of something else first, but they often show no symptoms until the disease is quite advanced.

Skilled ultrasound screening with a high-quality scanner can detect the cysts, and many breeders have screened their cats for years, but this involves considerable cost and in some cases travel. The dominant gene responsible for PKD has been identified, so DNA testing should now allow wider screening and help breeders to eliminate carriers from breeding programmes. However, if the proportion of cats carrying the gene is anything like as high as it is in the Persian, this could only happen slowly unless the gene pool were to be almost halved.

SHORTENED FACE
Because it shares the breed standard for a brachycephalic face with the Persian, the Exotic also shares the eye problems and breathing difficulties associated with the look. Breathing and sinus problems are reported, as well as jaw abnormalities. The flattening causes kinked tear ducts and prominent eyes, often enough to cause persistently watering eyes, or 'tearing'. This leaves red-brown tear stains on the face (more apparent in pale-coloured cats). The shortened face can also make it hard for a cat to eat tidily.

CREAM With red and cream cats always showing some tabby markings, the distinction between self and tabby cats can be tricky.

British Shorthair

ORIGIN United Kingdom (1800s)
SYNONYM None
WEIGHT 4–8 kg (9–18 lb)
BUILD
TEMPERAMENT
COAT CARE 🖊

COLOURS All colours in self, tortie, bi-colour, smoke, and tipped; blotched, striped, and spotted tabby; pointed pattern

One of the very first breeds to be given a standard and actively bred, the British Shorthair is an elder statesman of the feline fancy. And this is about as masculine as a cat breed can get: chunky and robust, it is a no-nonsense, cobby cat that scorns flashy features or fluffy coats.

BLUE SELF

RED SELF

BLACK & WHITE

CREAM STRIPED TABBY

SILVER STRIPED TABBY

SILVER SHADED

BREED ORIGINS

The ancestors of the British Shorthair were generations of working cats, from urban mousers and street cats to rural farm cats. When deliberate breeding began, this was the natural starting stock. The founder of the cat fancy and organizer of the first cat show at Crystal Palace, Harrison Weir, bred British Shorthairs – specifically British Blues – and it was the most popular breed at those early shows. At this time different colours of cats were treated almost as separate breeds.

After this early popularity, however, the British Shorthair began to decline during the 20th century, when other, more striking, exotics appeared on the scene. Two World Wars had a devastating effect on breeding, and by 1950, the breed was almost extinct. Dedicated breeders in Britain and throughout the Commonwealth began working to bring it back from the brink. By the 1970s, it was back in business, and those original British Blues were even becoming known in the United States.

Today, the British Shorthair is once again top cat in its homeland. It toppled the Persian from the number one spot in 2001, and has stayed there ever since, with almost twice as many cats registered as the next most popular breed. It is also popular in the United States, where it holds its own just outside the top ten.

RED TABBY POINT The pointed colours are still something of a novelty, with some breeders specializing in them.

SILVER TABBY Silvers were among the very first examples of the breed shown in the 1880s, and remain popular today.

BLACK SELF The combination of lustrous jet black coat with the copper eye colour so rarely seen in non-pedigrees is one of the most popular types today.

IF LOOKS COULD KILL

The British Shorthair is muscular, neither extremely cobby nor lean, suited to the rough-and-tumble life of a mouser or street fighter – although today, of course, it can look forward to a rather more regular and secure lifestyle. The legs are short and strong; the rounded head is carried on a short, sturdy neck; and everything is clothed in a dense, weatherproof plush that feels crisp rather than soft.

Because there was such a small gene pool left after World War II, outcrosses were made. The breeds used included Oriental Shorthairs (see pp 224–27) and Persians; it took considerable work to eliminate the long noses and coats that came with these and return to the original look.

BLUE SELF This, more than any other colour, typifies the British Shorthair. It was among the first colours bred and shown in Victorian Britain, and it remains the most widely shown colour today.

maintenance and nothing more than a quick brush and rub to bring out its lustre. Because it is so thick, a little extra combing or brushing to remove dead hair when moulting is advisable in order to avoid hairballs.

The stocky build of the British Shorthair does hint at one weakness: this is a breed inclined to obesity. Although as a large cat it does need a substantial amount of food, if you own one you are well advised to read the guidelines on the packaging of the food you buy and then stick to them. Avoid giving in to appeals or pestering, and steer clear of free feeding.

SELF-CONTAINED CATS

In character, the British Shorthair is literally down to earth: these cats dislike being picked up and handled all the time. They may play with you, and they may choose to snooze in your presence rather than a snug, hidden-away spot, but this breed is not a dependent type that wants constant attention, stroking, and to use you as its personal cushion. This is just as well, perhaps, given its substantial size and weight.

These cats have the intelligence of a natural survivor, but not the insatiable inquisitiveness that drives some breeds to investigate all the household cupboards, learn to open doors, and get stuck in unlikely places. British Shorthairs are essentially sensible, reliable, perhaps rather stolid cats.

CARING FOR A BRIT

The British Shorthair remains very close to its roots. The coat is easy-care, needing no day-to-day

TORTOISESHELL This, together with the dilute tortie or blue-cream, is one of the oldest colours in the breed. It has recently been joined by new versions in the Oriental shades.

There are no general health problems associated with the breed, but it does have one medical curiosity. While the blood type B is rare in the British moggie, it is the blood type of around 40 per cent of all British Shorthairs. Although transfusions remain an unusual form of treatment for cats, this would limit the options. It is likely this trait came from the outcrosses to revive the breed in the 20th century.

TORTIE AND WHITE The breed standard of the United Kingdom requires one-third to half the coat to be white. This coat is called calico in US standards.

ODD-EYED WHITE The blue-eyed white was the first colour to be recognized, and the orange-eyed white was developed from it.

Holding a mirror to nature

As the cat spread across Europe, self or solid-coloured cats came to form an ever higher proportion of the moggie population, reaching their highest levels in Britain. Hundreds of years later, it seems that the blotched tabby mutation appeared in Britain and spread to Europe and farther flung colonial settlements. These traditional colours remain popular in the British Shorthair, although there is now an enormous variety of colours and patterns accepted. In part this broadening of the spectrum reflects the range of breeds that was used to inject new blood into the breed, but it also fittingly mirrors the changing make-up of the British moggie population.

BRITISH SHORTHAIR (*see* pp 188–91) This tipped coat was for a time called chinchilla. It still carries that name in the United States, but in the United Kingdom colours of the British Shorthair have more prosaic, descriptive names.

European Shorthair

ORIGIN Mainland Europe (1980s)
SYNONYM None
WEIGHT 3.5–7 kg (8–15 lb)
BUILD
TEMPERAMENT
COAT CARE
COLOURS Western colours in self, tortie, bi-colour, and smoke; blotched, striped, and spotted tabby patterns

Most often seen in a brown striped tabby pattern, this breed is said to be the quintessential example of a north European feline. Moderate in build and looks, it has a dense, springy, slightly harsh coat to withstand continental winters, and a breed standard designed to ensure moderation in all its parts.

BLACK SELF	BLUE SELF	BLUE & WHITE	BROWN CLASSIC TABBY	RED STRIPED TABBY	TORTIE & WHITE

BREED ORIGINS

While there have been cats in Europe for two thousand or so years, this breed is a relative newcomer. National breeds gripped the imagination first, with the British Shorthair (see pp 188–93) and Manx (see pp 332–37) holding sway in the United Kingdom, and the Chartreux (see pp 196–97) in France. The

European Shorthair also began its existence as a national breed: in 1946 the registration and breeding to type of domestic cats began in Sweden under the name of 'Swedish housecat'. This name was later changed, and the cats were shown more widely across Europe.

Development was hampered, however, by showing these cats

against the British Shorthair and conforming to the same standard. This changed in 1981 when FIFé formally separated the breed and created a new standard for the European. The split gave the breed a fresh start, but with a ready-made breeding stock of registered cats; crosses to British Shorthairs are no longer allowed.

CREAM SELF Although eye colour was a weakness in early European Shorthair show cats, today, excellent, clear copper eyes are found in many of the coat colours.

Cats from Scandinavia

The history of the European domesticated cat is patchy, being pieced together from historical documents, archaeological finds, and genetic mapping. Between early trade and the Roman army bringing the cat with it on campaigns, it seems to have been established in even the northernmost reaches of Europe in little over a thousand years after first leaving Egypt for Greece. In Scandinavia, the cat was helped by its association with the goddess Freya, and the region has eventually given the world two cat breeds: the European and the rather more successful export, the Norwegian Forest Cat (*see* pp 268–73).

Some speculate that cats from Scandinavia may be behind other breeds, with mousers that accompanied Viking expeditions to North America around a thousand years ago forming an initial population there. While this is not substantiated, the distribution of the red gene does show some crossover between cats in Scandinavia and those in islands off the British coast.

TORTIE SMOKE The most popular colours are the black-based ones. The tortoiseshell mix of black and red is also popular; here it is softened by the white undercoat found in smokes.

Despite the separate recognition and having the freedom to perfect its own style, the breed remains unrecognized by other major registries, and is relatively rare beyond mainland European countries. It has won particular popularity in Finland.

PERSONALITY AND LOOKS

Like most of the older European breeds, this one is affectionate but quiet and self-contained in demeanour. It is playful, but when the toys are put away or the hunting done, it is happy just to be around people without needing to be involved in their every activity.

The European is an all-weather, all-purpose kind of cat. The body is medium long, not as cobby as the British Shorthair but never rangy, and every part is firm and neat: limbs and tail thick and gently tapering, the ears as wide as they are tall, the eyes rounded. The coat requires next to no care except when moulting.

The word 'medium' appears frequently in the breed profile, and perhaps this is why the breed has not caught the imagination of the public. It has no very distinctive feature to make it stand out from the crowd, but simply represents the best of a natural cat type, bred for consistency.

Chartreux

ORIGIN France (before 1700s)
SYNONYM None
WEIGHT 3–7.5 kg (7–17 lb)
BUILD 🐈
TEMPERAMENT 🐈
COAT CARE ✂️
COLOURS Blue self only

This cloud-coloured cat is the French Shorthair in everything but name. The Chartreux was named 'cat of France' and *Felis catus coeruleus* by the 18th-century naturalist Buffon, and was the pet chosen by the French President General de Gaulle and championed by the flamboyant author Colette. Despite lapses in its fortunes during the 20th century, the breed survived to stage a comeback, and the 'smiling cat' remains an icon of its homeland today.

CHARTREUX SHADES The coat may be any shade of blue from a pale ashy shade to a deep slate, although the brighter shades are preferred on the show bench in all the registries.

BREED ORIGINS

The origins of this breed are wrapped in legends. It has been claimed to be descended from cats that lived with Carthusian monks in the Chartreuse monastery, but there are no records of any such blue cats in the monastery archives. Another tale says that the ancestors of the Chartreux were brought to France from Syria in the 13th century by returning crusaders, many of whom became Carthusian monks. Stocky grey cats with copper eyes are referred to as 'the cats of Syria' in 16th-century French sources. But it seems likely that the name in fact comes from a Spanish woollen fabric called 'pile de Chartreux', just as the tabby pattern was named after a cloth. This hints at a darker past for these cats: they were prized by furriers for their luxuriant pelts.

Chartreux cats lived in small, natural colonies scattered across France, notably in Paris and on Belle Île, off the coast of Brittany. Two

World Wars were hard on the numbers, and outcrosses were made to other cats, based almost entirely on their colour: blue Persians (*see* pp 258–61), blue British Shorthairs (*see* pp 188–93) and blue Russians (*see* pp 198–99). The breed was considered so close to the British in type that FIFé declared the two to be one in 1970: concerted work and campaigning by breeders saw this reversed by 1977.

FRENCH BLUE

The Chartreux coat is a soft plush of an even blue, with an overall silvery sheen, setting off eyes in shades from gold to deepest copper. The build has been called 'primitive', and likened to a potato on matchsticks, due to the slender legs.

This seems to have been ignored by the creators of Ste-Cat, a mascot of the Montreal Jazz Festival in Canada. Ste-Cat is said to be a Chartreux, but the cartoons that appear on T-shirts show a truly bright blue cat made up of musical notes; the slender legs are still there, but she seems to have lost a lot around the midriff and acquired a rather more Oriental face.

TRUE TO TYPE Old photographs highlight the sheen of the coat and the smile so typical of the breed, which is due to its prominent, rounded whisker pads.

SLOW STARTER The Chartreux is far from a precocious breed. It can take two years or more to reach maturity, going through a gawky 'teenage' stage.

OWNING A CHARTREUX

The Chartreux is a flâneur, an observer rather than an active participant in events. Its high, chirping voice is never used to excess, and while it is affectionate and can be playful, it needs personal space.

Grooming is minimal: brushing is discouraged, but rubbing and stroking are recommended to bring out the best in the coat. There is a slight health concern with slipping kneecaps (patellar luxation); breeders should screen for this.

The naming of Chartreux cats is a curious matter. There is a convention that all kittens born in a particular year are given names starting with the same letter, although K, Q, W, X, Y, and Z are omitted from the sequence to save breeders' sanity.

Russian Shorthair

ORIGIN Russia (before 1800s)

SYNONYM Russian Blue, Foreign Blue, Maltese Cat, Spanish Blue, Archangel Cat

WEIGHT 3–5.5 kg (7–12 lb)

BUILD

TEMPERAMENT

COAT CARE 🖊

COLOURS Blue, black, and white self only; blue self only in CFA

Considered a lucky cat in Russia, these cats or images of them were traditionally given to brides, perhaps as a charm to ensure children. They may also have been put in new babies' cradles to drive out malign influences. This old and naturally occurring breed was Russia's first feline export, and a highly successful one.

BLACK SELF   WHITE   BLUE SELF

BREED ORIGINS

Rumours had it that the Russian Blue was the favoured cat of the Russian Czars. Less romantic tales with more evidence on their side tell us they were valued for their skins. The old name of Archangel Cat alludes to their supposed origins around the Russian port of Archangel, and the tradition that these cats were brought to Britain by Russian sailors in the 1860s. The alternative names of Spanish Blue and Maltese Cat muddy the waters somewhat, but the Russian sailors seem to win in the credibility stakes.

The Russian Blue was shown at Crystal Palace in 1875 under the name Archangel Cat, and exported to the United States by 1900. Early breed work was concentrated in Europe. Today the breed is recognized by all the major registries, but there are some differences. In the 1970s, Australian breeder Mavis Jones created a Russian White, and a Russian Black has followed. These are recognized in Australia, New Zealand, and South Africa, and have preliminary status in the GCCF, but elsewhere resistance has seen them remain outside the fold. Because of this, the breed is known as the Russian or Russian Shorthair in some places and the Russian Blue in others; the GCCF lists the three colours separately.

BEAUTIFUL BLUES

The Russian is generally semi-foreign in type, with a lean, muscular, slightly

SILVER TIPPING The coat is hard to describe: the CFA standard calls for 'distinctly silver tipped' guard hairs, the GCCF standard specifies no silver tipping, and FIFé settles for 'a silver sheen'.

Royal kitties?

It is sometimes claimed that Queen Victoria favoured Russian Blues, but the same claim is also made on behalf of the British Shorthair and even the Chartreux. The first show-classes pitted all blue cats against each other, and if the Queen owned a blue cat it would be easy for anyone wanting the royal seal of approval to claim it was their breed that sat on the palace cushions. The Russian got its own class at British cat shows in 1912, but the public inclination to see all blue cats as one still exists today.

angular look. The original Russian is is distinguished by the recessive blue coat. Early Russians shown in the United Kingdom had yellow eyes, and it was not until the 1930s that a green eye colour was written into the breed standard.

The coat is silky and double. The GCCF standard describes it as 'very different in texture from any other breed and the truest criterion of the Russian'. It is tipped with silver, giving a sparkling, shimmering appearance.

OWNING A RUSSIAN

Russians are easy to care for: indeed, some breeders claim that the less the coat is groomed, the deeper its sheen will become. They are best suited to a quiet home without upheavals; while affectionate, they are dignified, quiet, slightly shy cats that do not appreciate too much hurly burly. They are unlikely to react aggressively to overmuch handling, but tend to wriggle away and seek quiet elsewhere, so can be a disappointing pet for children or others who want to cuddle a cat frequently. In all ways, this is a very grown-up breed.

MONA LISA SMILE
Standards call for a moderately long, blunt wedge. The large ears are generally upright, the eyes almond-shaped and widely spaced. The muzzle and whisker pads can give the cat a mysterious smile.

American Shorthair

ORIGIN United States (1900s)
SYNONYM Once called Domestic Shorthair
WEIGHT 3.5–7 kg (8–15 lb)
BUILD 🐈
TEMPERAMENT 🐱
COAT CARE ✂✂
COLOURS Western colours in self, tortie, bi-colour, smoke, shaded, and tipped; blotched and striped tabby patterns

Although its name declares this no-nonsense breed to be the national American cat, it has been a less successful ambassador than the hugely popular Maine Coon (*see* pp 262–67). At home, it still enjoys a high profile, although other shorthaired breeds have overtaken it over the years.

BLACK SELF   BLACK & WHITE   RED STRIPED TABBY   SILVER STRIPED TABBY   TORTIE & WHITE   BLUE TORTIE & WHITE

BREED ORIGINS

Domestic cats have been present on the North American mainland for at least five centuries, since the first European settlers landed with their ships' cats. They spread across the continent just as the settlers did, although perhaps more slowly than dogs: a cat does not take easily to a shifting territory centred on a moving vehicle.

For the first four hundred years of American feline history, cats were simply working animals: mousers protecting homes, farms, and businesses from rodents, just as they did the world over. They developed into large cats, the better to cope with the predators and prey on this new continent, with a thick, dense, and hard coat to keep out cold and moisture.

In the late 19th century, people began to show and breed cats, although at the start the definition of a breed was hazier and the rules about what kinds of cats were judged against each other much broader than they are in today's highly organized fancy. At the second cat show in Madison Square Gardens, New York, in 1896, a brown tabby American shorthair, not yet quite a breed, was offered for sale for $2,500. When the Cat Fanciers' Association (CFA) was established a decade later, the Domestic Shorthair was one of just five recognized breeds.

It was established by a cross in 1904 with the British Shorthair (*see* pp 188–93). British cats were regarded as higher quality than American cats, and crosses helped to strengthen desired traits by using lines that had already been selectively bred for some time.

Renamed American Shorthair in 1966, the breed remains in the top ten in the United States. The American fancy, however, seems to have a preference for longhaired and more exotic breeds, which claim the very top spots. Overseas, the breed is virtually unknown.

OWNING AN AMERICAN SHORTHAIR

This is a cat for those who want a breed still close to its working roots. With a breed standard that calls for no part 'so exaggerated as to foster weakness', it is a robust, sturdy cat. In character, it is alert, intelligent, and friendly, tending more towards quiet companionship than demonstrative dependency.

SILVER CLASSIC TABBY It was when a cat of this colour won the title of Cat of the Year that the breed name was changed from Domestic Shorthair to American Shorthair.

RED MACKEREL TABBY The breed standard for the American Shorthair tends to favour males, with a large, full-cheeked face and solidly built, powerful body. Females are always lighter and slightly more finely boned.

AMERICAN SHORTHAIR (*see* pp 200–201) This muscular breed with the build of a prizefighter was one of the first breeds to be recognized. It is a distillation of the qualities of the true American working cat: robust, intelligent, and calm.

Snowshoe

ORIGIN United States (1960s)
SYNONYM None
WEIGHT 2.5–5.5 kg (6–12 lb)
BUILD 🐈
TEMPERAMENT 🐈
COAT CARE 🖌
COLOURS All colours in self and tortie (eumelanistic only in CFA); all tabby patterns (no tabby in CFA); always in pointed pattern and with white spotting

Beauty is truly in the eye of the beholder, and what some breeders scorn others will love. The white toes that were regarded as a fault in the early Siamese (*see* pp 220–23) have been cherished as a distinctive feature in other breeds, and they even sparked the creation of the Snowshoe.

LILAC POINT

CARAMEL POINT

CHOCOLATE POINT

FAWN POINT

SEAL TABBY POINT

RED TABBY POINT & WHITE

BREED ORIGINS

Early Siamese breeders in the west tried to eradicate the genes behind the white toes or paws that sometimes appeared in their kittens. In the 1950s, some American breeders tried to reverse this trend and create a white-footed Siamese under the attractive name of Silver Laces, but their efforts faded into obscurity. Then in the 1960s, Philadelphia breeder Dorothy Hinds-Daugherty noticed white feet in Siamese kittens and attempted to stabilize the 'fault' into a feature. After much frustration, the Siamese were crossed with American Shorthairs (*see* pp 200–203), giving a reliable bi-colour trait, and the Snowshoe was on its way.

BI-COLOUR In TICA, a cat with an inverted 'V' of white on its face is a bi-colour. Less than two thirds of the coat, on the lower half, should be white.

NOT JUST A COPYCAT

There was, naturally enough, opposition to the very existence of the Snowshoe from some Siamese breeders, who had spent decades reducing the appearances of white feet. This was also the first shorthaired cat breed to adopt the pointing pattern that was virtually the trademark of the Siamese, and the possibility of confusion in the public mind caused concern.

SEAL MITTED A mitted Snowshoe may have any pattern of white except an inverted 'V' in TICA; in the other registries, an inverted 'V' is preferred.

The longhaired Birman (*see* pp 276–79) had of course had the pattern for decades, and the Snowshoe was for a time described as a shorthaired Birman. The Birman now has its own, genuine shorthaired counterpart in the Templecat (*see* p 206).

The Snowshoe was originally quite similar to the Siamese in looks, although a little more solid due to the American Shorthair input. As the Siamese has become more slender and elongated, the two have diverged until nobody could confuse them.

The Snowshoe has a muscular, semi-foreign body and a modified wedge for a head. FIFé and the GCCF both allow a wider range of colours than North American registries, but prefer the mitted look, while TICA allows bi-colours with more white; CFA still does not show the breed.

KITTENS Like all pointed cats, Snowshoe kittens are born white. The breeder must wait some weeks to be sure of the coat patterns that will emerge.

OWNING A SNOWSHOE
Physically, Snowshoes are very low maintenance. The coat is single, like that of Oriental breeds, and needs no day-to-day care. This is a healthy breed, with no major inherited problems or physiological weaknesses.

The Snowshoe shows its Oriental heritage in more than just its coat. It is a playful, outgoing breed, and easily bored: not the best choice for someone who wants to leave a snoozing pet alone for much of the day. Snowshoes are gregarious, and a two-cat household may work better than a lone cat. They can also be talkative, but have a softer voice than some Oriental breeds, making them ideal for those who like a responsive pet but don't want one that will talk their ears off.

LILAC TABBY MITTED The most liberal registry of all with regard to colours and pattern, FIFé recognizes tabby patterns in the Snowshoe. Like all colours, the difference between the body and point colours is strong.

Templecat

ORIGIN New Zealand (2001)
SYNONYM Initially called Birman Shorthair
WEIGHT 4.5–8 kg (10–18 lb)
BUILD
TEMPERAMENT
COAT CARE
COLOURS All colours in self and tortie; all tabby patterns; always in pointed pattern with white mittens

Sooner or later, it seems, every shorthaired breed is subject to some breeder trying out a longhaired version, and for every longhaired breed there is someone who wants to see it in a short coat. Some experiments flourish, others fade: the fate of the Templecat remains to be seen.

SEAL POINT

CARAMEL POINT

CREAM POINT

BLUE TABBY POINT

RED TABBY POINT & WHITE

LILAC TABBY POINT

WORK IN PROGRESS The ideal conformation is a broad, strong head with a slight Roman nose and rounded eyes, set on a strong body with fairly thick-set legs. Eliminating traits brought in by the Oriental type is a painstaking process.

BREED ORIGINS

The Templecat is one of the small but growing number of breeds to emerge from Australia and New Zealand. In essence, it is a shorthaired Birman (*see* pp 276–79), and it was the creation of June Mateer. She bred a Birman to a cinnamon spotted tabby Oriental Shorthair (*see* pp 224–27). The resulting shorthaired litter included both a pointed kitten (showing the Oriental carried pointing under its solid coat, *see* pp 166–67) and a classic tabby (showing the Birman carried this pattern beneath its pointing, *see* pp 160–61).

These offspring were mated back to purebred Birmans in eumelanistic colours (*see* pp 158–59). Because the shorthair gene is dominant, the Templecat continues to produce longhaired kittens from carrying the hidden recessive gene.

Just like the Exotic (*see* pp 184–87), which has no long coat to cover any shortcomings in its build, the Templecat has to show proper Birman conformation in every exposed line. This is why crosses were all back to Birmans after the shorthair gene had been imported. Although longhair crosses might slow down the progress to a reliably shorthaired breed, this trait is easily and quickly spotted in a kitten and traceable through breeding lines. Conformation is a more subtle quality, controlled by a broad array of genetic influences, that is much harder to pin down.

Initially known as the Birman Shorthair, the breed has been named Templecat as a reference to the romantic tale of the Birman's origins. So far, it has only been recognized by Catz Inc., a young and adventurous association in New Zealand.

TEMPLECAT COMPANIONS

Anyone outside New Zealand is unlikely to find these cats available in the near future. They are said to be sociable, mellow types, just as relaxing to be around as their forebears. Such a tractable nature wrapped in a short, silky, easy-care coat sounds like an irresistible combination, however, so this breed may yet become more popular and spread abroad.

Temple cats

Monastic orders are credited in popular legend with the creation of a range of alcoholic drinks and a number of canine and feline breeds. Some of these legends don't stand up to scrutiny, but there is an element of truth to the breeds. Religious orders tend to be singular, self-sufficient communities, often surrounded by their own lands and so slightly isolated. Any cats (or dogs) brought into such a community as working animals or companions tend to form a closed breeding colony, in which otherwise rare characteristics can, over time, become the normal look of the group.

Antipodean

ORIGIN New Zealand and Australia (1990s)

SYNONYM Initially called New Zealand Shorthair

WEIGHT 3.5–7 kg (8–15 lb)

BUILD 🐈

TEMPERAMENT 🐈

COAT CARE 🖌

COLOURS Western colours in self, tortie, bi-colour, smoke, shaded, and tipped; all tabby patterns

The cat fancy began by recognizing national types as breeds – almost all of the early breeds had regional or national names. In the 20th century, much attention turned to creating breeds based on distinctive features instead. Around the world, however, breeds continue to crystallize out of national types.

 BLACK SELF

 RED & WHITE

 BROWN CLASSIC TABBY

 CREAM STRIPED TABBY

 TORTIE & WHITE

 TORTIE TABBY

BREED ORIGINS

One of the latest breeds to graduate from the class of domestic moggie is the Antipodean. This was at first called the New Zealand Shorthair, but the name was altered to reflect the work done by breeders in Australia, simultaneously giving the breed a broader base of appeal.

The Antipodean's ancestors arrived in the region with the Europeans. Nobody is quite sure when – it has been suggested that ships' cats were left on the Australian mainland before settlement – but certainly by the mid-18th century. The intervening century and a half has allowed time for generations of cats to breed and develop their own distinct type.

ANTIPODEAN CHARACTERISTICS

The type is moderate, muscular, and medium-bodied, with a wedge-shaped head that is neither elongated into a foreign type, nor shortened (*see* pp 178–79). While the climate in its homeland varies from cool, mountainous terrain to desert, no part of it is inhospitably cold; there is a longhaired version, but the shorthair is more often seen.

These are lively, intelligent and self-sufficient cats. Whether they catch the imagination or suffer the obscurity of other moderate breeds, such as the European (*see* pp 194–95), remains to be seen.

HELPING HAND A robust type with a large initial gene pool, the Antipodean could be of use as an outcross for other breeds. Once a type is stabilized and all the genes known, it is attractive to other breeders as a known quantity.

Asians

ORIGIN United Kingdom (1981)
SYNONYM Smokes were called Burmoires
WEIGHT 4–7 kg (9–15 lb)
BUILD
TEMPERAMENT
COAT CARE
COLOURS Western and Eastern colours in self, tortie, smoke, and shaded; tabby and sepia patterns

The Asians are distinguished as a group, rather than a single breed, by the GCCF registry. This reflects the fact that, although the cats share a common ancestry and type, the coats and the rules about what is allowed for each coat type are perhaps more diverse than for any other breed.

WHITE   BLUE TICKED TABBY   RED TICKED TABBY   SILVER SHADED   LILAC POINT   FAWN POINT

BREED ORIGINS

The origin of the Asian breed group lies in the accidental mating of two distinguished breeds. Breeder Miranda Bickford-Smith (née von Kirchberg) had bought a chinchilla Persian (*see* pp 258–61). The Persian was due to be neutered, but in the kind of mishap that owners are always warned about, he met a lilac Burmese (*see* pp 212–13) and ensured the survival of his line before human intervention.

The resulting litter of four female kittens had the Burmese type but sparkling silver-shaded coats. Their appearance and temperament were striking enough for the Persian male

to be given a second chance with another Burmese, resulting in a male kitten, and a breeding programme followed, outcrossing to Burmese to increase the gene pool.

The initial name of Burmilla for these shaded cats was a natural 'portmanteau' from Burmese

CHOCOLATE TABBY This blotched tabby shows the sepia pattern, with the markings on the body gently faded.

ROOM FOR CONFUSION Black Asian selfs are called Bombays, but are completely unrelated to the American breed of the same name (*see* p 232).

and chinchilla. The GCCF initially recognized the Burmilla, officially called the Asian Shaded, in 1989, and also shows all the other coats in the group. FIFé recognized the Burmilla alone in 1994; under FIFé breed standards, the breed is also being developed in Australia.

CHOCOLATE SMOKE The ideal smoke Asian appears solid-coloured when still, with the white undercoat only revealed in movement.

BLACK SILVER SHADED Shaded cats may have a creamy 'standard' or pure white 'silver' undercoat. Any degree of tipping is allowed.

TORTIE The GCCF recognizes all possible colours in Asian Selfs including the 'dilute modifier' shades and five torties, giving 13 in total.

A DIVERSITY OF COATS

All Asians are similar in type to the European Burmese, with a muscular, lithe body and medium legs and tail, all cloaked in a fine, short, sleek coat. The head is a relatively short wedge, with gently curved planes, and medium to large, fairly tall ears that are angled slightly out. The eyes are large and intermediate in shape – between rounded and oval. The range of coats, however, is much wide than in the Burmese.

The first generation of crosses always produced cats with short and shaded coats, because these dominant genes masked the sepia pointing of the Burmese and the long coat of the Persian. Later generations saw new coats emerging: longhaired, self, smoke, sepia patterned, and even tabby, because any shaded cat is genetically an agouti (*see* pp 164–65). The selfs and the tabbies had to content themselves with the relatively plain labels of Asian Selfs and Asian Tabbies, but the smokes were for a time called Burmoires and the longhairs are known as Tiffanies (*see* pp 288–91).

OWNING AN ASIAN

Asians are healthy and easy to care for; their coats need little routine grooming. But this cat first appealed to breeders for its temperament as much as its looks. While all show standards call for aggression or other undesirable behaviour in the show ring to be penalized, this was the first cat to include points for temperament in the breed standard. Livelier and more inquisitive than the typical Persian personality, Asians stop short of the full-tilt inquisitiveness and attention-seeking of the pure-blooded Burmese. Truly the best of both worlds, they make easygoing, friendly companions with a relaxed outlook on life.

The long haul

The journey to recognition can be a protracted one, with many stages. First, cats' pedigrees are recorded in a stage that may be called Preliminary or Miscellaneous, with cats exhibited at shows, but not competing. After this comes a stage often called Provisional, where cats compete against each other but perhaps not against other breeds. Only at what is usually called Championship level is a breed 'fully' accepted. Asians were registered by the GCCF from 1989, but only achieved Championship status in 1997.

LILAC This is the most common tabby pattern in the Asian. This is because most Burmese cats in the United Kingdom carry two copies of the ticked gene.

American Burmese

ORIGIN Burma, now Myanmar (before 1930s)

SYNONYM Some colours once called Mandaly

WEIGHT 3.5–6.5 kg (8–14 lb)

BUILD

TEMPERAMENT

COAT CARE

COLOURS All colours in self and tortie in TICA (sable, blue, chocolate, and lilac only in CFA); always in sepia pattern

The Burmese breed has had a short but eventful history. Although it only arrived in the West well into the twentieth century, within fifty years it split into two distinct types. This distinctly round-headed type is one of them: the other, with a more wedge-shaped head, is the European Burmese (*see* p 212–15).

LILAC POINT

CHOCOLATE POINT

FAWN POINT

The head fault

The lines of Good Fortune Fortunatus (*see* p 180), now found on almost every pedigree, carry a gene for a severe malformation called the Burmese craniofacial deformity. There is one lower jaw but two upper muzzles and noses, the eyes and ears are deformed, and the top of the head is incomplete, with a bulging brain covered by skin but no skull. Geneticists have identified the chromosome and the area of it that is responsible for the deformity: they hope they are close to finding the gene and developing a genetic test to allow the fault to be bred out. Until then, kittens die at birth or must be euthanized.

SABLE The look of the American Burmese is summed up by the words compact and rounded. Sable is genetically black degraded by the sepia gene.

BREED ORIGINS
The defining characteristic of all Burmese is the sepia pattern (*see* pp 166–67). This was widespread throughout southeast Asia: the copper-coloured Thong Daeng in the historic Thai *Cat Book Poems* or *Tamra Maew* are probably Burmese.

The mother of the breed was Wong Mau, brought to the United States in 1930. She was a natural Tonkinese (*see* pp 218–19); mated to a Siamese (*see* pp 220–23) she produced pointed and mink kittens. Only when bred to one of the latter did she produce sepia-pattern Burmese.

The breed's early history was turbulent: it was first recognized by CFA and then demoted in the 1930s. Reinstated in the 1950s, it had a new look and breed standard by the 1970s, when cats with a very rounded, short-muzzled head won all the prizes. This 'contemporary' head is now the standard look of the American Burmese, but it carries a price (*see* box).

OWNING A BURMESE
They may look sleek, but that muscular body is surprisingly heavy; the classic description is 'bricks wrapped in silk'. The glossy silk of the coat is fine and flat, without an undercoat, and virtually maintenance free. Burmese are less vocal than many of the other Oriental breeds, but still absurdly gregarious and affectionate.

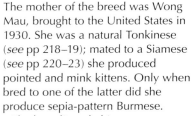
CHAMPAGNE This is genetically a chocolate; Burmese colours are still named as they were before their genetics were understood.

European Burmese

ORIGIN Burma, now Myanmar (before 1930s)

SYNONYM Red colours called Foreign Burmese in Canada

WEIGHT 3.5–6.5 kg (8–14 lb)

BUILD 🐈

TEMPERAMENT 🐾

COAT CARE 🖌

COLOURS Brown, blue, chocolate, lilac, red, and cream in self and tortie; always in sepia pattern

There are essentially two separate Burmese breeds, each referred to in their respective homelands simply as Burmese. The European type is now shown in North America, but the American type is not bred or shown abroad. This was one of the first breeds to suffer a schism over type, although others show signs of following in its footsteps.

LILAC POINT

CHOCOLATE POINT

FAWN POINT

BREED ORIGINS

The European Burmese was originally the same breed as the American Burmese (*see* pp 210–11), and all Burmese can trace their ancestry back to Wong Mau, the cat who brought the sepia-pointing pattern to the West from Burma (now Myanmar) in 1930. The breed was recognized in the United Kingdom in 1952 in the original brown colour.

After this, the breed diverged until it had two completely different looks: one in the United States and one in Europe. More colours were recognized in the European Burmese, and eventually differences over the shape of the head and health issues led to American cats being barred from European breeding lines. For many years, associations recognized either the American or the European Burmese, but not both. This changed in the 1990s, when CFA shows in Europe were suffering a dearth of entries in the Burmese class. CFA began to allow European Burmese to be shown and, in 2002,

gave the European Burmese full Championship status. There is some strife over whether or not the breed as shown in CFA is beginning to look too much like the American Burmese.

COMING TO A HEAD

The split between the American and the European versions of this breed began in 1959, when CFA revised their standard for the Burmese, requiring a round head with a short

LILAC TORTIE Torties arrived in the Burmese in the 1960s, at first through an accidental mating, followed by a planned cross.

CHOCOLATE This colour was brought into the European Burmese from cats imported from the United States in the late 1960s, when the two types still interbred.

First records

The *Tamra Maew* or *Cat Book Poems*, dating from 1350–1767, describes the many types of cat found in Thailand and the kinds of luck they could bring. Although Wong Mau came from Burma, the Burmese breed is believed to be present in the *Tamra Maew* in the shape of either the brown Supalak or the copper-coloured Thong Daeng.

muzzle. European breeders, on the other hand, kept a generally 'foreign' type, with a wedge-shaped head.

The issue became more urgent in the 1970s, when the 'contemporary' look took hold in the United States. Because of the lethal gene carried in the lines associated with this look, Burmese from American lines that might carry the fault cannot even be registered in the GCCF and many other associations.

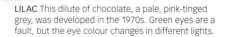

LILAC This dilute of chocolate, a pale, pink-tinged grey, was developed in the 1970s. Green eyes are a fault, but the eye colour changes in different lights.

THE EUROPEAN BURMESE TODAY

Like the American Burmese, the European breed is still characterized by the sepia pattern, with colour shading softly from dark points to a lighter body. A wide range of colours has been developed and is recognized in the European Burmese, but no shaded forms or tabby patterns. Those seeking a wider range of coats on a body of this type should look at the Asian group (see pp 208–209).

The European standards of points differ from the standards for both the American Burmese and, interestingly, the CFA standard for the European Burmese. American standards put more emphasis on colour, while the points in the FIFé standard are evenly distributed between colour and type. The GCCF standard puts the least emphasis on colour, and includes points for temperament, which is given as much weight as eye colour.

The wedge-shaped head is the most obvious factor distinguishing the European from the American Burmese, but the differences extend to other aspects of the build as well. The legs are slender, but still strong in appearance, and the tail is medium in thickness and the same length as the body. The body is lean, but picking up one of these cats can be a surprising experience; a dense, muscular build makes them heavier than they look.

BROWN Genetically, this is the same colour that is black in a self cat and seal in a pointed cat; it is called seal brown in breed standards. It was for many years the only Burmese colour.

All this is wrapped in a fine, short coat that lies flat against the body, with no insulating undercoat to pad it out.

OWNING A BURMESE

The Burmese is a low-maintenance breed, generally sound in health and needing no day-to-day care to keep it sleek and glossy. In personality, it is a gregarious and active companion, which is well suited to either a family home or a household with more than one cat. It is less vocal and inquisitive than the breeds derived from the Siamese (see pp 220–23), however, and makes a peaceable choice for those who find the chattier Oriental types a bit overwhelming.

RED Tabby markings on the face are allowed, and small indeterminate markings elsewhere, but the body colour should be an even, tangerine shade.

SEPIA SHADING In the sepia pattern of the Burmese, the underparts are lighter than the back, and this in turn is slightly lighter than the points; the face may be the darkest.

EUROPEAN BURMESE (*see* pp 212–15) The chocolate colour shows sepia shading more strongly than many other shades. Although the European head is a moderate wedge, breeding males, like the cat on the right, inevitably develop 'stud jowls'.

Tonkinese

ORIGIN United States and Canada (1960s)
SYNONYM Tonkanese, Golden Siamese
WEIGHT 2.5–5.5 kg (6–12 lb)
BUILD 🐈
TEMPERAMENT 🐾
COAT CARE 🪥
COLOURS All colours except cinnamon and fawn in self and tortie (only eumelanistic in CFA); all tabby patterns (not in CFA or TICA); always mink

The pattern that defines the Tonkinese had been in existence long before the breed itself was recognized – or created, depending on your point of view. This breed was a first in the feline world because it was accepted from the start as an inevitable part of its genetic make-up that it would never breed true.

LILAC POINT

CARAMEL POINT

CHOCOLATE POINT

FAWN POINT

SEAL TABBY POINT

BREED ORIGINS

The Tonkinese is a hybrid of the Siamese (*see* pp 220–23) and the Burmese (*see* pp 210–15). Two mutations of the same gene are responsible for the different pointing patterns seen in these breeds (*see* pp 166–67), but neither form is dominant over the other. The result is that if a cat carries one copy of each form (a state called heterozygous), it will show an intermediate pattern that is less dramatically pointed than the Siamese, but more pointed than the Burmese: this is the distinguishing pattern of the Tonkinese, known as mink.

It is possible that some of the unacceptably dark 'chocolate Siamese' mentioned in British sources of the 1880s may have been minks. But the very first Tonkinese reliably recorded in the West was in fact Wong Mau, the founder of the Burmese breed. When bred to a

Siamese, she produced kittens of a Siamese coat type (showing she carried the pointing gene) and kittens of her own type (showing she carried the sepia gene). Only when she was mated to one of her kittens with the same coat as herself did she produce the all-sepia Burmese.

In the 1950s breeders deliberately recreated this hybrid as the Golden Siamese in the United States, and then in the 1960s as the Tonkinese in Canada, where it was finally recognized. Today it is accepted by most major registries; efforts to create a longhair under the name Silkanese or Himbur have come to nothing.

Because both forms of the mutation are needed in any Tonkinese meeting the breed standard, a litter of kittens from two Tonkinese will inevitably include some pointed and some

LILAC TORTIE The mixture of colours in the tortie coat tends to obscure the shading of the mink pattern, even more so with dilute shades.

sepia types; TICA and CFA show these, but not the GCCF. Most breeds seek to eliminate variants and breed true to the standard, so the fact that this is impossible in the Tonkinese has led some people to question whether it is a breed at all.

CHOCOLATE Mixing two breeds with different characteristics leaves some undesirable traits. Eyes from blue to green are accepted in minks, but golden eyes only in sepia cats.

OWNING A TONKINESE

Whatever the misgivings of the pedants, the Tonkinese has become a popular breed, although it lurks outside the top ten that are annually recorded in the United Kingdom and United States. Indeed, it is a very attractive cat: less angular than one parent but more lithe than the other, with a unique eye colour that is described as 'aqua'.

They are affectionate and lively cats, always on the move through the home, and remarkably tolerant of even the unpredictable nature of children's play, with melodious voices that are used in moderation.

BLUE The blue of the Tonkinese is allowed to have warm undertones, rather than the crisp, cool colour seen in some other breeds.

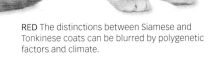

RED The distinctions between Siamese and Tonkinese coats can be blurred by polygenetic factors and climate.

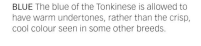

CHOCOLATE TORTIE The base colour should be a warm chocolate, well broken up with varying shades of red, which should show no tabby markings.

Siamese (including Colorpoint Shorthair)

ORIGIN Siam, now Thailand (before 1800s)
SYNONYM Once called Royal Cat of Siam
WEIGHT 2.5–5.5 kg (6–12 lb)
BUILD 🐈
TEMPERAMENT 🐈
COAT CARE 🖌
COLOURS All colours in self and tortie (some called Colorpoint Shorthair in CFA); all tabby patterns (called Colorpoint Shorthair in CFA); always in pointed pattern

As if its extraordinary looks were not enough to get it noticed, the Siamese arrived in Europe embellished with tales of both a royal heritage and a past as a sacred temple cat. In fact, the Siamese has probably had more extravagant legends attached to it than any other breed in feline history.

RED POINT

CREAM POINT

BLUE TABBY POINT

LILAC TABBY POINT

BREED ORIGINS

The mutation that causes the pointed coat pattern arose at least five centuries ago, somewhere in Asia, and it was most strongly associated with the Far East: beyond these generalities, nothing specific has yet been ascertained.

Cats of Siamese type appear in Thai manuscript books. The original *Tamra Maew*, or *Cat Book Poems*, was compiled sometime between 1350 and 1767, and a new *Smud Khoi* copy was made from the old texts between 1868 and 1910. The folded sections bear illustrations of various cat types, together with advice as to what kind

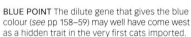
BLUE POINT The dilute gene that gives the blue colour (*see* pp 158–59) may well have come west as a hidden trait in the very first cats imported.

of luck they may bring and how to treat them. The Siamese is called the Wichien-Maat (the translated spellings vary).

Despite trade between West and East for centuries, no record of Siamese pointed cats reaching the West can be found before the 19th century, although a description of one in eastern Russia was written in 1793. The first British mention is in a catalogue from the first Crystal Palace Show in 1871. In 1879, the American Consul in Bangkok brought cats to the United States from Thailand, and in 1884, the British Vice Consul in Bangkok sent a breeding pair back to Britain as a gift for his sister, Lilian Jane Veley.

Although the story goes that these cats were a royal gift, and they were dubbed the Royal Cats of Siam, Lilian Jane Veley wrote that at least

SEAL POINT Today's Siamese breed standards call for deep blue eyes, strikingly large ears, and long legs and tail.

Breed standards or buyer's guide?

The *Tamra Maew* is rather like a field guide to cats. Verses accompanying each cat's picture give details of the coat and type very similar to a modern breed standard. In some cases they also outline the cat's behaviour, and how one should behave towards the cat. There is no reference to breeding as such, only advice to seek out the desirable types. And not all are desirable: there are evil, bad-luck cats to avoid. These often look as if they have congenital or other health problems, and their texts could be seen as simple husbandry advice.

one of them was bought from a street vendor for a relatively modest price. No real evidence has been found to back up the romantic tale that pointed cats enjoyed royal privileges. The Thai king of the day, Rama V or King Chulalongkorn, was enthusiastic about cats, and he had the *Tamra Maew* copied, but he is said to have preferred the odd-eyed

white cats now being bred as the Khao Manee (*see* box p 231).

Whatever their origins, these two cats and their three kittens were shown at the Crystal Palace Show in 1885. Their exotic appearance and emphatic voices were not an immediate hit with everybody; one observer described them as 'an unnatural nightmare of a cat'.

SIAMESE KITTENS All pointed cats come out of the warmth of their mother's body completely white and will develop their points over the first few months.

However enough people were taken with them, including the founder of the cat fancy, Harrison Weir, for this line to become the start of the Siamese breed in Europe.

CHOCOLATE POINT This is one of the four colours first established in the breed: chocolate, seal, and their dilute forms of lilac and blue.

CHOCOLATE TORTIE POINT Chocolate and lilac may have been carried from the start, with chocolates explained as 'poor' seals.

APRICOT TABBY POINT This is the modified dilute form of red, and one of the later colours to be understood and recognized in many cats.

TORTIE POINT Bringing the red shades into the colour palette made tortoiseshell points possible. The colouring need not be even, but all the points must show some mix of colours.

CARAMEL TABBY POINT The dilute modifier gene turns both blue and lilac to a caramel shade.

CREAM POINT The red colours have always been present in Oriental cats, but were introduced into the Western Siamese by outcrossing to other breeds.

THE CHANGING SIAMESE

Self cats were excluded in the 1920s, eventually becoming the Oriental Shorthairs (*see* pp 224–29). Similarly, unwanted longhairs became the Balinese (*see* pp 300–301). When 'new' colours appeared, only some associations accepted them; CFA still calls them Colorpoint Shorthairs.

But the most controversial change is more subtle. The Siamese has become 'ultra-typed' – so slender that it makes size zero supermodels look curvaceous. Advocates claim this was always the ideal; detractors claim it is nothing like photographs of the early show winners. In response, TICA began the process in 2007 of recognizing a less etiolated type under the name of Thai.

OWNING A SIAMESE

On one level, Siamese are fairly low maintenance, with a fine, short coat that needs no grooming. The lack of an undercoat and insulating fat means an outdoor lifestyle in a cooler climate may not be suitable. But in personality, this is a high-maintenance pet. Vocal, sticking its long nose into everything, playful, and gregarious, the Siamese is the original all-singing, all-dancing party animal.

Oriental Shorthair

ORIGIN United Kingdom (1950s)

SYNONYM Once called Foreign Shorthair in Britain

WEIGHT 4–6.5 kg (9–14 lb)

BUILD

TEMPERAMENT

COAT CARE

COLOURS All colours in self, tortie, smoke, shaded, and tipped; all tabby patterns

Burdened with a multitude of names down the decades, Oriental cats have suffered a few identity crises since they first appeared in the West. But, despite it all, today they hover in or just outside the top ten breeds in both the United Kingdom and the United States, and hold their own elsewhere.

| BLACK SELF | WHITE | LILAC STRIPED TABBY | RED TICKED TABBY | RED STRIPED TABBY & WHITE | BLUE TORTIE TABBY & WHITE |

RED SELF It took a long time for this colour to be accepted, because of the markings exposed by the red gene. Markings are now accepted in the colour.

BREED ORIGINS

These solid-coloured cats were at first included within the Siamese breed (*see* pp 220–23). But in the 1920s the Siamese Club of Great Britain changed the standard, deciding that the name Siamese excluded 'any but blue-eyed' (and therefore pointed, *see* pp 166–67) cats.

Following their expulsion, the elegant but now unrecognized cats languished, their numbers declining. Breeding of black and blue selfs may have continued until World War II in Europe, and here, in the early 1950s, a revival began. It started with Baroness Edit von Ullmann and Mrs A Hargreaves, both seeking to produce self brown cats of a foreign type; they were joined by other breeders, and after crosses of Siamese and non-pedigree cats (both shorthair

LILAC SELF Carried as a recessive gene by many cats used in developing the Havana, lilac was shown as 'any other variety', together with blacks and blues until in 1977.

and longhair) succeeded in developing a chocolate self cat.

This was initially (and again later) known as Havana, but it was first recognized in 1958 in the United Kingdom as the Chestnut Brown Foreign; the name Havana had unfortunate connections to the fur trade, due to there being a rabbit of the same name. This cat contributed to the development of the Havana Brown breed (*see* pp 232–33) in the United States, but should not be confused with it – the two are quite separate. In the United Kingdom, this was the start of the Foreigns, the name given to all the self-coloured cats at first; it was accepted that they were essentially colours of one type, rather than separate breeds.

Foreigns caught the eye of the Marksteins, Siamese breeders from the United States, who had travelled to England in 1972 looking for new Siamese lines. In the course of the 1970s, Foreigns were accepted in CFA and other American registries, but under the name Oriental Shorthair.

In the United Kingdom, tabbies were accepted in the late 1970s, but under the name of Orientals. At the start of the 1990s, almost all Foreigns were rechristened Oriental Shorthairs in the United Kingdom, removing some confusion. In the United States,

CFA classes the shorthairs and the longhairs (see pp 302–303) as one breed with two divisions, an approach that has not been taken up by other registries. The status of bi-colours (see pp 230–31) varies internationally.

BLUE SELF Blue cats of Siamese descent produced during development of the Havana colour were registered as Russian Blues in the 1950s.

SILVER SHADED Recognition of shaded Orientals in the United Kingdom took eighteen years from 1978. It was feared that the varied expression of the silver gene would lead to unpredictable coats.

SLEEK AND SLENDER

Oriental Shorthairs have a distinctly Art Deco look: they are all long lines and svelte sophistication. The head is a long, triangular wedge, topped by large ears that flare outward at an angle. The eyes, in vivid shades of clear, unflecked green, are slanted and widely set.

The coat, like that of the Siamese, is short, fine, and lacking an insulating undercoat; this is not a cold-weather breed. In good condition, the coat is smooth and has a glossy sheen, as if polished.

OWNING AN ORIENTAL SHORTHAIR

This is one of a quartet of Oriental breeds, all tracing back to the introduction of the Siamese. The pointed Siamese has a longhaired counterpart in the Balinese (*see* pp

Siamese in disguise

When the Foreigns became Oriental Shorthairs in the United Kingdom, some colours retained individual names: one was the Foreign White. Three breeders, including geneticist Patricia Turner, began working towards a blue-eyed cat of Foreign type in the late 1950s. This Siamese in a white overcoat was shown in the 'any other variety' class from 1966; it was highly popular and gained recognition in the 1970s. It is a blue-eyed cat with reliably good hearing: the deafness associated with the white coat (*see* pp 168–69) has been virtually bred out (the original whites were copper-eyed), and the blue eyes come from their hidden Siamese gene. The colour retained its 'Foreign' name because Oriental whites in other registries have green eyes.

300–301), and the solid-coloured Oriental Shorthair has the Oriental Longhair. All are long-lived and generally healthy, although there is a tendency to heart attacks. Between the four, there is a look to please

SPOTTED TABBY These coats were recognized in the 1970s. They were developed under the name of Mau, but should not be confused with the spotted Egyptian Mau breed.

everyone. The shorthairs need no routine maintenance of the coat, although brushing it to a shine can be a pleasure for both owner and cat.

Beneath the varied hues and patterns, the Oriental personality reflects its ancestry. It loves nothing so much as to be the centre of attention, and will do its level best to achieve this. If that means physically getting between you and whatever else is occupying you, so much the better. It also has a loud voice, used liberally to remind you of its needs.

Those needs include not just attention but plenty of activity. These gregarious characters are also athletic achievers, ready to scale the heights in your home and explore its farthest corners. Be prepared to devote time to playing with an Oriental, and consider getting more than one cat, because the likelihood is that they will wear you out faster than you can tire them.

TICKED TABBY The striped, blotched, and ticked tabbies all followed the spotted tabbies in the 1980s.

ORIENTAL SHORTHAIR (*see* pp 224–27) This elegant breed presents the lean, angular Oriental body type in a wide range of colours and patterns, from sleek selfs to wild-looking spotted tabbies like this. There is also a longhaired version of the look.

Seychellois

ORIGIN Europe (2000s)

SYNONYM None

WEIGHT 4–6.5 kg (9–14 lb)

BUILD 🐈

TEMPERAMENT 🐈

COAT CARE ✏

COLOURS All solid eumelanistic colours except dilute-modifier shades in self and tortie; red and cream in tabby patterns; always with white; always in pointed pattern

When is a breed not a breed? When it is a colour or pattern in another breed. The Oriental breeds have between them stirred up enough international naming anomalies to confuse everyone for years. And it isn't over yet: this European breed is an example of registry independence for the new millennium.

RED TABBY POINT & WHITE

BLUE POINT

LILAC POINT

CHOCOLATE POINT

FAWN POINT

SEAL BI-COLOUR There are three different classes of coat: the bi-colour, the harlequin, and the van. All have colour on the head and tail; the harlequin also has colour on the legs, and the bi-colour on the legs and body.

BREED ORIGINS

The Seychellois looks like a Siamese (*see* pp 220–23) in a bi-colour coat, and that is pretty much what it is. These are included in the Oriental Shorthair (*see* pp 224–39) and Longhair (*see* pp 302–303) by CFA and TICA, but not in Europe.

In the 1980s, British geneticist Pat Turner set out to achieve cats of Oriental type in a white coat with patches of colour and a solid-coloured tail, working with another breeder, Julie Smith. In 1988, they showed two cats auspiciously named Victoria and Félicité.

Getting colours recognized within an existing breed is often harder than getting a new breed recognized. Clearly these cats would not be accepted as Siamese: Siamese breeders have devoted decades to getting rid of the spotting gene, and did not want it back. Recognition within the Oriental Shorthair was also resisted – GCCF did not even recognize bi-coloured Orientals. And so FIFé has given these cats the name Seychellois, in reference to the cats of the Seychelles said to have inspired the breed, but also following the tradition of using the names of islands for offshoots of the Siamese, as in the Balinese and Javanese (*see* pp 300–301). In the United Kingdom, the GCCF has instead started the process of recognition for Oriental bi-colours and includes the pointed colours within this, following the US lead.

OWNING A SEYCHELLOIS

The Seychellois is typically Oriental, ideal for those who want a new twist on that elongated face, slender body, and long legs. There is a longhair as well as the shorthair but, like the Balinese and the Oriental Longhair, the difference is seen mostly in a plume-like tail and a neck ruff.

While the official Seychellois breed is likely to remain a European idiosyncrasy, those smitten with the patchwork look can find pointed Oriental bi-colours elsewhere. They are easy to run, with minimal grooming and health problems, and described by breeders as sensitive, athletic, loving, and demonstrative.

EARLY FORERUNNERS The name Seychelles was suggested for Oriental bi-colours like this, before they were given Preliminary status by the GCCF.

Royal Cat of Siam?

There is another breed out of the Thai gene pool currently gaining ground in the West: an all white cat, but distinct from white Orientals or Foreign Whites. The Khao Manee or 'white jewel' cat is a minor breed, but still being raised by people in Thailand. It can have eyes of any colour, but often has one yellow and one blue, sometimes called the 'diamond eye'. Adherents of the breed, including Thais, claim that it was the true Royal Cat of Siam, and the consul who sent home two Siamese was fobbed off with a substitute; in his book *Siamese Cats*, author Sydney W France reported that this seemed true when he visited Thailand in the 1930s. As a contemporary of the Thai King at Eton, he was granted special access to the palace, and found the cats to lack points. The breed is present in the United States and recognized by FIFé in Europe, but remains rare at present.

POINTED NOSE White spotting is unpredictable, except that it tends to 'spread' from the bottom of the cat up. Some breeds favour a white nose, often with a spot of colour.

Havana Brown

ORIGIN United Kingdom and United States (1950s)

SYNONYM Once called Chestnut Brown Foreign in United Kingdom

WEIGHT 2.5–4.5 kg (6–10 lb)

BUILD 🐈

TEMPERAMENT 🐾

COAT CARE 🖌

COLOURS Chocolate self only

This is one of a handful of single-colour breeds in the world. These cats can have a hard time winning fans: you have to love not just the type but the one coat colour available, and none of these breeds make regular appearances in the top-ten breeds. The Havana Brown is further hampered by confusion with an ancestor of the same name, and remains virtually unknown beyond its homeland.

BREED ORIGINS

Brown cats were known and shown in Europe as far back as the late 19th century. Some of these were solid-coloured Siamese (*see* pp 220–23), but the name 'Swiss Mountain Cat' was also used. When these solid-coloured cats were barred from the Siamese breed, they soon faded from view and almost from existence.

In the 1950s, they were taken up again by breeders in the United Kingdom, starting with a self brown termed the Havana – a genetic chocolate eventually recognized in the United Kingdom as the Chestnut Brown Foreign. In the mid-1950s, one of these cats was imported into the United States by a Mrs Elsie Quinn. Other imports and breedings followed, and by 1959 a Havana Brown won Grand Champion status in CFA. While the Foreigns in the United Kingdom were bred to a more angular standard and became in general a solid-coloured counterpart to the Siamese, eventually becoming the Oriental Shorthair (*see* pp 224–29), the American breed retained a more moderate, sweet-faced look. It could not now be confused with the British cat when seen, only by the name of the colour.

HAVANA FACE The head is a moderate wedge, with a distinctively rounded, somewhat narrow muzzle with a pronounced break.

OWNING A HAVANA BROWN

As a shorthair with a thin coat, the Havana Brown is as low-maintenance as a breed can get – in terms of grooming, anyway. Their insatiable curiosity and playful nature can be harder to keep up with.

However, finding a Havana Brown may be a problem. Known only in North America, it is close to the bottom of the rankings in numbers of cats registered each year. Outcrosses were closed in the 1970s, and appeals to allow them again fell on deaf ears within CFA for some time. Although limited outcrossing is now once again underway, the breed still teeters on the brink of viability.

HAVANA BROWN Every hair, including the whiskers, is a warm, even shade of brown. The shade is a rich mahogany, brighter and warmer than chocolate in some other breeds.

Bombay

ORIGIN United States (1960s)
SYNONYM None
WEIGHT 2.5–5 kg (6–11 lb)
BUILD 🐈
TEMPERAMENT 🐾
COAT CARE 🖌
COLOURS Black self only

The desire to breed a domestic cat that resembles one of its wild brethren may seem like a new phenomenon, but in fact such ideas have a long history in the cat fancy. The Bombay, designed to be a 'mini black panther', was the first of these attempts to win any serious recognition. While it looks relatively tame compared with some of the creations and even hybrids that have followed since, this was the pioneer of the class.

BREED ORIGINS

In the 1950s, Nikki Horner, a breeder from Kentucky in the United States, set out to create a domestic cat resembling a melanistic leopard (*see* p 14). Starting with a black American Shorthair (*see* pp 200–203) with deep copper eyes and a show-winning sable Burmese (*see* pp 210–11) with a fine, glossy coat, she was disappointed with a lack of progress at

BOMBAY BUILD The conformation of the Bombay is fairly close to that of the Burmese, with a substantial, muscular body, and a well-rounded chest.

Eye colour

The Bombay breed standards call for brilliant copper eyes, but this is a hard colour to achieve, and many must settle for gold instead. Eye colour can vary considerably, not just across the breed, but in the lifetime of an individual cat. Full, intense colour can take some time to develop in kittens, and then it may fade or even gradually become greenish, particularly in male cats, once they reach maturity at three to five years.

first. A change in breeding lines provided better results, and she succeeded in her aim by the 1960s.

The Bombay caught the eye of breeders and the public, and was recognized in North America during the 1970s. However, it has now been eclipsed by more recent arrivals, has never won widespread popularity abroad, and remains unrecognized by European registries. There is room for confusion in the United Kingdom, where the name Bombay is used for the black self colour within the Asian breed group (see pp 208–209).

Outcrossing to the parent breeds is still allowed, but this is usually to Burmese for the desired conformation; the dominant black colour of the American Shorthair needs no reinforcing. The recessive Burmese sepia gene means sable variants are still produced. One drawback of this outcrossing is that Bombay lines carry the lethal Burmese head fault.

OWNING A BOMBAY

Bombays have been described as the perfect cat for anyone who wants a dog – or a monkey. Showing their Oriental origins, they are gregarious, playful and outgoing, and some owners successfully train them to fetch or to walk on a leash. They are heat-seekers, and find no seat so

ROUNDED OR WEDGE Standards vary between CFA and TICA. Cats with a head shape closer to the European Burmese might do well in TICA but be heavily marked down in CFA.

INTENSE CONTRAST The Bombay should have a coat like black patent leather, with copper eyes shining out of it. The glossiness is due to a fine topcoat that lies flat, with no fluffy undercoat.

comfortable as the human lap. Their American Shorthair input tempers the Oriental side of their nature, making them self-reliant and laid back.

Korat

ORIGIN Siam, now Thailand (before 1800s)
SYNONYM Si-Sawat
WEIGHT 2.5–4.5 kg (6–10 lb)
BUILD 🐈
TEMPERAMENT 🐆
COAT CARE 🖌
COLOURS Blue self only

It is said that a cat may look at a king, but few can claim to have been named by one. This ancient breed from Thailand claims just such a distinction, as well as a rainmaking role and one of the most poetic breed standards ever written. The Korat was a relative latecomer to the West, and remains something of a rarity, but in looks and personality this is a cat to remember.

BREED ORIGINS

The earliest record of the Korat is found in the Thai manuscript, the *Tamra Maew* or *Cat Book Poems* (1350–1767). This describes the silver-blue Si-Sawat: it was renamed Korat by King Chulalongkorn or Rama V (1853–1910) in order to commemorate the province of Thailand that is its homeland.

To call for rains in the Korat's homeland, a cat in a bamboo cage was paraded through the village; the cat was sprinkled with water, and then set free. Such ritualistic processions persisted into the 1980s, but rocket displays are now more favoured.

It is possible that the breed came to the West as early as the 19th century; a 'blue Siamese' (*see* pp 220–23) at an early show in London may have been either the type that became Oriental Shorthairs (*see* pp 224–29) or a Korat. A more certain date is 1959, when Mrs Jean Johnson brought Korats to the United States, where the breed was recognized by 1965. It was first brought to the United Kingdom in 1972, and was recognized by 1975.

OWNING A KORAT

The issue with a Korat is whether one owns it, or is owned by it. The large, rounded eyes and heart-shaped face

KORAT EYES The eyes should, according to the *Tamra Maew*, 'shine like dewdrops on a lotus leaf'.

look appealing and gentle, but this is an opinionated breed that will join in with whatever its owner is doing and then praise or criticize with equal enthusiasm. Whether with cats or people, the Korat wants to be top cat.

ALL HEART The Korat is said to have five hearts. The first is its face, the second its head seen from above, and the third the nose leather. The muscular chest forms a fourth and encloses the fifth, beating heart.

COAT COLOUR The *Tamra Maew*'s lyrical description says the coat is 'as the flower of the pampas grass, smooth and orderly'.

KORAT (*see* pp 236–37) Thailand's second most famous breed is a shimmering blue cat with a reputation as both a lucky cat and a rainmaker. The coat is described as cloud-coloured at the base turning to silver at the tip.

Abyssinian

ORIGIN Ethiopia (1800s)
SYNONYM None
WEIGHT 4–7.5 kg (9–17 lb)
BUILD 🐈
TEMPERAMENT 🐆
COAT CARE 🖌

COLOURS All colours in self, tortie, and shaded (brown, blue, cinnamon, and fawn only in CFA); always in ticked tabby pattern

Distinguished by the ticked tabby pattern, this was for many decades the only cat for which the pattern was essential. Only with the arrival of the Singapura (*see* pp 246–47) did the field widen. But for those seeking the translucent shimmer of the ticked coat with the look of the wild, the Abyssinian is still the breed of choice.

BLUE TICKED TABBY

RED TICKED TABBY

BROWN TICKED TABBY

BREED ORIGINS

The history of this striking breed is something of a riddle. It may come from Abyssinia (now Ethiopia), as its name implies, but it may not. Certainly cats of this type were brought back from Africa to the United Kingdom by returning troops: one 'captured in the late Abyssinian War' (which ended in 1868) took third prize at the Crystal Palace cat show of 1871. The founder of the cat fancy, Harrison Weir, wrote a breed standard in 1889. These early records should put the Abyssinian among the oldest known breeds.

But then the trail disappears. No recorded pedigree traces the later ticked cats back to the earliest imports, and the early pedigrees, going back as far as 1896, show mostly one or both parents as unknown. However, some also show crosses to other cats, which gives weight to the belief held by some breeders that the Abyssinian was in fact a British

BLUE The darker bands of slate-blue ticking alternate with beige, producing a warm dark blue coat, with very subtle shading.

LILAC This colour is allowed by TICA and the GCCF only. The coat is of warm, pinkish cream ticked with pinkish dove-grey.

SORREL The second colour to be recognized, this is also called red, but is genetically a cinnamon, not phaeomelanistic red.

native masquerading as an exotic foreigner, actually created from crosses of existing silver and brown tabbies with native British ticked cats. The crosses do explain some of the recessive colours that surfaced later in the breed, not to mention the gene for long hair that eventually led to the creation of the Somali (*see* pp 304–307). However, the ticked pattern is not a European one; it may have been in the British feline population by this time, but it must have arrived from somewhere.

The advent of genetic studies has shed some light on the business: most probable that the ancestors of the modern Abyssinian, and the origin of the ticked tabby gene, came from

SILVER BLUE All the major associations except CFA accept and show the silver colours.

Southeast Asia and the coast of the Indian Ocean. A stuffed cat with a ruddy ticked coat, identified as an Indian housecat, was acquired by the Zoological Museum in Leiden, in the Netherlands, in the 1830s, and it is possible that the ticked gene came to Europe not only as the spoils of war in Africa, but through trade with India. The breed has another genetic distinction: a four-year-old Aby named Cinnamon was chosen for the mapping of the feline genome, completed in 2007. She was chosen because her highly inbred genome made mapping the sequence easier.

OVERSEAS SUCCESS

After its early success at the London shows, the Abyssinian faded from view, and it barely existed

as a breed by the turn of the 20th century. In 1907 the first Abys were exported to the United States, but the breed did not really get off the ground there either. In the 1930s, after the founding of a dedicated breed club in the United Kingdom, top-quality cats sent overseas formed the foundation of a successful breeding programme and the Abyssinian was established as a breed on both sides of the Atlantic, as well as in Australia and New Zealand.

Unfortunately for British breeders, World War II put paid to cat showing and breeding, and by the end of the war there were only a dozen or so surviving Abys. Although importing cats has helped the breed recover, it has never achieved the same levels of popularity in the United Kingdom as it has in the United States, where it consistently sits somewhere in the middle of the top ten breeds.

CHOCOLATE Like its dilute, lilac, this is a relative latecomer to the Aby palette. The base coat is apricot, ticked with bands of dark chocolate to give an impression of a rich copper-brown.

FAWN The dilute of sorrel, fawn is one of the four basic colours that are recognized by CFA. The base colour of warm, rosy beige is ticked with cocoa-brown bands.

SILVER This is the usual, or brown, tabby seen below, with the warm base coat turned to shining, silvery white by the inhibitor gene.

THE ABYSSINIAN COAT

The ticked pattern is a dominant tabby gene (*see* pp 162–63). Beneath the subtle ticked coat there may be self or striped, blotched, or spotted tabby genes. The first colour recognized in the breed was a brown (genetically black) tabby, given the name of 'usual', unique to the Abyssinian breed. This is a dominant colour, and beneath it there can be the genes for blue, chocolate, or cinnamon, and their dilute versions. Early Abys did produce a lot of 'variant' kittens in these not-quite-usual coats. It is hard to breed

Ancient looks

Perhaps one of the reasons that the African name and supposed origins have stuck to this breed is that Abyssinians bear such a strong resemblance to the cats depicted in the wall paintings and sculptures of ancient Egypt. Of course, those in the wall paintings usually have the spotted coats that are a feature of the other 'African' breed that was created to emulate them, the Egyptian Mau (*see* pp 248–49). However, some paintings depicting hunting scenes show unspotted cats among the reeds, probably the jungle cat (*Felis chaus*, *see* p 27), and before DNA evidence pinpointed the origins of the domestic cat, some people thought that this might have been an ancestor. The shape of the Aby is also a good match, right down to the ear-tufts that it often sports.

The recessive genes have also produced some interesting results in late cross-breedings. Apart from the Somali (essentially an Aby in a luxury coat), the Aby has contributed to the spotted Ocicat (*see* pp 250–51) and the Australian Mist (*see* p 254).

OWNING AN ABY

The Aby, while low-maintenance, does have a few health problems. A pyruvate kinase (PK) deficiency causing intermittent anaemia is carried as a recessive trait: there is a genetic test. Patellar luxation or slipping kneecaps, renal amyloidosis (deposits in the kidneys), and retinal atrophy (causing impaired vision) may also be found; good breeders are aware of these and work to eliminate them.

As to personality, this is a people-oriented cat, but not a lap cat: it doesn't want to sit

on you so much as play with you or, failing that, follow you around and 'help you out'. They are intelligent and loyal, but their curiosity can make them a disaster for ornaments.

out recessive genes, but dedicated work by early breeders vastly reduced the variation to produce a consistent brown ticked tabby. Ironically, most of the colours they were working so hard to eliminate have now been recognized in the breed, although this varies from one registry to another.

CREAM Once, the name cream was used for the colour that is genetically fawn (*see* opposite), just as the genetically cinnamon sorrel was called red.

USUAL This original brown tabby is also known as ruddy. In French it is still called *lièvre*, or hare, and early cats were much less warmly coloured.

ABYSSINIAN (*see* pp 240–43) The wild looks of the Abyssinian proved more popular when it was revived in the 20th century than when the breed first emerged in the 1860s. There is also a longhaired version: the Somali.

Singapura

ORIGIN Singapore and United States (1970s)

SYNONYM The Malay word *Kucinta* ('sweet little cat') is sometimes used

WEIGHT 2–4 kg (4–9 lb)

BUILD 🐈

TEMPERAMENT 🐱

COAT CARE 🖌

COLOURS Brown ticked tabby in sepia pattern only

This is one of those breeds that provoked a flurry of excited publicity, which in turn brought not a little grumpiness from breeders weary of the public appetite for novelty. And there was a little bit of cloak and dagger to the story of the Singapura's origins. As time has passed, other novelties have distracted the crowd, but these charming, small cats have become an established, if minority, interest in the cat world.

BREED ORIGINS

The name Singapura is the Malay name for the island of Singapore. The original breeders and champions of the Singapura, Hal and Tommy Meadow, said that they brought three local cats back from Singapore in 1975, which were the foundation of the breed. These were said to be strays, and they were markedly smaller than cats found in the West. The three cats were named Ticle and Tes, male and female littermate kittens, and Puss'e, a young female. The Meadows presented the Singapura to CFA as a natural breed in 1981 and it was fully recognized by 1988.

However, Tommy had been a breeder of Abyssinians (*see* pp 240–45), Burmese (*see* pp 210–211), and Siamese (*see* pp 220–23) since 1955, and as the Singapura was distinguished not only by its size, but also by the innate characteristics of two of these breeds, pointed

SMALL SIZE The smallest feline breed, Singapuras are still larger than the ferals of Singapore: household cats are usually healthier and larger than ferals.

FACIAL MARKINGS The face is elegantly defined with dark brown eyeliner, lips, nose outline, and whisker roots. Dark lines extend over the brow and from the corners of the eyes.

SEPIA AGOUTI This combination is not the most commonly found coat pattern in Singapore, but it is still the only one allowed in the breed.

COMBINED PATTERNS Southeast Asia has the highest incidence of the ticked tabby gene, and the sepia trait was already known from Burma and possibly recorded in the Thai *Tamra Maew*.

questions were asked. Some concerned documents showing that the Meadows had imported three cats into Singapore in 1974 that had the same names as those they brought back in 1975. In 1990 the CFA board looked into the issue and the Meadows admitted that Malay cats had been brought back earlier, without proper import papers. However, since the ticked tabby and sepia genes both originated from southeast Asia, and since another important Singapura ancestor was known to have come from a Singapore cat shelter, the Singapura breed was allowed to stand.

SINGAPORE MASCOT
Having won recognition abroad, it has latterly caught the imagination back in Singapore. In 1990, the Singapore Tourist Promotion Board nominated the cat as a mascot, and held a 'Name the Singapore River Cats' contest. The winner was

kucinta, meaning 'sweet little cat', a name that can, confusingly, be found on products bearing images of cats with no resemblance to a Singapura. Life-size statues of cats and kittens now stroll and play among other sculptures along the Singapore river.

OWNING A SINGAPURA
The first issue when it comes to owning a Singapura is finding one. This breed has never achieved stellar popularity, and remains rare, especially in Europe, where it is not recognized by FIFé.

If you locate and obtain one, it will not be an overwhelming presence in your home. The Singapura is a quiet, retiring cat – said to be a relic of its feral evolution, where going unnoticed could save a lot of trouble. If a softly spoken, demure little cat is your aim, it may be worth seeking a Singapura.

KITTEN COATS The coat of the adult Singapura is single, silky, fine, and flat, but, like the correct yellow to green eye colour, takes time to develop fully.

Egyptian Mau

ORIGIN Egypt and Italy (1950s)

SYNONYM None

WEIGHT 2.5–5 kg (6–11 lb)

BUILD 🐈

TEMPERAMENT 🐁

COAT CARE ✐

COLOURS Brown and silver in spotted tabby pattern, black smoke with 'ghost' spotted tabby markings

The Egyptian Mau was the first breed to be defined by a spotted coat pattern; previous natural breeds had been defined by solid colours or pointing. Based on near-wild ancient cats, it was the first in a trend that persisted through the late 20th century, with the Ocicat (*see* pp 250–51) bred to resemble a wild cat and then hybrid breeds including real wild blood (*see* pp 360–69).

BREED ORIGINS

Extreme romantics will claim that this breed dates back to the ancient Egyptian dynasties because it can trace its ancestry directly back to those cats. Of course, all cats' ancestry goes back to ancient Egypt: the Mau is simply the cat that stayed at home.

Deliberate breeding began with Nathalie Troubetskoy, an exiled Russian living in Italy after World War II. Struck by the appearance of spotted street cats in Cairo, she imported two and began breeding and showing the cats. She moved to the United States in 1956 and continued her work there. It took twenty years for the breed to win major recognition. Acceptance came latest in the United Kingdom, where early spotted Oriental Shorthairs (*see* p 224–29) had been called Maus; the naming conflict probably contributed to a lack of enthusiasm, and the breed was not recognized by the GCCF until after the turn of the century. It remains rare in Europe, although it is growing in popularity, and it sits somewhere in the middle of American breed rankings.

MAU LOOKS

The Mau has the looks of a natural cat from a warm climate. The long, athletic body is clad in fine, silky fur that lies close to

Egyptian ancestry

Mau is simply the Egyptian word for cat, descended directly from the very first name for the cat, *miu*, used in ancient Egyptian writings. It seems an apt name for a cat that resembles the depictions of cats in ancient wall paintings and scrolls more than any other modern feline. Such a look could have been recreated by careful choice of cats from anywhere in the world and a great deal of work, because all cats are descended from the same original Egyptian ancestors, and will carry those same original genes. But using street cats from Egypt undoubtedly gave the best chances of rapidly stabilizing the desired look, because unlike cats elsewhere, these descendants have not been subjected to the selection pressures of other environments that favoured other adaptations alongside the original features. For example, there was no cold climate to favour the development of a dense undercoat, or more dramatically, a long topcoat.

SILVER The Mau comes in silver and smoke as well as bronze. The silver, seen here, is like all others, but uniquely, the smoke is a tabby with much less white undercoat than silver tabbies.

BRONZE This brown tabby coat is visually and genetically closest to the original cat at domestication. The eyes should be almond-shaped and gooseberry green in the mature cat.

the skin, but is not as short as that of Oriental breeds. Its head is a moderate wedge, defined by smooth curves with no flat planes, topped with medium to large, fairly upright ears.

The spots on the Mau, unlike those generally prized in cats of older breeds, do not follow the lines of a striped or mackerel tabby. The gene that is generally thought to be responsible for the spotted pattern can act on both striped and blotched patterns (*see* pp 160–61), and like the similarly spotted Ocicat, the Mau does throw classic or blotched tabby variants – a rather un-Egyptian trait. There is a whole range of other genes suggested that may have an effect on the pattern, however.

OWNING A MAU

The short coat is easy-care, and this is a robust breed. They have a soft, slightly chirping voice and friendly if busy natures. The Mau has a 'belly flap' of skin at the back of the abdomen, which is generally not seen in pedigree breeds. It may not give a sleek line, but it nevertheless allows great extension of the body in a flat-out gallop, and the active Mau will put it to use. This is a natural hunter: owners who keep it indoors should be sure to provide suitable 'prey' – before it chooses its own.

Ocicat

ORIGIN United States (1960s)
SYNONYM Ocelotte, Accicat
WEIGHT 2.5–6.5 kg (6–14 lb)
BUILD 🐈
TEMPERAMENT 🐆
COAT CARE 🖌
COLOURS Eumelanistic colours in solid and silver spotted tabby pattern only

Breeding today often seems to be divided into those who treat genetic traits like a pick-and-mix counter, and create some very odd combinations, and those who disapprove of any changes or crossing of breeds. The Ocicat is the product of a less divided era, the accidental outcome of a dare between breeders that won over the world with ease.

BREED ORIGINS

The main difference between a pedigree breed and a lookalike moggie is what happens when the cat produces kittens. Breeds should 'breed true', producing kittens like themselves – their type, coat, and colour stabilized through generations of careful breeding. A lookalike moggie can be a random coincidence, and just how diverse the results can be is shown by comparing the Ocicat with the Oriental Longhair (*see* pp 302–303). No immediate similarity is apparent, but the Ocicat comes from a cross identical to that which started the Oriental Longhair in the United Kingdom: a Siamese (*see* pp 220–23) and an Abyssinian (*see* pp 240–45), with the aim of producing Siamese with ticked points. Virginia Daly, a breeder from Michigan, made the cross in the early 1960s, and in the second generation she got not only her hoped-for Aby-pointed Siamese but also selfs, classic tabbies, tabby points, and one spotted kitten, which Daly's daughter called an Ocicat. This was sold as a pet and neutered, but after communicating with Dr Clyde Keeler of Georgia University, who wanted to produce a cat similar to the extinct Egyptian spotted fishing cat, Daly repeated the mating and a new breed was underway. Throughout the 1970s the breed was slow to develop, but interest was increasing. By the mid-1980s the Ocicat was

BLACK SILVER SPOTTED The Ocicat head is broadly wedge-shaped, with a broad muzzle and widely spaced, slightly slanted, almond-shaped eyes.

LILAC SILVER The silver gene was introduced into the breed quite early in its development through outcrosses to American Shorthairs, made by breeder Tom Brown.

recognized in CFA and TICA. It started to spread around the world in the same decade, and is now recognized by all major international registries. Other wild-looking breeds followed (*see* pp 252–55), culminating in the hybrid Bengal (*see* pp 362–67).

OWNING AN OCICAT

The spotted tabby pattern of the Ocicat is the feature that first distinguished it. The spots do not follow the lines of the striped or mackerel tabby pattern, but the blotched or classic tabby. Blotched tabby, self, and smoke variants still appear. But the other vital element of the Ocicat's look is its muscular, powerful build. There is nothing cobby about the breed, but it is no lightweight built for elegant lounging: first and foremost it should resemble a wild cat.

The muscular body of the Ocicat is clothed in short, fine fur that needs no attention beyond the cat's own,

TAWNY This brown tabby colour with large, well-scattered, oval spots is the original and classic Ocicat look, called tawny by CFA.

and this is a generally healthy breed, although inherited problems in the parent breeds may obviously also turn up in this breed. The wild looks are belied by a gregarious and playful personality, and Ocicats will follow owners around their homes apparently finding any activity interesting – this is definitely a cat that enjoys company.

CHOCOLATE All hairs except the tip of the tail are banded, tipped with a darker colour in the markings, a lighter colour elsewhere.

CLASSIC KITTEN Because its pattern is produced by the spotting gene breaking up the classic tabby pattern, blotched or classic tabby kittens like this are born.

California Spangled

ORIGIN United States (1971)
SYNONYM None
WEIGHT 4–7 kg (9–15 lb)
BUILD
TEMPERAMENT
COAT CARE
COLOURS Western colours in self, smoke, and silver in spotted tabby pattern only

Born from the mind of a Hollywood scriptwriter, this unusual and attractive cat should have had a happier ending. Arriving in a blaze of glory, today it is effectively a ghost breed. It blazed a trail, bringing wild-looking cats right to the forefront of public attention, but those who followed after trod more cautiously.

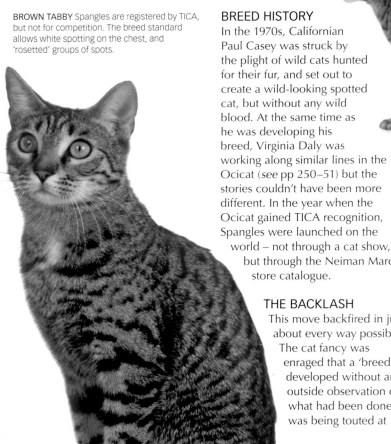

BROWN TABBY Spangles are registered by TICA, but not for competition. The breed standard allows white spotting on the chest, and 'rosetted' groups of spots.

BREED HISTORY
In the 1970s, Californian Paul Casey was struck by the plight of wild cats hunted for their fur, and set out to create a wild-looking spotted cat, but without any wild blood. At the same time as he was developing his breed, Virginia Daly was working along similar lines in the Ocicat (*see* pp 250–51) but the stories couldn't have been more different. In the year when the Ocicat gained TICA recognition, Spangles were launched on the world – not through a cat show, but through the Neiman Marcus store catalogue.

THE BACKLASH
This move backfired in just about every way possible. The cat fancy was enraged that a 'breed' developed without any outside observation of what had been done was being touted at

SPANGLED BUILD The long, lean, muscular body is carried level on strong legs, giving a 'hunter-like' quality to the cat's stride. Everything is meant to closely resemble a wild, natural cat.

premium prices. Campaigners were incensed that an 'anti-fur' cat was for sale in a catalogue that included fur coats. Neiman Marcus themselves were less than pleased when they realized – apparently belatedly – that their furs were being criticized.

The Spangle never recovered from this disastrous start, and today it is mostly a reminder that a beautiful and even healthy cat is not enough for success. Breeding has been all but abandoned, although occasionally new interest leads to rumours of a return.

SPANGLED HEAD Rounded in shape, equal in width and length, the head has a strong, heavy muzzle. It is topped by ears as tall as they are wide, carried with a slight outwards twist.

Australian Mist

ORIGIN Australia (1970s)

SYNONYM Initially called Spotted Mist

WEIGHT 3.5–6 kg (8–13 lb)

BUILD

TEMPERAMENT

COAT CARE

COLOURS Eumelanistic colours in spotted or blotched tabby pattern overlaid with ticking only

This cat has been a long time coming. It has hovered on the edge of obscurity for a considerable period, and was occasionally said to be defunct. But reports of its demise were exaggerated, and recently it has been taken up by breeders beyond its homeland. Genial, relaxed, and tantalizingly patterned, the Mist is spreading.

BREED ORIGINS

There are fashions in cats over the decades, and one of these was for spotted cats. The Egyptian Mau (*see* pp 248–49), the Ocicat (*see* pp 250–51), the ill-fated California Spangled (*see* pp 252–53), and this breed, which was originally called the Spotted Mist, were all developed and recognized through the 1970s and 1980s.

What made this cat different is that it was the first breed to be developed in Australia rather than the traditional breed hotspots of western Europe and North America. Founder Trude Staede also had a particularly Australian goal in mind. Just as important as the physical type and coat of the cat was the aim of a cat with a 'redirected' hunting instinct that would be content with an indoor life. The Burmese (*see* pp 212–13) gave its type and personality, the ticked Abyssinian (*see* pp 240–45) gave the coat its 'mist', and domestic moggies contributed spots.

OWNING A MIST

For many years, this was not possible in most of the world, but in the 2000s, the breed has spread to Europe and is recognized by some international registries, so they may be worth seeking out. Like its Burmese ancestor, this is a short-coated, easy-care breed. It is gregarious and affectionate. It may not feel a strong urge to hunt small mammals, but it will pursue owners around the house for company and play.

Healthy kittens

The breed began with over 30 foundation cats, giving it a large gene pool. A quarter of the original cats were domestic moggies, bringing in a fresh array of genes selected only by nature, to ensure that these cats had no unusually high incidence of hereditary problems. As a result, this is a healthy breed with litter sizes and ease of birth equivalent to the natural cat. The breed spread to Hungary in 2005 and the first kittens were born in the United Kingdom in 2007.

BROWN SPOTTED The Mist coat is short and glossy. This spotted and ticked tabby was the original pattern. Blotched kittens kept appearing, and the breed name was changed to include them.

Sokoke

ORIGIN Kenya (1970s)
SYNONYM Kadzonzos
WEIGHT 3.5–6.5 kg (8–14 lb)
BUILD 🐈
TEMPERAMENT 🐈
COAT CARE ✏
COLOURS Brown blotched tabby only

This breed was at first called the Sokoke Forest Cat. While it does come from a forest, that name conjures up to northern-hemisphere minds a shaggy, burly cat built to survive in snowy woodlands. But this is a cat of the rainforest, and unique as the first recognized breed to emerge from sub-Saharan Africa.

BREED ORIGINS

This breed takes its name from a National Park, the Arabuko-Sokoke Forest in Kenya. The largest remnant of coastal rainforest left in Africa, it is home to a number of rare endemic birds, amphibians, and mammals – including, as it turns out, a cat.

Local farmer Jeni Slater found a litter of unusual feral kittens in her garden in 1978. Unlike the cobby, spotted local cats, these were slender and had distinctively blotched coats, in which the markings were not solid, but 'hollowed out' (*see* p 163), with ticked areas inside them. The cats were known to locals and soberingly described as 'very sweet to eat'; they were seen as wild animals of the forest, and not pets. Gloria Moeldrup, a friend of Slater, imported breeding cats to Denmark first in 1984 and then again in 1990,

and the breed was recognized by FIFé in 1993. The main centre of breeding for the Sokoke is in Denmark, with a few cats in the Netherlands and Italy.

OWNING A SOKOKE

The Sokoke has an unusual coat. Like that of warm-climate breeds from southeast Asia, it lacks an insulating undercoat, and this is not a cold-weather cat. But unlike those Oriental types, its coat is not silky, but elastic in texture.

They are an intelligent and lively breed, friendly and talkative but self-reliant; they tend to hang around their owners and chat, rather than sit on laps. Curiously, they lack the cat's traditional aversion to water, and will swim across anything in their way.

BROWN TABBY The softened tabby markings give an effect like dappled shade and wonderful camouflage. The local name for these cats is *Kadzonzo*, which translates as 'looks like tree bark'.

Where did they come from?

Unknown wild origins have been suggested for this breed, based on the 'African tabby' coat. One is a separate descent from wildcats, another the possibility that this is the origin of the blotched tabby pattern. But hollowed-out markings are occasionally seen in random-bred cats the world over and, like a similar effect in Australian Mists (*see* opposite), may be caused by a gene provisionally named *Chaos*. The blotched pattern is frequent in the United Kingdom, which was a major colonial power in eastern Africa: this and the appearance of pointed 'snow Sokokes' suggest that these may be the descendants of imported pets, honed to camouflaged perfection by survival in the African forest.

LONGHAIR BREEDS

Longhairs have always been the prestige pets of the cat world. The coat may be practical in a cold climate, but in the first widely recognized longhair, the Persian, it was simply glamorous. Longhaired cats were brought to Europe from both Persia and Turkey in the 16th and 17th centuries, and it is generally thought the mutation for long hair arose there, but the trait may have appeared independently in several places: some genes are 'hotspots' for mutation. Because the gene for long hair is recessive, most free-breeding cats are shorthaired. This means longhairs stand out from the crowd.

SOMETHING FOR EVERYONE Breeds vary from this chocolate-box Persian to the slinky Balinese, so whatever your tastes, there is a longhair to tickle your fancy.

Persian

ORIGIN United Kingdom (1800s)
SYNONYM Longhair, Himalayan
WEIGHT 3.5–7 kg (8–15 lb)
BUILD
TEMPERAMENT
COAT CARE

COLOURS All colours and bi-colours in all shades; all but ticked tabby pattern (not spotted in CFA); pointed pattern (also sepia and mink in TICA)

The first distinctive feature of the Persian is its luxurious coat, far longer than it was in the original cats brought from the East. The second distinctive feature is the short nose, which gives the breed a brachycephalic face described as 'pansy-like' by its fans, but associated with breathing and eye problems.

BLUE SELF (LONG)   RED & WHITE   BLUE SILVER TABBY   BLACK SMOKE   SEAL POINT   BLUE POINT

BREED ORIGINS

Longhaired cats may have been brought to the West during the Crusades, but the first imports to be reliably recorded took place in the 17th century. Pietro della Valle brought longhaired cats from Persia to Italy, and Nicolas-Claude Fabri de Pieresc brought them from Turkey to France. Although today we have the Persian and Turkish Angora (*see* pp 294–99) breeds, they did not descend separately from these two imports. The longhaired cats were interbred, and the 18th-century naturalist the Comte de Buffon wrote that the Persian and Angora were one and the same. When they first arrived in England in the 19th century they were even known as French cats.

Khmers and Himalayans

In the 1930s, American geneticists investigating coat patterns crossed Siamese cats (*see* pp 220–23) with Persians. The resulting pointed longhairs were called Himalayans, after Himalayan rabbits with a similar pointing pattern, but were not pursued as a breed. In Europe there was a pointed longhair called the Khmer, and separate efforts were made to create a pointed Persian. The GCCF recognized the Colourpoint pattern as part of the Persian breed in 1955, and the Khmer was absorbed into the group. Renewed interest in North America led to acceptance there by 1961, as the Himalayan.

CHOCOLATE TORTIE The Oriental range of colours naturally accompanied the pointed pattern. Because of the genetics, all-female torties must be created anew in each generation.

POINTED PERSIANS Persians like this lilac point have softer shading and lighter eyes than a Siamese.

margin. Elsewhere its star has faded, and in the United Kingdom, for example, it now trails in fourth place in the GCCF's list of most popular breeds.

APPEARANCE

Everything about the Persian is soft and rounded. The coat is about 10 cm (4 in) long, longer on the ruff and in some top show cats. It wraps a body that is broad and cobby, and carried on short legs.

BREED DEVELOPMENT

Persians were one of the first breeds to be recognized by the cat fancy and given their own written standard in the late 19th century. However, the standards in both the United States and United Kingdom classed all types of longhaired cats as Longhairs, and each colour as a separate breed. This has changed over the years, as other distinctive longhaired cats have been recognized, and now the breed, in all colours, is recognized by all major registries internationally and known by the Persian name everywhere.

Persians have been perceived as high-status pets ever since they first appeared. Although less popular than the Maine Coon (*see* pp 262–67) in the United States when showing began, it became the most popular breed by far in the 20th century and still leads by a four-to-one

SILVER TABBY This blotched or classic tabby is the traditional tabby pattern of the Persian, with others only being allowed much later. Cats with silvered coats have green eyes.

The head is rounded, and the ears have rounded tips. Cats in North America tend to have the shortest noses, and the CFA breed standard calls for forehead, nose, and chin to be in vertical alignment, while in the United Kingdom the GCCF standard calls for a 'short, broad nose with a stop'.

All colours are now accepted internationally, in solid, tortie, pointed, or bi-colour, and smoke, shaded, and tipped, although some of these colours may be given different names by different registries: for example, shaded colours are often called cameo, and tipped colours are called shell cameos in CFA. The GCCF allows blotched, striped, and spotted tabby patterns, but CFA does not recognize the spotted pattern. TICA also allows sepia and mink pointing.

LIVING WITH A PERSIAN

Whatever its colour or pattern, the long coat is fine and matts easily, making this a breed that demands a considerable investment of time in grooming. Show cats are sometimes clipped outside the showing season, and resemble the increasingly popular easy-care Exotic (*see* pp 184–87). In personality, the Persian is undemanding. It is quiet,

RED NOSES Red and cream Persians tend to have the shortest noses. 'Peke-faced' Persians, briefly in vogue in the United States, were usually red.

BLACK SMOKE A smoke Persian may seem to be solid in colour when still, but with movement the white undercoat shimmers through.

DOLL-FACED Health concerns have led some breeders to breed for longer noses. The Traditional Cat Association has its own standard for Traditional or Doll Face Persians.

sweet-voiced, and content to lounge around, although clipped cats are more active. The short face can cause breathing problems and kinked tear ducts, and there is a high incidence of polycystic kidney disease and retained testicles.

Maine Coon

ORIGIN United States (1800s)

SYNONYM American Longhair, Maine Cat, Maine Shag

WEIGHT 4–10 kg (9–22 lb)

BUILD

TEMPERAMENT

COAT CARE

COLOURS Western colours in self, tortie, bi-colour, solid, smoke, and shaded; classic and mackerel tabby patterns

This is the first, most famous, and still most popular national breed of the United States. It is the gentle giant of the cat world, renowned for its size, its sociable nature, and its reputation for enjoying a swim. Its history is not one long success story, however: the Maine Coon made perhaps the greatest comeback in feline history.

BLACK SELF   BLUE SELF (LONG)   BLUE & WHITE   BROWN STRIPED TABBY   SILVER TABBY   BROWN TABBY & WHITE

BREED MYTHS

The early origins of the Maine Coon are the subject to many colourful legends. It was suggested that it was the hybrid offspring of domestic cats and the bobcat (*Lynx rufus, see pp 18–19*). A more outlandish early legend concerns cats interbreeding with raccoons – the striped tail may have inspired this particular flight of fancy. Other tales, from human history, are scarcely more believable.

One popular tale holds that this longhair is descended from ancestral Norwegian Forest Cats (*see pp 268–73*) brought over to North America by ancient Vikings. Another gives it

classier ancestors: the royal pets of Marie Antoinette. These cats would have been breeds like the Persian (*see pp 258–61*) or Turkish Angora (*see pp 294–99*). Perhaps the most charming, but least likely, tale involves a sea captain named Coon who sailed the New England coast with a bevy of Persian and Angora-type cats, whose longhaired progeny became known as 'Coon's cats'.

BREED ORIGINS

The truth is more prosaic. The Maine Coon is undoubtedly descended from cats that came in ships, but probably from those that arrived in waves with successive groups of settlers. Somewhere in this founder population was the longhaired gene, and in the harsh continental winters, cats with a thick coat had a clear survival advantage.

TABBY BI-COLOURS Originally only cats of tabby pattern were called coon cats. Tufted ears, like a bobcat, are part of the Maine 'look'.

A large size also made them less attractive as prey for local wildlife, and enabled them as hunters to tackle larger animals such as hares, supplementing whatever pickings were already available from human households.

By the 1860s, farmers held a Maine Coon cat show at the Skowhegan State Fair. In 1878, a dozen Maine Coons were entered in a show held in Boston. The Madison Square show of 1895 was won by a brown tabby Maine Coon by the name of Cosey, although all the longhaired cats were classed together in the entries, so it is hard to know exactly how many entered.

In the early 20th century, showing of breeds in North America spread out from New England, but more exotic breeds held sway, with the Persian establishing an early and apparently unassailable position as 'the' longhaired cat. By the end of the first decade of the new century, the Maine Coon was starting to slip into a forty-year period of obscurity.

RED TABBY Only the blotched and striped tabby patterns are allowed in the Maine Coon. This is in keeping with its origins among early exports from Europe.

CREAM TABBY AND WHITE Bi-colour cats must have white on the bib, the belly, and all four paws. The cream tabby has buff markings on a very pale cream ground.

THE COMEBACK KID

In the early 1950s, a club was formed to revive the breed. Relentless showing and publicity brought measurable success by the early 1960s, with the Maine again being bred to a written standard and shown in competitions. In the early 1970s, breeders began to petition for new recognition of the breed, but numbers were still low. A new breed club was formed, and by 1976, this big, square-jawed breed was back in business. Show successes followed, with the revived breed holding its own against other cats in national rankings. By the end of the millennium, it was second only to the Persian in popularity.

In the 1980s, the breed crossed the Atlantic, together with some quite exaggerated tales about its size and weight; some wilder pieces of journalism claimed that this was the cat that could beat up dogs. Unlike many other American breeds, the Maine Coon was a highly successful export. It was recognized by both FIFé and the GCCF; in the United Kingdom it started from scratch in the 1980s to sit comfortably in the top ten breeds within a decade. Numbers are still rising, and it seems that the Maine Coon's star is unlikely to fall again.

BLACK Selfs are less common in the Maine than in many other breeds, and do not have the 'classic' look of the breed.

OWNING A MAINE COON

Although it is longhaired, the Maine Coon does not require painstaking grooming. Its coat was not bred for decoration but evolved for survival; a fluffy coat that snarls quickly is little use in vicious winter weather. It has a shaggy look (hence the

RED AND WHITE Perhaps because they look so natural, bi-colours are popular in this breed, along with tabbies. Many of the top show winners of recent years have been bi-colours.

RED SHADED Also called the shaded cameo, this has a white undercoat with a warm red shaded top coat, which may be darker on the face and legs.

TORTOISESHELL TABBY AND WHITE The first national winning Maine Coon in CFA after the breed was re-established was a cat of this pattern, GC NW Tufpaws Rosette.

alternative name of Maine Shag) and needs piecemeal attention to trouble spots rather than all-over, every-day grooming. However, there is an inherited tendency to heart trouble.

Maines are described by their owners as gentle, loyal, and reliably good with children and other pets – and yes, they are bigger than some family dogs. They are sociable but not intrusive, and active but laid back.

MAINE COON (*see* pp 262–65) This hardy, friendly breed is a loyal companion that will join in family activities with gusto, and then relax just as thoroughly when eventually the time comes to wind down.

Norwegian Forest Cat

ORIGIN Norway (1930s)
SYNONYM Skaukatt, Norsk Skogkatt, Wegie
WEIGHT 3–9 kg (7–20 lb)
BUILD
TEMPERAMENT
COAT CARE
COLOURS Western colours in self, tortie, bi-colour, solid, smoke, shaded, and tipped; blotched, striped, and spotted tabby patterns

Scandinavia's 'little lynx' is a self-contained, self-reliant, hardy longhair, equally comfortable in the snowy forests of its homeland or more moderate climes abroad. Popular across Europe and in North America, it is seen by its fans as the cat sacred to the Norse goddess Freya, powerful enough to draw her chariot.

BLUE SELF (LONG)

RED SELF

RED & WHITE

BROWN CLASSIC TABBY

SILVER STRIPED TABBY

BLACK SMOKE

BREED ORIGINS

It is known from archaeological evidence that the domestic cat was well established in Scandinavia before 1000AD. The Vikings had traded and raided widely throughout Europe, and even had direct links to the Ottoman Empire, so there were a number of routes through which the cat could have arrived. The distribution of phaeomelanistic colours (*see* pp 158–59) suggest that direct trade with the Ottomans was an important influence. It may well be that the longhaired mutation, thought to have arisen somewhere in the near East, arrived in Scandinavia well before it was imported into western Europe in the ancestors of the Persian (*see* pp 258–61).

Some even suggest that the forebears of the modern Norwegian Forest

travelled to North America with the expeditions of Leif Erikson, thought to have reached Newfoundland in about 1000AD, forming a foundation stock that later became the Maine Coon (*see* pp 262–67), but evidence is sadly lacking. It is also not sure that the longhair gene was prevalent in Scandinavia by this time; as a recessive trait, it would have started from a small number of imports.

Wherever it may have wandered, at home, the ancestors of today's breed had a distinct advantage over smaller, shorthaired arrivals in the country. Their long, glossy, water-repellent coat is a perfect protection from the worst a Scandinavian winter can throw at them, and their muscular, imposing build makes them both unattractive prey for wildlife and fearsome predators in their own right. Over time, long hair became a more common characteristic of Scandinavian farm and household

SILVER TORTIE TABBY AND WHITE The face is an equilateral triangle, with large, tufted ears, and almond-shaped eyes. The body is substantial, with the hind legs longer than the front, and large feet turned out at the toe.

BLACK SELF Self colours are not seen as often as tabbies and bi-colours. FIFé and the GCCF, unlike North American registries, allocate no points for colour or pattern.

cats, but nobody really regarded the hardy longhairs of Norway as a distinct breed until the 20th century.

FORMAL RECOGNITION

In the late 1930s, examples of the Skaukatt or Norsk Skogkatt (literally Norwegian forest cat) were shown to

BLUE (LEFT) AND CREAM (RIGHT) The gene for blue is distributed across the feline world. The gene for red and cream is most common at the Nile delta, on the Scottish isles and in Scandinavia.

great acclaim in Germany. A group of breeders made efforts to preserve the type that had evolved, before it faded into the general feline population – always a risk for an unrecognized breed, especially one with a recessive trait such as long hair that would be lost in any crossbreeding with shorthairs. World War II interrupted these efforts, however, as it did for many breeds across Europe.

In the 1950s, the task was taken up again by breeders who eventually established a formal breed club in 1975. Two of these breeders, Egil and Else Nyland, bred the legendary Pan's Truls. This maginificent male is regarded as the epitome of the breed, and served as the model for the written breed standard. This was adopted by FIFé, and the Norwegian Forest Cat reached full Championship recognition in the association in 1977. It was also designated the official cat of Norway by King Olaf.

COPPER-EYED WHITE The ruff remains full year-round. Its characteristic parts are mutton chops at the sides, a short collar around the neck itself, and a bib of longer hair on the chest.

INTERNATIONAL RECOGNITION

Two years after full recognition in Europe, Norwegians reached the United States, where they were soon nicknamed Wegies. They were recognized by TICA first, in the 1980s, then CFA and other associations. In the United Kingdom, the GCCF began registering cats in the 1980s; from a very small start the Norwegian rose to just outside the top ten breeds within twenty years.

The coat is double, with a woolly, insulating undercoat and long, glossy, water-repellant topcoat. It is given considerable importance in most breed standards, with the word 'coarse' being used of the topcoat; in CFA it commands fewer points.

STRANGE NEW COLOURS

The Norwegian is only allowed in the traditional Western colours (*see* p 158). So it was an unpleasant surprise when kittens that appeared to be in the Oriental shades of lilac and chocolate, but later looked more fawn and cinnamon, turned up in a litter in Sweden in 1993. As it turned out, these supposed Oriental colours were not what they seemed to be. These colours are something new: they change markedly as a cat matures, so that

SILVER TABBY The tabby pattern is characteristic of the breed. Some suggest that longhaired tabbies were particularly common among Scandinavian populations, but no survey has backed this up.

kittens born with black or blue in their coats later become reddish or yellowish, and have been called fox colours, x colours, or amber colours. FIFé has now settled on amber and included them within the colour classes, but only as the trait affects black and blue coats: it is generally felt that there needs to be more clarity on how the mutation affects other colours of coat and how it is to be distinguished from red and cream before there can be wider acceptance.

OWNING A WEGIE

The heavy coat is a triumph of functional design, and needs a bit of help every few days to look its best, not a full-body groom every day. The annual moults are a different matter, of course; brush daily unless you like vacuuming up cat hair instead.

The Norwegian is an enterprising breed that will rise to most situations: children, visitors, and other pets will not daunt it. It is a cool, calm, and collected breed, not a lap cat, intelligently cautious but perfectly sociable with those that it trusts.

BLUE-CREAM SMOKE AND WHITE This breed is slow to mature, and there is a marked difference in size between the males and the females, like this dilute tortie bi-colour.

NORWEGIAN FOREST CAT (*see* pp 268–71) This brown tabby shows the slightly wild look preferred in what is a natural breed. The lynx-tipping and long furnishings in the ear are key, and tabby coats are highly popular.

Siberian

ORIGIN Russia (1980s)
SYNONYM Neva Masquerade
WEIGHT 4.5–9 kg (10–20 lb)
BUILD
TEMPERAMENT
COAT CARE
COLOURS Western (and Eastern in TICA) colours in self, tortie, bi-colour, solid, smoke, shaded, and tipped; all tabby patterns; pointed pattern in CFA and TICA

For most of the 20th century, no new cat breeds came out of Russia, where Communist ideology scorned breeding. With the end of the Soviet era, not only people and ideas but animal breeds of all sorts began to move. The West gained the Siberian and Kurilean (*see* pp 342–43) and Russia has a fledgling cat fancy.

WHITE	BLUE SELF (LONG)	BLUE & WHITE	CREAM STRIPED TABBY	SILVER SHADED	SEAL TABBY POINT

PROVING GROUND The long, weatherproof coats and take-on-all-comers bravado of the Siberian are said to have been fostered by the extreme conditions of the taiga or boreal forest.

BREED ORIGINS

Finding the truth amid Siberian myths is like catching smoke. Anecdotal accounts have cats trekking to Siberia with Russian settlers, or living, like so many romanticized breeds, in monasteries. Their descendants made the long return trip to Moscow and Leningrad, where the new cat clubs could, apparently, distinguish them from other non-pedigree longhairs on sale for much less in the markets. In truth, the Siberian may not be Siberian at all, but it is certainly a Russian cat.

In 1990, three were shipped by a Russian breed club to Elizabeth Terrell, a breeder in the United States, and fifteen were imported by David

SIBERIAN HEAD Breed standards for the head differentiate the Siberian from similar breeds, being curved rather than square-muzzled like the Maine or distinctly triangular like the Wegie.

Boehm, who visited Leningrad and Moscow to buy cats at a show and in markets. It is recognized in North America, and by FIFé in Europe, but not yet by the GCCF.

OWNING A SIBERIAN

First, is the Siberian hypoallergenic? Breeders say test results for Fel D1 in saliva showed less of the protein in Siberians, but scientists say the results were misinterpreted, and this breed is not the long-sought hypoallergenic cat.

The Siberian has much the same appeal as the Maine Coon (*see* pp 262–267 and the Norwegian Forest Cat (*see* pp 268–73). It is usually seen in the same naturally Western colours: pointed cats, sometimes called Neva Masquerades, are rarely seen. The original importer is quoted as saying that 'we've never found anything they're afraid of' and that they are 'the most affectionate things I've ever seen'.

SIBERIAN COAT The Siberian is described as possessing a triple coat, adults having a particularly tight, dense undercoat beneath the longer layers.

Birman

ORIGIN France or Burma, now Myanmar (1920s)

SYNONYM Sacred Cat of Burma

WEIGHT 4.5–8 kg (10–18 lb)

BUILD 🐱

TEMPERAMENT 🐱

COAT CARE 🖌🖌🖌

COLOURS All colours in self and tortie; all tabby patterns; always in pointed pattern with white mittens

The first pointed longhair breed, the Birman is a silky, elegant cat with an angelic expression, and it has a religious history to match. Or has it? From its very first appearance, suspicion has been attached to the official version of its origins, with many suspecting that French creative flair lies behind those glamourpuss looks.

BLUE POINT

CARAMEL POINT

CHOCOLATE POINT

BLUE TABBY POINT

BREED LEGEND

The legend of the Birman starts in a temple in Burma (now Myanmar). It is set in a temple to Tsun Kyan-Kse, a goddess of the Khmer people who presided over the passage of souls. The temple held a magnificent golden statue of her with sapphires for eyes. Here one hundred pure white cats lived; when a priest died, his soul entered the body of such a sacred animal, to be reborn when it died. One particular golden-eyed cat, named Sinh, was the companion of the head priest, Mun-Ha.

One night, the temple was attacked by forces from what is now Thailand; that same night, the head priest died. But as Mun-Ha lay dying, Sinh leapt onto him, his eyes fixed on the statue of the goddess. His coat took on the golden tones of the statue and the brown shades of the earth, except where his feet touched the head of Mun-Ha, and his eyes became sapphire blue, reflecting those of the goddess. Sinh then turned and stared at the south door of the temple; the priests rushed to secure it and managed to hold off the invaders.

Sinh remained on Mun-Ha's body for the next seven days, refusing all sustenance, gazing at the statue, until he died, carrying the soul of the head priest to the goddess. Seven days later, when the priests were assembled to decide who should succeed Mun-Ha, the remaining temple cats entered, all transformed just as Sinh had been. They surrounded the youngest of the priests, and he was declared Mun-Ha's successor.

SEAL POINT This is the original colour of the Birman, but as the Siamese arrived carrying the genes blue and possibly chocolate, such genes probably also lay in the Birman.

COMING WEST

So far, so poetic. But how did the breed get from the mountains of Burma to the show halls of Europe? This part of the story is scarcely less romantic.

In the most popular story, two Europeans, Major Gordon Russell and August Pavie, were given two cats for saving a temple from being destroyed by Brahmins. The male cat died on the way to France, but the female, Sita, was pregnant on arrival in Paris, and founded the breed in Europe. The main problem with this is that Russell and Pavie appear to have been in southeast Asia in 1898, but the cats were sent to France in 1919. A gap of two decades seems implausible.

LILAC POINT This recessive of chocolate was among the four 'traditional' colours that were the only ones accepted by CFA until relatively recently.

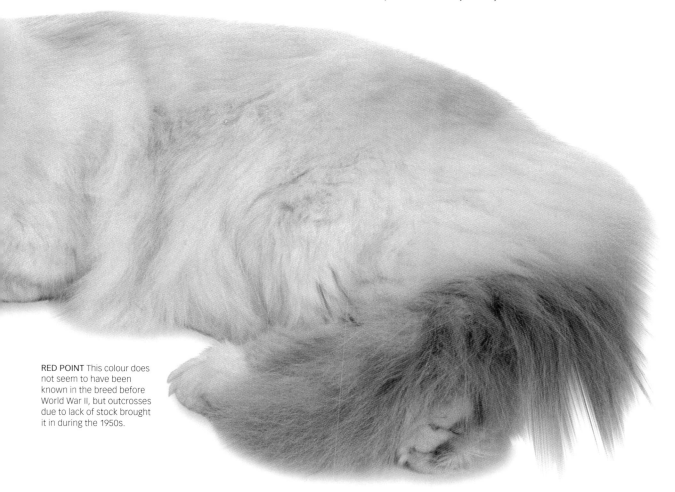

RED POINT This colour does not seem to have been known in the breed before World War II, but outcrosses due to lack of stock brought it in during the 1950s.

SEAL TORTIE POINT The tortie points is hard to breed to show quality. The points and the shading on the body must show some mixing of colours.

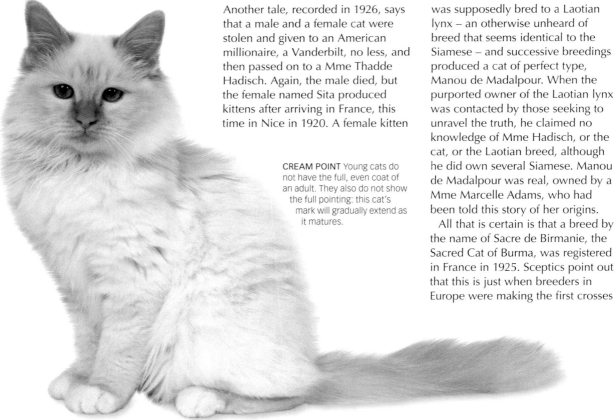

CREAM POINT Young cats do not have the full, even coat of an adult. They also do not show the full pointing: this cat's mark will gradually extend as it matures.

Another tale, recorded in 1926, says that a male and a female cat were stolen and given to an American millionaire, a Vanderbilt, no less, and then passed on to a Mme Thadde Hadisch. Again, the male died, but the female named Sita produced kittens after arriving in France, this time in Nice in 1920. A female kitten was supposedly bred to a Laotian lynx – an otherwise unheard of breed that seems identical to the Siamese – and successive breedings produced a cat of perfect type, Manou de Madalpour. When the purported owner of the Laotian lynx was contacted by those seeking to unravel the truth, he claimed no knowledge of Mme Hadisch, or the cat, or the Laotian breed, although he did own several Siamese. Manou de Madalpour was real, owned by a Mme Marcelle Adams, who had been told this story of her origins.

All that is certain is that a breed by the name of Sacre de Birmanie, the Sacred Cat of Burma, was registered in France in 1925. Sceptics point out that this is just when breeders in Europe were making the first crosses of Persians (*see* pp 258–61) with Siamese (*see* pp 220–23) to create the forerunners of the Colourpoint or Himalayan Persians. Another pointed longhair breed was first recorded in France in the 1920s: this was called the Khmer, and the story behind it was that a soldier returning from Indochina brought a breeding pair to Paris.

Whatever its origins, the breed almost died out in World War II: ironically, it is reported to have been reduced to just two cats before outcrossing to appropriate breeds was undertaken. The revived breed was accepted on both sides of the Atlantic during the 1960s; today it is in the top ten breeds in the United Kingdom and United States. The Birman and its legend are well established around the world, and unlikely to fade away again.

OWNING A BIRMAN

The Birman requires a little devotion. The long, soft coat needs regular care to keep it sleek and tangle-free. The breed is fairly healthy, with no major hereditary disorders.

In personality, this dedicated companion is described as quiet but sociable. It is said to prefer not to be the only pet in the home – a hundred cats may be too many for most people, but do consider two.

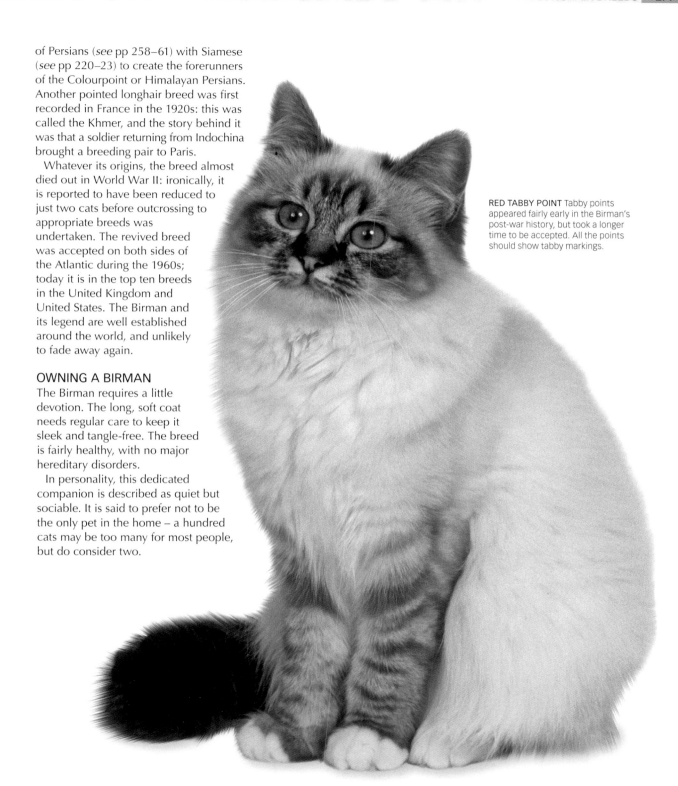

RED TABBY POINT Tabby points appeared fairly early in the Birman's post-war history, but took a longer time to be accepted. All the points should show tabby markings.

Ragdoll

ORIGIN United States (1960s)

SYNONYM None

WEIGHT 4.5–9 kg (10–20 lb)

BUILD 🐈

TEMPERAMENT 🐈

COAT CARE 🖌️

COLOURS All colours except cinnamon and fawn in self and tortie; all tabby patterns; always in pointed pattern and either mitted or bi-colour

It's hard to believe that such a charming-looking cat as this could have been at the centre of decades of controversy and feuding, much less that it could be a link between humans and aliens. But all of these are elements in the story of the Ragdoll and its quite extraordinary founding breeder.

SEAL POINT   BLUE POINT   LILAC POINT   CHOCOLATE POINT   RED TABBY POINT & WHITE   LILAC TABBY POINT

BREED ORIGINS

Genetically, the breed began when Ann Baker, a breeder of Persians (*see* pp 258–61), began selecting kittens out of Josephine, a white, non-pedigree, longhair cat who ran free in her neighbourhood of Riverside, California. These kittens were by a number of non-pedigree sires, mostly unknown, but some of Burmese (*see* pp 210–11) and Birman (*see* pp 276–79) type. Josephine was mated to two of her sons. Among the offspring of these matings were two females. All

subsequent Ragdolls are descended from these two males and two females.

Ann Baker began registering Ragdolls in 1965, and started selling them by the end of the decade. She began working with other breeders, but kept control over all breeding decisions. In 1971, she founded

her own registry, the International Ragdoll Cat Association (IRCA). She also trademarked Cherubim cats, a rubric that included the Ragdoll, which entitled her to demand royalties from other breeders for using it, and looked into setting up other breeders as franchisees in a nationwide business.

POINTED AND MITTED One of the founder males, Daddy Warbucks, was a mitted Birman-type cat, and some registries resisted the breed in part because of this 'lookalike' trait.

TWO KINDS OF RAGDOLL

Breeders who were chafing under Ann Baker's restrictive regime started another association, the Ragdoll Fanciers' Club International (RFCI). Chief among them were Denny and Laura Dayton. By 1975, the breeders had split into two camps: those who wanted major registry recognition were members of RFCI, and those happy with Ann Baker's way of doing things were members of IRCA.

BLUE BI-COLOUR One of Ann Baker's early cats, which was registered as a lilac, turned out to be a blue, and the colour was clearly quite warm at the start. The standard now calls for a colder-toned blue.

Over the years, the number of breeders in the IRCA camp dwindled, while the efforts of the Daytons and others saw the breed achieve some recognition. CFA remained resolutely opposed to the breed, but by the end of the decade, it was established within the newly formed TICA. In the 1980s, RFCI cats were sent to Europe – Ann Baker would not export cats –

SEAL BI-COLOUR Seal is still the most commonly found colour of Ragdoll. Most of the cats used by the Daytons were eumelanistic, and these lines have had the most lasting influence.

and by 1990, Ragdolls were recognized in the United Kingdom. Now shown by all major registries, this popular breed sits in the top ten cats on both sides of the Atlantic.

RAGDOLL MYTHOLOGY

Ann Baker made claims that the breed in fact had its roots before she began to breed from Josephine, and these claims were not only too outlandish to accept in themselves, but they effectively kept the cats from wider acceptance for decades. According to Baker, the Ragdoll began before the selective breeding started, through something that happened to Josephine. The cat was injured in a road accident, and Baker claimed that after she recovered, she began producing kittens that were cuddly, placid, and passive, with an unusually high pain threshold, and flopped like ragdolls when picked up. This new trait was caused by the accident, she said, and inspired both the breed and its name.

That is one story. Others were that the cats were the result of

TORTIE BI-COLOUR Some people feel that the red and cream shades are not quite traditional in the Ragdoll, but they have been accepted by all the major breed associations that recognize Ragdolls.

Business and pleasure

When people wince at the price of a pedigree kitten, breeders explain that given the costs (*see* p 148), their hobby may never even pay for itself. Ann Baker wanted more than a hobby: she charged for tours of her cattery, and wanted breeders to buy not just cats but the rights to a breeding franchise from her, at prices that ran into thousands of dollars, limiting numbers so that supply never outstripped demand. The animosity this roused certainly sets the boundaries on commercial breeding. But she did spot a gap in the market: her cuddly, dog-like cats were ahead of the trend. Since the 1980s, it has become almost ubiquitous to describe cats as 'love-babies' and 'faithful lap cats' that bond with their owners. The cats have not changed, but owner expectations have.

LILAC One Ann Baker's claims was that her cats came in seal and lilac without blue and chocolate. A glance at the genes behind these colours (*see* pp 158–59) shows the strangeness of this idea.

secret genetic mutation work carried out by the government, and contained either alien or skunk DNA, depending on when you heard the story. The skunk DNA claim turned up in another context. Another of Ann Baker's Cherubim developments was a breed she called Honey Bears, but registered with CFA as Persians. She said they did not have a cat skeleton, and in the late 1970s, she told CFA that although they were Persian, they were genetically modified and part skunk. The registry's response to this was understandable: they decided to look again at all her past registrations, and accept no further registrations from her.

It would be safe to say that Ann Baker understood little about genetics, but rather made it up as she went along. While her wild stories certainly gained publicity, they won more notoriety than fame, and brought the breed into disrepute at least as much as they promoted it.

OWNING A RAGDOLL
Ann Baker made five claims for the Ragdoll (apart from the many surrounding its origins). These were that they are relatively large, have almost magically non-matting fur,

lack the skills and instincts for self-preservation, go limp when you hold them, and are less sensitive to pain than other cats.

So which of these hold any truth? They are large, imposing cats, but not outrageously so. Their fur lacks a dense undercoat and is certainly less prone to matting than the coat of a Persian, but this should not be taken to mean the Ragdoll is a longhair that will look great with no grooming.

As for the supposed character traits, it seems that one car accident wasn't really enough to undo the basic common sense of the free-ranging Josephine and her loose-living paramours. While breeders, especially in the United States, often stipulate that all cats should be kept indoors, Ragdolls are no more vulnerable than any other breed. They do tend to relax when picked up – at least by those they trust – to a greater degree than other breeds, sprawling with the abandon of those in deep sleep when they are fully awake. The most irresponsible claim, that they do not feel pain like other cats, is utterly false, and one can only hope that few were traumatized by foolish owners testing this.

SEAL TORTIE POINT Ragdolls mature slowly, not reaching their full adult size and coat for some three to four years. One of the appeals of the breed is its enduring kittenish nature.

RAGDOLL (*see* pp 280–83) This large, cuddly, soft-coated breed has a sweet face with a distinctly retroussé nose and sparkling blue eyes. Its gentle personality is said to be a perfect match for these innocent looks.

RagaMuffin

ORIGIN United States (1990s)
SYNONYM None
WEIGHT 4.5–9 kg (10–20 lb)
BUILD 🐈
TEMPERAMENT 🐈
COAT CARE ✂️
COLOURS All colours in self, tortie, and bi-colours; all tabby patterns

This cheekily named breed was developed for over twenty years outside the registry system before it 'came in from the cold'. It has suffered something of an identity crisis; for a long time the cats behind this breed shared their name with an established breed, and then they had to give it up and find a new name to win recognition.

BLUE & WHITE   RED & WHITE   LILAC STRIPED TABBY   BLACK SMOKE   CHINCHILLA   BLUE TORTIE & WHITE

BREED ORIGINS

The RagaMuffin has essentially the same early story as the Ragdoll (*see* pp 280–85). In the 1970s, when the Daytons' RFCI Ragdolls split from Ann Baker's IRCA, some of the breeders opted to stay with Ann Baker's association. Over the years, the turnover was relatively high, as Baker's idiosyncrasies tested the patience of many breeders beyond endurance. She herself suffered setbacks when she had to change her cattery name and asked her registering association, the National Cat Fanciers' Association (NCFA), to change all her Ragdoll registrations to match the new name; they refused and dropped all registrations from her cattery.

By the mid-1990s, breeders who had been working with her were again seeking to set up on their own and work within major registries, just as in the 1970s. And so, in 1994, they broke away and petitioned for recognition of their cats in several associations. Because of the trademark held by Ann Baker on the name Ragdoll, these breeders chose the name RagaMuffin for their breakaway breed. Although Ann Baker died in 1997, and her trademark on the Ragdoll name has now lapsed, the RagaMuffin name is still attached to this breed.

OWNING A RAGAMUFFIN

The easy-going personality and easy-care coat of this breed are essentially the same as those of the Ragdoll. Given the common origins of the two breeds, this is only to be expected.

What's the difference?

The breeders who originally split from Ann Baker were working with only the pointed, blue-eyed cats. There had always been other colours in the gene pool – Josephine herself was white, after all, which could mask anything – and RagaMuffins come in non-pointed colours. Among the major registries, the breed is in the preliminary stages of the recognition process in CFA, and the pointed and mitted colours are relegated to 'Any Other Variety' when showing, providing some distance between the breeds.

BLUE BI-COLOUR The RagaMuffin is shown in two types of coat; this bi-colour has an inverted V of white over the nose, and in the van colour is restricted to the tail, ears, and mask.

Nebelung

ORIGIN United States (1980s)
SYNONYM None
WEIGHT 2.5–5 kg (6–11 lb)
BUILD
TEMPERAMENT
COAT CARE
COLOURS Blue self only

While longhaired cats stand out from the crowd, most of the breeds regarded as national and natural types are shorthaired, be they British, American, French, Thai, or Russian. Some of these breeds have carried longhaired versions: although naturally present they did not fit the tidy minds of those who drew up early breed profiles. But breeders who know their genetics will tell you 'recessives are forever', and this is what happens when they pop up again.

BREED HISTORY

This breed is an American recreation of a Russian natural breed. When blue cats from Russia were first shown in the United Kingdom in the 19th century, there were some longhairs among the shorthairs. The shorthaired cats became the Russian Shorthair (*see* pp 198–99), but the longhaired ones faded.

In the early 1980s, Cora Cobb in Colorado mated a shorthaired blue cat, believed to be a Russian, to a black shorthaired domestic cat, and there were longhaired blue kittens in the resulting litters. Two of them, Siegfried and Brunhilde, were mated to each other in 1986, and produced further longhaired blue kittens. She outcrossed to Russian Blues (sometimes promising anonymity to their owners) to achieve the desired type; longhair is still carried as a recessive trait within the breed.

After the end of the Soviet system, similar cats emerged from Russia, and the breed is essentially a longhaired Russian Blue, but the name tactfully avoids this. Nebelung both continues the Wagnerian theme of the first cats' names by echoing the Nibelung, and also includes the German word for mist, Nebel, so can be translated as 'creature of the mist'.

OWNING A NEBELUNG

The cat is recognized by TICA, and remains rare, bred in just a handful of American states, Russia, and France. They are intelligent and resourceful felines, loving with their family but reserved with strangers, and may be affronted by the antics of children.

NEBELUNG Everything about this cat is long: the silver-tipped coat, the body, the legs, and the tail, which is a plume of longer hair. Cobb herself wrote: 'The overall effect is that of a romanticized 1900 cat picture.'

Tiffanie

ORIGIN United Kingdom (1970s)
SYNONYM Longhair Burmilla
WEIGHT 3.5–6.5 kg (8–14 lb)
BUILD 🐈
TEMPERAMENT 🐆
COAT CARE 🖌️
COLOURS All colours in self, tortie, and shaded; all tabby patterns; sepia pattern

This gorgeous cat is of a type that remains unusual in the feline breed spectrum: a longhaired cat of moderately foreign type. While there are a few big, wild, farm-cat type longhairs, even more cute and cuddly fluffy ones, and a choice of slender, slinky Oriental types, the Tiffanie stands almost without competition in its homeland.

RED SELF

LILAC SELF

SILVER TABBY

BLACK TICKED TABBY

BLACK SMOKE

CHINCHILLA

BREED ORIGINS

The Tiffanie is a member of the otherwise shorthaired Asian group (*see* pp 208–209) and so shares their initial parentage, which was the unplanned alliance of a young chinchilla Persian male (*see* pp 258–61) and a Burmese female (*see* pp 212–15) in 1981. The Persian obviously contributed his longhaired trait to the offspring, but in the first generation it was masked by the dominant shorthaired trait of their mother. From the second generation of kittens on, fluffy coats appeared, and although disregarded at first, they eventually progressed with the rest of the Asian group.

The breed reached full Championship status a little later than the shorthaired members of the group, just after the turn of the millennium. It is still only recognized in the United Kingdom. In Europe, FIFé recognized only the Asian shaded, under its original name of Burmilla. There is also an Australian Tiffanie, first recognized in 1999. This was created out of longhaired kittens that turned up in litters from Asian cats; ultimately, it shares the same origins as the British breed, but its immediate parents are different, and it remains to be seen how similar these two Tiffanies on opposite sides of the globe will prove to be.

In North America, there has always been a problem of confusion between this cat and another longhaired breed that was at first called the Tiffany. This chocolate-coloured cat, often described as a longhaired Burmese although its origins were in fact unknown, was

LILAC SMOKE In the Australian Tiffanie, which is officially listed by the Australian Cat Federation as the longhaired Burmilla, shades of lilac are the rarest of the colours seen.

later renamed the Chantilly/Tiffany, but to no avail. Although recognized by the Canadian Cat Association, it has faded into obscurity.

OWNING A TIFFANIE

For Brits who want an elegant but not supermodel longhair, this is a good choice; elsewhere, the Turkish Angora (*see* pp 294–99) provides similar grace. The coat needs grooming a few times a week, more during moulting. Polycystic kidney disease came into the breed from the Persian heritage, but a test allows this to be detected and eliminated from breeding lines.

In personality, the Tiffanie is a reasonable medium between the extrovert Burmese and the placid Persian, with an outgoing but easygoing nature.

BLUE SMOKE The most common coats, even within the broad range recognized in the United Kingdom, are smokes, shaded, which are heavily mantled with colour, and tipped.

RED SHADED SILVER The red colours were developed rather later in the Asian group than the eumelanistic shades (*see* pp 158–59), and are judged separately in FIFé and Australian registries.

CHOCOLATE SHADED SILVER Solid, sepia, and tabby patterned Tiffanies are accepted in the United Kingdom, reflecting the whole Asian coat spectrum.

ASIANS AND TIFFANIE (*see* pp 208–209, 288–89) Because the
longhair gene is recessive, litters of Asian kittens will always
produce the occasional variants. Other breeds have found it best
to have a longhair version, and so the Asian has the Tiffanie.

Turkish Van

ORIGIN Turkey (before 1700s)
SYNONYM Turkish swimming cat; Vankedisi
WEIGHT 3–8.5 kg (7–19 lb)
BUILD
TEMPERAMENT
COAT CARE
COLOURS Western colours in self and tortie; all tabby patterns; always Van pattern bi-colour; all-white cats known as Vankedisi in GCCF

One of two breeds to come out of Turkey, this cat looks a big softie. It has a sweet, rounded face; big eyes, sometimes in baby blue; and a soft, long coat that constantly shifts and flows as it moves. But it is a natural breed from a harsh, rugged terrain, and although exotic, it is no lap cat.

 WHITE
 BLACK & WHITE
 BLUE & WHITE
 TORTIE TABBY & WHITE
 BLUE TORTIE & WHITE

CREAM AND WHITE The ideal Van is completely white on the body with a coloured tail and head markings. One or more markings are allowed on the body, and some white on the tail.

BREED ORIGINS

The Turkish Van is a naturally distilled breed, originating around Lake Van in the mountains of eastern Turkey, where it can still be found breeding true without human intervention. The region is relatively isolated, exactly the circumstances that favour the development of a distinctive local type.

The bi-colour pattern, predominantly white with isolated colour on the head and tail, is generally known in the cat fancy as the van pattern, after this breed. Although claims that cats of this pattern appear in Hittite art may be pushing the bounds of possibility back too far, it can be seen in old works of art from the near East, both local and painted by foreigners who clearly saw it as characteristic of the

place. Later studies have confirmed this: the pattern is found in a relatively high percentage of cats here, but is rare elsewhere in the world.

In 1955, two British women visiting Turkey, Laura Lushington and Sonia Halliday, brought some of the cats home with them. Laura's kittens endured a car tour and camping en route,

showing them to be fairly adaptable creatures. They bred true, confirming they were a true natural variety, not a mere coincidence.

Lushington worked for recognition of the cats in the United Kingdom, where they became known at first as Turkish cats. The Turkish Angora (*see* pp 294–99) not being a recognized breed in the country, this name seemed to make perfect sense. The breed arrived on the shores of the United States in 1982, and had Championship showing status in TICA and CFA by 1994. It remains rare in both North America and

TORTIE AND WHITE Unusually, the eumelanistic colours (*see* pp 158–59) were recognized in this breed after the phaeomelanistic. The markings above the tail are known as thumbprints.

Europe, however, with only a hundred cats registered each year. Their numbers have also diminished in recent years in their homeland but, like the Turkish Angora, they have government protection and are bred in Ankhara zoo. In the United Kingdom, the GCCF has begun the process of recognizing an all-white strain of the cat under the name Vankedisi; the name Van Kedi has also been applied to the bi-colour Van.

OWNING A TURKISH VAN

Bred by nature in an uncompromising environment, these are resourceful, intelligent, and fairly independent cats. They are gregarious, but prefer joint activities to lounging around simply purring, and have seemingly unlimited energy. The original breeder, Laura Lushington, noted that 'their outstanding characteristic is their liking for water … they not only dabble in water and play with it, but have been known to enter ponds and even horse-troughs for a swim'.

AUBURN AND WHITE
Auburn is the breed name for red, and this is the 'classic' Van colour and pattern. The markings on the head should be symmetrical.

Turkish Angora

ORIGIN Turkey (before 1700s)
SYNONYM None
WEIGHT 2.5–5 kg (6–11 lb)
BUILD 🐱
TEMPERAMENT 🐾
COAT CARE 🖐️🖐️
COLOURS Western colours in self, tortie, bi-colour, smoke, and shaded; blotched and striped tabby patterns

Possibly the oldest longhaired breed in the world, the Angora found fame in Europe, nearly went extinct, was rescued by a zoo and the government, found a new life in the United States, and spread back to Europe and beyond. At the end of this rocky ride, it still closely resembles the cats depicted in old artworks.

BLACK SELF   BLUE SELF   RED SELF   BROWN CLASSIC TABBY   SILVER TABBY   CHINCHILLA

BREED ORIGINS

The Turkish Angora shares with the Persian (*see* pp 258–61) the reputation of being an ancestor of all the longhaired cat breeds. The mutation for long hair is generally thought to have arisen many centuries ago in central Asia and spread outwards. The first recorded imports into Europe, in the 17th century, came from Persia to Italy with Pietro della Valle, and from Turkey to France

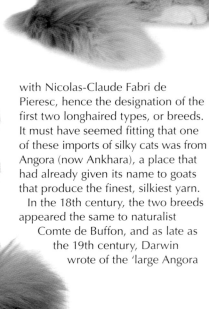

CREAM AND WHITE Bi-colours and red shades are common in Turkey. The inverted V on the face is also a classic marking and noted as desirable in the CFA standard.

with Nicolas-Claude Fabri de Pieresc, hence the designation of the first two longhaired types, or breeds. It must have seemed fitting that one of these imports of silky cats was from Angora (now Ankhara), a place that had already given its name to goats that produce the finest, silkiest yarn.

In the 18th century, the two breeds appeared the same to naturalist Comte de Buffon, and as late as the 19th century, Darwin wrote of the 'large Angora

TORTOISESHELL SMOKE Smokes were recorded in 19th-century writings. The shimmer of the silver undercoat is seen at its best in winter when the coat is longest.

or Persian cat' that was 'believed by Pallas, but on no distinct evidence, to be descended from the *F. manul* of middle Asia'. This theory, that the long hair is a result of a cross with Pallas's cat (*see* p 25) has now been disproved by genetic studies, but it persisted well into the 20th century.

Late 19th-century breeders could distinguish between them well enough, however, and it was the Persian that took off and passed on the longhair trait to most of the other longhaired breeds created in the 20th century. The Angora languished in obscurity, becoming virtually extinct beyond and even within its homeland.

REVIVAL OF THE BREED

Fortunately, there was a small breeding population kept in the zoo at Ankhara. Starting in 1917, the zoo undertook a concerted breeding scheme to save the cats. Efforts concentrated on saving whites, with blue, golden, or odd eyes, which were and still are regarded as a national treasure, although the breed has historically contained a wide range of coat colours and patterns. As with all zoo conservation efforts, the breedings were carefully controlled and recorded, with great care taken to establish as broad a genetic base as possible, and the zoo staff were very reluctant to part with any cats.

Finally, in 1962, Walter and Liesa Fallon Grant did manage to wrest a breeding pair of unrelated cats from the Ankhara zoo: an odd-eyed white male named Yildiz (meaning star) and an amber-eyed white female named Yildicek (meaning starlet, though not in the movie sense). In the United States, these two cats bred, but without any other cats to breed to, the kittens were at first simply sold as pets. In 1966, the Grants visited Turkey and brought another two unrelated cats home with them to supplement their breeding stocks: again, an odd-eyed white male and an amber-eyed white female.

CREAM TABBY As the dilute form of red, this shade is common in the Angora's homeland. In pedigree cats, the colours must be warm and rich, never sandy.

BLUE-CREAM The breed standards allow for the colours of torties and blue torties to be either patchy or softly and evenly intermingled across the cat's body.

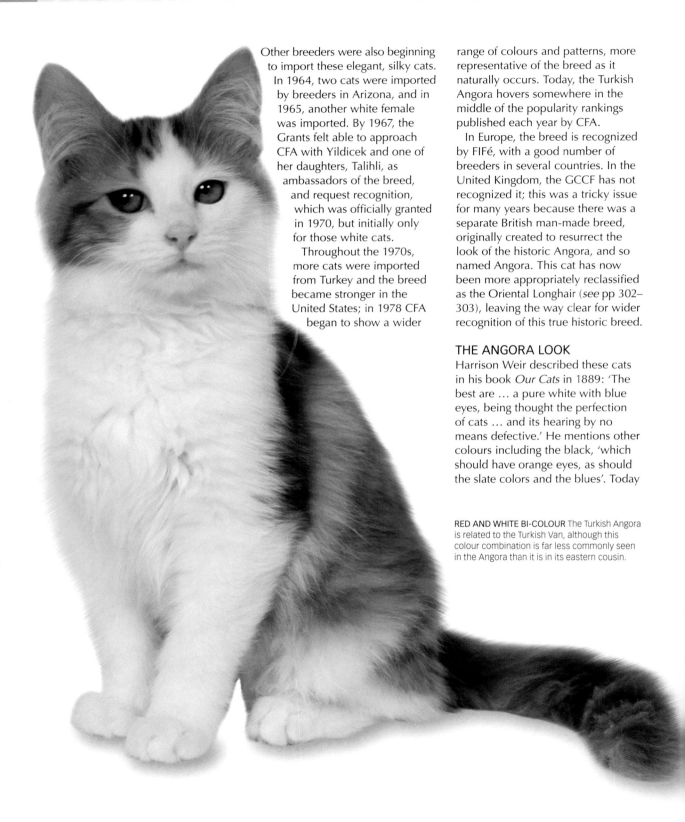

Other breeders were also beginning to import these elegant, silky cats. In 1964, two cats were imported by breeders in Arizona, and in 1965, another white female was imported. By 1967, the Grants felt able to approach CFA with Yildicek and one of her daughters, Talihli, as ambassadors of the breed, and request recognition, which was officially granted in 1970, but initially only for those white cats.

Throughout the 1970s, more cats were imported from Turkey and the breed became stronger in the United States; in 1978 CFA began to show a wider range of colours and patterns, more representative of the breed as it naturally occurs. Today, the Turkish Angora hovers somewhere in the middle of the popularity rankings published each year by CFA.

In Europe, the breed is recognized by FIFé, with a good number of breeders in several countries. In the United Kingdom, the GCCF has not recognized it; this was a tricky issue for many years because there was a separate British man-made breed, originally created to resurrect the look of the historic Angora, and so named Angora. This cat has now been more appropriately reclassified as the Oriental Longhair (*see* pp 302–303), leaving the way clear for wider recognition of this true historic breed.

THE ANGORA LOOK

Harrison Weir described these cats in his book *Our Cats* in 1889: 'The best are ... a pure white with blue eyes, being thought the perfection of cats ... and its hearing by no means defective.' He mentions other colours including the black, 'which should have orange eyes, as should the slate colors and the blues'. Today

RED AND WHITE BI-COLOUR The Turkish Angora is related to the Turkish Van, although this colour combination is far less commonly seen in the Angora than it is in its eastern cousin.

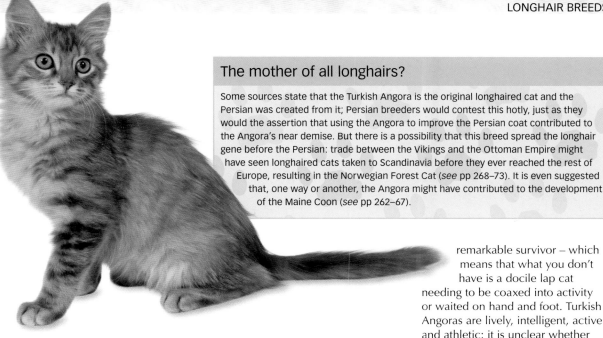

ANGORA KITTEN Occasionally Angora kittens suffer a form of ataxia – their nervous systems do not develop as they should. They never learn to move, and are euthanized.

The mother of all longhairs?

Some sources state that the Turkish Angora is the original longhaired cat and the Persian was created from it; Persian breeders would contest this hotly, just as they would the assertion that using the Angora to improve the Persian coat contributed to the Angora's near demise. But there is a possibility that this breed spread the longhair gene before the Persian: trade between the Vikings and the Ottoman Empire might have seen longhaired cats taken to Scandinavia before they ever reached the rest of Europe, resulting in the Norwegian Forest Cat (*see* pp 268–73). It is even suggested that, one way or another, the Angora might have contributed to the development of the Maine Coon (*see* pp 262–67).

all these are once more recognized; only colours that hint at an outcross to Oriental breeds are forbidden.

The silky, semi-long coat has no undercoat and lies smooth against the body, shimmering with every movement. The body is long and lithe, but not thin; these are muscular cats. The head is a moderate wedge of smooth lines, tapering evenly into a fairly narrow muzzle. It is topped by large ears which give the breed a characteristically alert, interested look.

OWNING A TURKISH ANGORA

Depending on where you are, finding one of these cats may at first make you feel like the early breeders trying to import one of those prized specimens. Breeders can be thin on the ground in some places.

Should you find one, you have a true piece of living history, and a remarkable survivor – which means that what you don't have is a docile lap cat needing to be coaxed into activity or waited on hand and foot. Turkish Angoras are lively, intelligent, active and athletic; it is unclear whether their minds or their bodies work fastest, but either one will prove an enjoyable challenge to keep up with.

BLACK These must be a dense, coal black from the roots to the tips. The eyes need not be orange, but deeper, richer tones are preferred.

TURKISH ANGORA (*see* pp 294–97) This young cat shows how the typically high placing of the large ears gives every Turkish Angora the look of a highly focused hunter on the move – even if the prey is no more than a wind-blown leaf.

Balinese (including Javanese)

ORIGIN United States (1950s)

SYNONYM Javanese

WEIGHT 2.5–5 kg (6–11 lb)

BUILD 🐈

TEMPERAMENT 🐈

COAT CARE 🖌🖌

COLOURS All colours in self and tortie; all tabby patterns; always in pointed pattern

This breed – or these breeds, depending on your registry – arrived late on the scene. By the time they were developed, the pointing gene was already available in two longhaired breeds, both of them at the chunky-and-cuddly end of the scale. The Balinese finally presented a pointed, longhaired cat for those who prefer svelte.

 LILAC POINT

 CREAM POINT

 CHOCOLATE POINT

 FAWN POINT

 SEAL TABBY POINT

 RED TABBY POINT & WHITE

BREED ORIGINS

It is impossible to know when or how the longhaired gene entered the make-up of the Siamese (*see* pp 220–23). It may have been present when the cats first arrived from their Oriental home; it may have appeared through an accidental or deliberate outcrossing early in its history as a breed.

The usual practice with variants that could not be shown is to sell them as pets. In the years following World War II, however, one breeder in California started to breed these longhaired cats instead. Marion Dorsey first showed her 'Longhaired Siamese' in 1955 and they were recognized in American registries by 1961. Siamese breeders objected to the name, and it was changed to

RED TABBY OR LYNX POINT This is a Balinese in most registries, but a Javanese in CFA. The Javanese breed is less popular than the Balinese.

Balinese, inspired by the sinuous, elegant dancers of the island's temples. The breed spread from North America in the 1970s, and is recognized by all major registries around the world today.

THE JAVANESE

Just as in the Siamese breed, there is some division over colours between registries. TICA and registries in Europe and elsewhere recognize both eumelanistic and phaeomelanistic colours (*see* pp 158–59), as well as tabby patterns. But CFA accepts only four colours in the Balinese – seal, blue, chocolate, and lilac – and classifies all other colours and patterns in a separate offshoot called Javanese. This name caused some confusion between American and European sources, because FIFé used the name Javanese for the breed

SEAL TORTIE TABBY POINT In a show-quality tortie tabby, each of the points must show mingled tortie colours and some tabby markings.

Red cats in Thailand

Although chocolate and cinnamon originated in the East, it would be wrong to think that the colours and patterns regarded as 'not traditional' in the Siamese and Balinese are solely Western. Reds and tabbies are frequently seen in Asia – although their only appearance in the *Tamra Maew* copied in the 19th century is the bad-luck 'tiger breed' cat, the Phan Phayak or Lai Seua.

CHOCOLATE TORTIE POINT In tortie points, all the points must show some mingling of colours, but the balance of the two need not be even.

that is now known as the Oriental Longhair (*see* pp 302–303).

OWNING A BALINESE

The silky coat is fairly low maintenance, and when it is shed in summer, cats can appear shorthaired apart from their plume-like tail. Like the Siamese, they are long-lived cats, and more robust than their delicate build would seem to imply.

Like all the Oriental breeds, it has a loud voice which it will use to remind you that it needs your attention and admiration. The Balinese is also an active and inquisitive breed, and will get everywhere – but most often you will find it right in front of you.

BLUE POINT Dilute colours are more liable to be confused than dense ones. Blue points should be cool – impossible to mistake for the warmer lilac points.

Oriental Longhair

ORIGIN United Kingdom and United States (1970s on)
SYNONYM Angora, Javanese, Mandarin
WEIGHT 4.5–6 kg (10–13 lb)
BUILD
TEMPERAMENT
COAT CARE
COLOURS All colours in self, tortie, bi-colour, solid, smoke, shaded, and tipped; all tabby patterns

This is the last of the quartet of Oriental breeds that first came to the West in the eye-catching pattern of the Siamese (*see* pp 220–23). Solid colours were barred, becoming the Oriental Shorthair (*see* pp 224–29), but the longhair gene eventually gave us both the Balinese (*see* pp 300–301) and this elegant breed.

BLACK SELF

WHITE

LILAC SELF

RED TICKED TABBY

BLACK SMOKE

BLUE TORTIE TABBY & WHITE

BREED ORIGINS

The Oriental Longhair has different origins on either side of the Atlantic. In the United Kingdom, breeder Maureen Silson mated a Siamese with an Abyssinian (*see* pp 240–45), hoping to get a ticked tabby point Siamese. Unexpectedly the kittens included longhairs. The longhairs began to appear at shows in the 1970s, but under the name Angora; they were seen as a recreation of the longhairs that had died out in Europe at the end of the 19th century, and the Turkish Angora (*see* pp 294–99) had not reached British shores. In Europe the new breed was recognized as the Javanese, to avoid confusion with the Turkish cats; this name has now changed in FIFé, but remains in use in New Zealand. Progress was slow: mating back to Siamese and

WHITE The United Kingdom has a longhaired equivalent of the Foreign White with its Siamese-blue eyes and avoidance of deafness problems.

Oriental Shorthairs meant many short-haired and pointed kittens. Angoras only achieved full Championship status in 2003, and at this point were officially renamed Oriental Longhairs.

In the United States, the breed had a later start, in 1985. Here the parents were an Oriental Shorthair and a Balinese at Sheryl Ann Boyle's Sholine Cattery. An accidental mating produced solid and pointed longhair and shorthair kittens. Boyle developed the solid longhairs as a breed, named Oriental Longhair, and it was rapidly

CINNAMON (LEFT) AND BLUE TABBY (RIGHT) The first important cat of the breed in the United Kingdom was a cinnamon. All variants of tabby patterns are shown.

ALL ORIENTALS Pointed members of the Oriental groups are still allowed as outcross breeds. A litter of solid kittens like this is what all breeders want, but occasional pointed offspring will turn up.

recognized by major registries across North America and Europe, except for the GCCF.

In these four linked breeds, the solid colours will produce pointed variants and the shorthairs will produce longhairs; the status of these for showing vary. TICA has one root standard for all, and in 1995 CFA merged the Oriental Shorthair and Longhair into one breed with two coat lengths, which upset breeders who feared that the longhair gene could subtly affect the quality of the shorthair coat.

OWNING AN ORIENTAL LONGHAIR

The coat of the Oriental Longhair is often not that long, especially in summer, a warm climate, or cats kept permanently indoors in warm homes; these may look like shorthairs but for a plumed tail. The fineness of the sleek coat makes it one of the easiest longhairs to care for.

Like all its Oriental sibling breeds, this is an active and athletic cat that likes to do rather than see things. It is also gregarious to the point of absurdity, and can gossip for hours.

BLUE SELF The blue of the Oriental Longhair should be free from any trace of the silver tipping that is prized in some other breeds.

Somali

ORIGIN North America (1960s)
SYNONYM Longhaired Abyssinian
WEIGHT 3.5–5.5 kg (8–12 lb)
BUILD
TEMPERAMENT
COAT CARE
COLOURS All colours in self, tortie, and shaded (brown, blue, cinnamon, and fawn only in CFA); always in ticked tabby pattern

Even harmless recessive genes sometimes seem like a dirty secret. The Russian (*see* pp 198–99), Siamese (*see* pp 220–23), and Abyssinian (*see* pp 240–45) all carried long hair, but it took decades for breeders to move to developing their attractive, fluffy kittens. They all did eventually, and the Somali is one of the happy results.

BROWN TICKED TABBY

BLUE TICKED TABBY

RED TICKED TABBY

BREED ORIGINS

It is not clear when the longhaired gene came into the Abyssinian breed, or whether it was present from the start; given the way that recessive genes can hide for many generations, it is quite possible that the very first cats carried it.

SORREL Most of the thick coat that makes a Somali look so magnificent in winter is shed in spring. Sorrel is the breed name for cinnamon.

For a long time, the slightly fuzzy kittens that turned up in litters were neutered and passed on as pets, and nobody talked about them – breeders can be cagey about recessive variants that seem to undermine the 'purity' of a breed if not properly understood.

One particular line of Abys, from British breeder Jean Robertson, seemed to consistently produce these variants. In the 1960s, Ken

Any colour you like

The colours that are allowed in the Somali vary greatly internationally. CFA is most restrictive in colours, allowing only ruddy (brown tabby), red (cinnamon), and their dilutes blue and fawn, and no silvers. FIFé follows the same palette of four colours, and TICA recognizes only the eumelanistic colours (*see* pp 158–59), so there are no reds, creams, or any torties, but both of these registries do allow silver cats. The GCCF in the United Kingdom, often quite a traditional registry, has the widest range, showing all colours in both solid and silver.

BLUE SILVER The pure white undercoats give silver Somalis quite a different, more dramatic effect. Most of the coat appears to have a veil of colour drawn over it.

McGill in Canada began breeding from these lines. Canadian breeder Don Richings then used McGill's cats and began working with American breeder Mary Mague, who was also developing the longhairs and calling them Somalis. By the late 1970s, the new breed was accepted in North American registries. In the 1980s, they were exported to Europe and beyond, and by the early 1990s, the breed was accepted by registries internationally.

SOMALI LOOKS
The ticking, combined with the tufted ears, luxuriant ruff, bottlebrush thickness of tail, and generally wild appearance of Somalis, has earned them the nickname of 'fox cats'. In their general build and appearance, they resemble their Abyssinian parents, muscular and athletic with a slightly arched back that

gives them the look of a cat about to spring at any moment.

The longer coat can accommodate more bands of ticking (see p 161), with up to twelve light and dark alternating bands on each hair. This gives a luminous depth and shimmer to the coat in a fully developed adult – the coat can take years to mature.

OWNING A SOMALI
The Somali is a fairly easy-care cat, although it is prone to the same

inherited problems as its Aby ancestors. It is intelligent, active, interested in all that goes on around it. Although more gregarious than older European breeds, it does not tend to try and join in with all your activities like Oriental types. If you have two of these cats, they will occupy themselves for much of the time, although you may find yourself checking up on exactly what they are doing, because their curiosity will lead them into strange places.

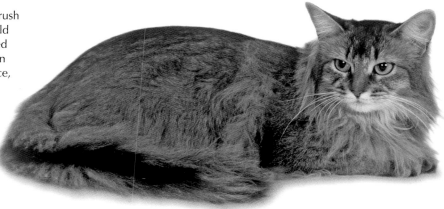

RUDDY OR USUAL Just as in the Aby, this coat has idiosyncratic names, being called usual in the United Kingdom and ruddy in North America.

SOMALI (*see* pp 304–305) Some aspects of the ticked tabby pattern, such as the white chin and the strong facial markings, are apparent from birth. But the coats of these kittens may take years to develop their full ticking potential.

REXED AND HAIRLESS BREEDS

Curly (rexed) and even absent coats have cropped up throughout history, but have usually remained relatively local oddities and died out over time, because they are a significant disadvantage to a self-supporting cat. Darwin recorded several in his writings, including one that over a period of eight weeks 'underwent a complete metamorphosis, having parted with its sandy-coloured fur'. Rexes have also cropped up within established breeds, although they are usually unwelcome: the curly-coated Persian named the Bohemian Rex and the Maine Wave were both regarded as a problem by the breed clubs, rather than welcomed as an opportunity.

SPHYNX This was not the first appearance of a hairless type, nor even the first attempt to turn one into a breed. However, it was the first, and for a long time the only, such breed to achieve recognition and popularity.

Cornish Rex (UK)

ORIGIN United Kingdom (1950s)

SYNONYM None

WEIGHT 2.5–4.5 kg (6–10 lb)

BUILD

TEMPERAMENT

COAT CARE

COLOURS All colours in all shades and all patterns

There have been earlier historical reports of cats with bristly or wavy hair, but the Cornish was the first such cat to be turned into a successful breed. Its velvety coat and elegant looks are well established now, but the breed had a rocky start in life when the demand for novelty was less pronounced than it is today.

BLUE & WHITE

CREAM STRIPED TABBY

BLUE TABBY & WHITE

BLUE TORTIE TABBY & WHITE

BLUE TABBY POINT

BREED ORIGINS

The first cat known with the mutation appeared in a litter born to a tortie-and-white female owned by Nina Ennismore of Bodmin in Cornwall. A cream male named Kallibunker, he had tight curls and a light, foreign body-type, long legs, and large ears.

Ennismore consulted geneticist AC Jude, who suggested the kitten should be bred back to his mother to confirm that the coat was a mutation rather than the result of some environmental factor. A litter of three kittens resulted, two of which had the same curled coat. Test breedings to other random-breed cats, and to Burmese (*see* pp 212–15) and Siamese (*see* pp 220–23), showed the mutation to be recessive, with two curly-coated cats always producing litters solely of curly-coated kittens. Familiar with a similar coat in Rex rabbits and mice, Ennismore chose this name for the breed.

The Cornish Rex was far from an instant success. By 1956, both Serena and Kallibunker had been euthanized, and Nina Ennismore gave up breeding. Breeder Brian Sterling-Webb continued the work, but by this time there were only two Cornish Rexes left, and both were male. One was Poldhu, a rare dilute tortie-and-white male. Poldhu had

CREAM Some accounts hold that Kallibunker was a cream, others that he was a red. Given his non-pedigree background, either is possible – a very cool red or warm cream might look similar.

CHOCOLATE TABBY New breeds with distinctive characteristics, such as rexed coats, are often recognized in any colours, as they are not 'historic' breeds.

CORNISH REX LOOKS

The curl is not the only thing that is odd about the Cornish coat. While a normal, straight coat contains guard, awn, and down hairs (*see* pp 54–55), the Cornish coat lacks guard hairs, and as a result feels noticeably softer.

The look is distinctly foreign, with a wedge-shaped head and mussel-shell ears. The body is slender, of medium length, and carried high on long legs, but is hard and muscular. The wave of the coat is less obvious and the build less whippet-like in British Cornish Rexes than in bred in the United States.

produced fertile kittens, and two had been sent to the United States, where they became the foundation of the American version of the breed (*see* pp 314–17). When a vet took a tissue sample from Poldhu for research, the cat was accidentally castrated, leaving the breed in more tenuous position.

This left Champagne Chas, a son of Poldhu. With just one surviving male carrying the gene, many feared that the breed was unsustainable. In 1960, a curly-coated kitten was found in Devon, but this turned out to be a separate mutation, and became the Devon Rex (*see* pp 318–19). The Cornish mutation was called Gene I and the Devon, Gene II; although some of the straight-coated offspring were included in the Cornish breeding programmes, the original experimental crosses were not repeated.

WHITE This cat is a typical example of the British type. The body is long and slender, but without a pronounced 'waist', and the nose is straight. The ears are large and erect, but not bat-like.

Outbreeding avoided a dangerously small gene pool, but led away from the original Oriental look. A male was imported from Canada in 1965 to get back to this slender type. In the same year, the GCCF approved a Provisional standard for the breed, and by 1967, the Cornish Rex finally had Championship recognition in the United Kingdom. Several breeds are still approved as outcrosses, to maintain a large, healthy gene pool.

RED The curl of the Cornish coat produces a regular series of 'waves' over the body, traditionally called a 'Marcel wave' after the once-fashionable hairstyle.

CHOCOLATE AND WHITE Any amount of white is permitted, from mittens to a van pattern, and eye colour is not related to coat colour.

Asthmatic attacks respond fairly well to placebos, so if anyone can convince themselves that the lovely breed they have fallen for just happens to be hypo-allergenic, they have about a 30 per cent chance of making it true. It is vital to be sure that any strategy works before getting the chosen cat, however, otherwise another cat will end up needing to be re-homed.

OWNING A CORNISH REX

Because of the minimal coat, these are easy-care cats. However, the same minimal coat means they are not the best cold-weather cats. If they are to be kept indoors, then the house will need to be fairly well cat-proofed.

Perhaps due to all the Oriental input, this is a high-energy breed, which never seems to grow up. Playful, adventurous, it is almost always on the move, and likes to

A HYPO-ALLERGENIC CAT?

As a rexed breed, there were hopes that it might be suitable for allergy sufferers. Dog breeds with curled coats, such as poodles, hold dead hair in the coat until it is brushed out, and so provoke fewer allergic responses.

Allergies to cats, however, are almost always to the protein Fel D1, produced in the hair and skin but also in the saliva that a cat leaves all over its coat every time it grooms itself, so coat type has no real influence on allergic responses. Any cat with a finer coat will shed less hair, and so provoke fewer problems. Some owners find that wiping their cat daily with a damp cloth can reduce allergies.

BLUE-CREAM SMOKE The anomalous male Poldhu was a dilute tortie, with white patches rather than the white undercoat just seen here where the hair parts.

BLACK SMOKE AND WHITE Because the Cornish coat is close and dense, the white undercoat of a smoke may not be seen when the cat is at rest.

LILAC POINT Pointed Cornish Rexes are sometimes called si-rexes, but are not a separate breed: the name is just shorthand for this sought-after, distinctive pattern.

CREAM AND WHITE The Cornish Rex breed was established in Australia in 1963 by Senty Twix Crispuss, a 'red' and white male – now thought to have been a very warm cream.

climb as much as it likes to run around. All that activity needs fuel, and these cats eat a surprising amount for their size; many owners allow them to free-feed without problems. Cornish Rexes have earned the nickname 'Velcro cats' for their tendency to be found attached to their owners at every opportunity.

The German Rex

This breed may start with a cat named Munk. Born in the 1930s to the Schneider family, near the Prussian town of Königsberg (now called Kaliningrad and in Russia), his curly-coated recessive trait spread throughout the local free-breeding feline population.

In 1951, Dr Rose Scheuer-Karpin noticed a black curly-coated cat in the garden of the Hufelandklinik hospital in Berlin. The cat was thought to have been brought there by a male nurse fleeing Königsberg after World War II. She named the cat Lämmchen (meaning 'little lamb'), and started to breed from her. When one of her straight-coated sons was bred back to her in 1957, she produced two curly-coated kittens, and became the founder cat of all the current German Rex breed.

In 1956, German Rexes were crossed with Cornish Rexes and produced curly kittens, so are assumed to possess the same mutation; being pipped at the post was almost a death knell for the breed, although they were used in Cornish Rex breeding. Enthusiasts kept the line going; today, a loyal and growing band of breeders, emphatic that this is the 'first' rex breed, ensure that it remains viable and have won recognition in FIFé.

Cornish Rex (US)

ORIGIN United Kingdom (1950s)

SYNONYM None

WEIGHT 2.5–4 kg (6–9 lb)

BUILD 🐈

TEMPERAMENT 🐾

COAT CARE 🖌

COLOURS All colours in all shades and all patterns

The Cornish Rex was developed in parallel in its native home, the United Kingdom, and in North America. Although all originally descended from the same mutation, the two strains developed in slightly different ways from the start, and today the looks are quite distinctly different.

BLACK SELF

BLUE & WHITE

BROWN CLASSIC TABBY

RED STRIPED TABBY

TORTIE TABBY

LILAC POINT

BREED ORIGINS

In 1957, a Californian breeder, Frances Blancheri, imported a son of Kallibunker, Pendennis Castle, and a daughter of Poldhu, Lamorna Cove, who had been bred to her sire before she was exported. Pendennis Castle had no offspring, but Lamorna Cove gave birth to four kittens, marking the start of the breed in the United States.

When breeders tried to import more of the cats, there were none to be had, and so outcrosses were made to Siamese, American Shorthairs, Burmese, and Havana Browns, starting a drift between the two types.

A rexed female who turned up in a California animal shelter proved to have the same mutation and was taken into the line; whether she had come from it or was a separate mutation is not known. Also, the German Rex (*see* p 313) arrived in the United States in 1961 and was judged in one class with the Cornish. The highest-ranked

Rex ever was Katzenreich's Bianka; as the name implies, Katzenreich bred German Rexes. The German Rex eventually merged into the Cornish and was forgotten. In 1962, CFA recognized Cornish Rexes and within two years they had full Championship status.

Despite the appearance of other native mutations since the 1960s, the Cornish remains popular in its adopted home. In fact, hovering a little outside the top ten breeds, it is more popular than it is in the United Kingdom.

IS IT A DIFFERENT CAT?

The American Cornish differs from the British type in its body shape, its head, and a little in the coat. Where it does not differ is in its appealingly lively, inquisitive, and gregarious personality.

TORTOISESHELL Standards call for a Roman nose, and the 'break' at the whisker pads is pronounced; the whole look is more chiselled than the British type.

CREAM AND WHITE The body type of the American cat is lean and racy, with an arched spine. The chest is deep, but then slims into a whippet-like, tucked-up tummy.

BLACK SMOKE AND WHITE American standards differ in the total points for the coat, but both CFA and TICA award most for waviness and call for more of the cat to be curled.

CORNISH REX (US) (*see* pp 314–15) The hair on the head of a cat is generally too short and fine to show any curls, except for the whiskers, but the chiselled cheekbones and strong nose mean this breed still stands out.

Devon Rex

ORIGIN United Kingdom (1960s)

SYNONYM None

WEIGHT 2.5–4 kg (6–9 lb)

BUILD 🐈

TEMPERAMENT 🐆

COAT CARE 🖌

COLOURS All colours in all shades and all patterns

Like so many modern breeds distinguished by a single striking feature, the Devon Rex mutation was first seen in a stray. Of course, mutations occur within breeds too, but they often have a hard time getting accepted. This breed, with its extraordinary elfin looks, had no such problems, and is a popular breed in many countries.

BLUE SELF

RED SELF

SILVER STRIPED TABBY

TORTIE & WHITE

RED POINT

CREAM POINT

BREED ORIGINS

In the 1950s, a curly-coated tomcat was active around Buckfastleigh in the west of England; in fact, cats of this type, locally called the 'Buckfast Blue', had been reported around Buckfast Abbey for some time. In 1960, a feral tortoiseshell-and-white female gave birth to a litter in the garden of Beryl Cox; the litter included a curly-coated kitten, which Cox adopted and named Kirlee.

That year, a newspaper article was published celebrating ten years of the Cornish Rex (see pp 310–13), with a picture of what was claimed to be the only curly-coated kitten in the country. Miss Cox contacted the newspaper to tell them about her kitten, and was put in touch with Cornish Rex breeder Brian Sterling-Webb. They arranged for Kirlee to be sent to Cornwall to be part of the breeding programme. However, when Kirlee was bred to several Cornish Rex females, the kittens were all straight-coated. Kirlee was recognized as a different rex mutation, called Gene II.

One breeder, Mrs P Hughes, had kept a straight-coated female, named Broughton Golden Rain, from one of the crossed litters. When she was bred back to Kirlee, she produced two straight-coated kittens and one curly female. This first curly-coated offspring of Kirlee showed the Devon Rex gene to be a simple recessive.

By 1967, the breed was recognized by the GCCF, and over the next decade it spread around the world. In 1968, breeder Marion White and her daughter Anita imported two cats to Texas after seeing them while in the United Kingdom, and in 1969, another Texas breeder, Shirley Lambert, imported a pair. These two

CREAM TABBY POINT There have been pointed Devons, sometimes called si-rexes, since the early days; two of the first cats imported into the United States were seal points.

breeders were the spearhead of interest that spread to other states and to Canada through the 1970s.

But in North America, the Devon was hampered by CFA rules. They were judged simply as rexed cats, against a standard drawn up for the Cornish Rex, which had arrived first. Unwilling to lose the distinctive looks of the Devon by breeding to another cat's standard, they looked elsewhere, and the breed was recognized and shown in ACFA and later TICA instead. In 1979, CFA had a change of heart, and the Devon was finally recognized as a breed in its own right, reaching Championship status by 1983.

OWNING A DEVON

The Devon has guard, awn, and down hairs. Although the guard hairs are sparse and short, they give the Devon coat a looser, more open-looking curl than the Cornish Rex. Like the Cornish, this is not a hypoallergenic cat, but it is low-maintenance. Early inbreeding resulted in some health problems –

BLUE SELF The original Devon Rex, Kirlee, is variously described as grey, black, or brownish-black. He is most likely to have been a blue, like his sire.

luxating patella (slipping kneecaps), coagulopathy, and inherited spasticity – but testing and outcrossing have been and still are used to reduce these.

As for personality, Devons look like mischief-makers, and they live up to their looks, but usually only enough to endear them to their owners.

TABBY POINT The pointed pattern can be combined with any other pattern in the Devon Rex, so tabby or lynx points, shaded silver points, and bi-colour points are all allowed.

TORTOISESHELL The Devon profile shows a curved forehead and a clear stop before the short muzzle. The breed has a broad chest, widely spaced front legs, and a muscular body.

RED TABBY The Devon 'look' favours females or younger cats. This face is too full and heavy for perfection, due to stud jowls that develop in males kept intact for breeding.

American Wirehair

ORIGIN United States (1960s)

SYNONYM None

WEIGHT 3.5–7 kg (8–15 lb)

BUILD 🐈

TEMPERAMENT 🐈

COAT CARE 🖌

COLOURS Western colours in self, tortie, bi-colour, smoke, shaded, and tipped; blotched and striped tabby patterns

As North America's first home-grown rexed cat, the Wirehair certainly did not win in the naming stakes. Such an unstrokable name may have helped hold the breed back from greater success, although today slightly painful puns about 'getting wired' are in play in an attempt to improve its fortunes with a new generation.

BLACK SELF

WHITE

CREAM STRIPED TABBY

BLUE SILVER TABBY

SILVER SHADED

TORTIE TABBY & WHITE

BREED ORIGINS

The first Wirehair was a red-and-white male, the only survivor in a litter of free-breeding barn cats in Verona, New York. The year

BROWN TABBY Tabbies and bi-colours predominate, but the haywire crimping of the coat produces some strange effects on tabby patterns, sometimes making identification hard.

was 1966, so the Cornish Rex (see pp 314–17) was already a Championship breed, raising the profile of unusual coats. The male, Council Rock Farm Adam, was bred to a straight-coated female, and the resulting kinked coats showed the mutation to be dominant.

Wirehairs were first accepted for CFA registration in 1967 and for Championship competition in 1978, and are also recognized by other North American associations including TICA. However, only a few tens of cats are registered each year, and they are rarer abroad.

AMERICAN WIREHAIR LOOKS

The breed was developed using the American Shorthair (see pp 200–203) as an outcross breed. As a result, the standard of the Wirehair is similar to that of the American Shorthair in type, the crimped coat being the main distinguishing feature. This has moved away from the founding father's wedge-shaped head, large ears, and slanted eyes.

The coat is generally coarse and springy. This rexing trait is an 'incomplete dominant', so cats may be anything from slightly wavy to tightly crimped, and litters usually contain at least one straight-coated kitten, making progress all the more difficult. The coat is rather unstable, with the hardest types breaking easily, and cats sometimes shed almost all their hair due to relatively minor stress, such as a change in the weather. Longhairs do appear from time to time, but are never shown: they are said to look like 'dust bunnies'.

OWNING A WIREHAIR

If you are lucky, the coat is low maintenance, and best without grooming. Wirehairs can be prone to skin allergies and heavy production of earwax, however, so regular cleaning and bathing without brushing may be necessary, although this is no more onerous than the grooming needs of several longer-haired breeds. Other than this, the breed is generally hardy and healthy.

In personality, Wirehairs are close to their Shorthair outcross: playful and friendly, but generally quiet and laid-back individuals.

BROWN TABBY AND WHITE All Wirehair colours are shown in one class. Cats with silver-shaded coats should have green eyes, but all other colours should have brilliant golden eyes.

LaPerm

ORIGIN United States (1980s)
SYNONYM Dalles LaPerm
WEIGHT 3.5–5.5 kg (8–12 lb)
BUILD 🐈
TEMPERAMENT 🐈
COAT CARE ✂️
COLOURS All colours in all shades and all patterns

Despite the quirky name, this breed is not the result of any human hairdressing or other tinkering, but a mutation that turned up in free-breeding rural American cats. Although it has not yet climbed the popularity tables in its homeland, it has become established overseas in Europe and as far afield as New Zealand.

BLACK SELF

WHITE

RED SELF

CREAM STRIPED TABBY

BLUE TORTIE TABBY & WHITE

SEAL TABBY POINT

BREED ORIGINS

The first LaPerm appeared on the cherry farm of Richard and Linda Koehl in the Dalles, Oregon, in 1982. She was in a litter of kittens born to a working barn cat: the rest of the litter was normal, but this one was bald, with a 'blueprint' of a tabby pattern on her skin. Despite her lack of hair, the kitten survived and grew, and within eight weeks she began to grow a coat, but one that was soft and full of curls. The Koehls named her Curly, and over the next ten years she bred to local toms, gradually increasing the numbers of curly-coated offspring in the cats on the farm. Finally, the Koehls sought guidance and began to control the breedings, establishing that the mutant gene was dominant.

Eventually the cats were entered in a show and generated enormous interest. The breed is recognized by CFA and has full Championship status within TICA. It arrived in the United Kingdom in 2002, and numbers have been climbing steadily since the GCCF started registering LaPerms in 2004, but it is not yet recognized by FIFé.

BLUE TICKED TABBY The texture of the shorthair coat is generally firmer and springier than the longhaired variety. The coat is light and airy, standing away from the body.

LAPERM LOOKS

Curly was a generally long, slender cat. This fits a strange pattern in the rexed breeds. With the exception of the Selkirk Rex (see pp 324–25), the cats in whom the mutation are first seen are distinguished not only by their curled coats but also by a look that is lighter, longer, and generally more Oriental than the stock from which they spring. Whether this is a real trend, or whether the additional unusual build simply helps to get the cat noticed is debatable.

The LaPerm coat is fairly soft, but differs greatly from cat to cat. It comes in long and short versions, and varies in curl from waves to ringlets; the favoured longhair coat is a tousled look called the 'gypsy shag'. Kittens may be born hairless, curly, or straight-coated, and often lose any hair at about two weeks, regrowing it over the next months.

OWNING A LAPERM

Springing from a large pool of free-breeding cats, the LaPerm had an excellent genetic start and cats from this breed are generally healthy. As might be expected from their barn-cat beginnings, they are also intelligent, inquisitive, and active, but they are noticeably more gregarious and people-oriented than their forebears. They enjoy being stroked every bit as much as their owners enjoy stroking the wild and wonderful coat.

Recessive traits

The first Rex breeds, the Cornish (see pp 310–17) and Devon (see pp 318–19), were both recessive traits. This meant that any outcross produced straight-coated kittens, with a lot of test-breeding needed to show which offspring carried the mutant gene, and could contribute to the breed. The American Wirehair (see pp 320–21), LaPerm, and Selkirk Rex are all dominant mutations. Useful cats from any outcross breeding are immediately identifiable, but the breeds will continue to produce recessive straight-coated variants.

RED TABBY Although the markings on the legs and face are clear, the random curls of the LaPerm coat can make the pattern on the body hard to discern.

Selkirk Rex

ORIGIN United States (1980s)

SYNONYM None

WEIGHT 3–5 kg (7–11 lb)

BUILD 🐈

TEMPERAMENT 🐈

COAT CARE 🪮🪮

COLOURS All colours in all shades and all patterns

There are fashions in feline breeds. Once, curly-coated cats were oddities to be shunned, an attitude that changed only with better understanding of genetics. The Selkirk is the most recent of the rexed breeds to be developed, and is proving to be both healthy and popular: the breed motto might be 'never be first, only be best'.

BLACK   WHITE   BLUE SELF   BLACK SMOKE   SEAL POINT   LILAC POINT

TORTIE SMOKE (LEFT) The ideal smoke should look like a self at rest, showing the undercoat when it moves. In rexed cats, a hint of the undercoat always shows.

BLUE-CREAM (RIGHT) Pest and her mother both wore this blue-cream coat with a little added white.

BREED ORIGINS

In 1987, a dilute tortie kitten with thick, curled hair unlike all her littermates appeared in a litter born at the home of Kitty Brown in Sheridan, Montana. Peggy Vorrhees of the Bozeman Humane Society took the young cat, named her Miss DePesto, and showed her to Jeri Newman, a breeder of Persians in Livingston, Montana, interested in genetics and unusual cats. Miss DePesto, or Pest, went home with Newman to become the mother of a new breed.

It seemed unlikely that Pest was the offspring of another pedigree rexed breed running around mating with local cats. Newman was taken by the thick coat and robust build of the cat, but felt that the head was not a good match. She described Pest as the 'world's worst Devon

BLACK SMOKE AND WHITE The Selkirk face is broad and full-cheeked, with a muzzle wider than it is long and convex in profile, and a rounded head.

The breed is accepted in all major North American registries, and is the most successful native rexed breed to date. Overseas, it is not recognized by FIFé, and European breeders show it in TICA. It is accepted by the GCCF and gaining in popularity. It is also a Championship breed in Australia.

SELKIRK LOOKS

In head and body, the Selkirk Rex is a cobby cat, similar to the British Shorthair. The build is sturdy, but the legs are longer than the British type.

The underlying coat quality is thick and soft, and feels plush to the touch. All three types of hair are present, showing a random arrangement of loose curls. The underside, flanks, and neck show the most curl, the back the least. There are both shorthaired and longhaired versions, the latter having an even more eye-catching, ringletted coat.

OWNING A SELKIRK REX

The soft Selkirk coat is much the better for being left in the care of its wearer, because too much grooming reduces the curls. This slightly unkempt appearance is part of the cat's appeal.

Their character is similar to that of their outcross breeds. Although they can be playful and inquisitive, these are easy-going cats, never in a hurry, and content to be near their owners.

with a Chartreux body'. Newman decided that a shorter, more rounded head, and slightly longer coat (to show off that curl) would be ideal, and so bred Pest to her own Persian (*see* pp 258–61).

The resultant litter contained three curly-coated and three straight-coated kittens, confirming the gene to be a dominant. One of these kittens was bred to Persians, Exotics (*see* pp 184–87), and British Shorthairs (*see* pp 188–93), all of which are still allowed as outcross breeds. He was also bred back to Pest. No serious problems connected with the gene came to light. The breedings also established that the gene was a simple dominant, eliminating the possibility that it was the same trait

as the American Wirehair (*see* pp 320–21). Newman named the breed after her father's family name and the Selkirk Mountains, and began to show the cats, finding instant popularity.

Early signs

Curly-coated Selkirk Rexes can be distinguished from their straight-coated littermates at birth by their curly whiskers. These are brittle, and the ends may break off as they grow. Sometimes, rexed coats change as kittens grow up, but this is not true of the Selkirk; if they are curly at birth, they will remain curly as an adult, although the adult coat may show less curl.

Sphynx

ORIGIN North America, Europe (1970s)
SYNONYM Canadian Hairless
WEIGHT 3.5–7 kg (8–15 lb)
BUILD
TEMPERAMENT
COAT CARE
COLOURS All colours in all shades and all patterns

Few breeds will divide those who see them into 'love them' and 'hate them' camps so starkly as the Sphynx. Although they are bred and shown in all major world registries, public opinion is more divided. To their fans, Sphynxes are amazing, even magical; to others they can seem unnatural, even monstrous.

LILAC SELF

BLACK & WHITE

BLUE TORTIE & WHITE

SEAL POINT

BLUE POINT

BREED ORIGINS

In 1966, a shorthaired domestic cat gave birth to a hairless kitten in Toronto, Canada. Aptly named Prune, he was mated to his mother and began the first hairless breeding programme.

CFA withdrew support for the breeding programme in 1971, believing the gene to carry lethal problems. It is hard to be certain whether the modern Sphynx is descended from Prune or from other hairless cats that appeared, apparently having the same mutation, and were taken into the

BLACK AND WHITE The Sphynx is medium sized and medium boned with a well-developed musculature. The torso and belly are rounded.

breeding programme. A breeding pair from Prune was sent to Dr Hugo Hernandez in the Netherlands, and in the late 1970s, he was sent two more females from a litter in Toronto. He bred the queens to a Devon Rex (*see* pp 318–319) to keep the line going.

From this foundation, the breed spread to France, the United Kingdom,

BLUE AND WHITE Although the head looks angular and Oriental, the build of the Sphynx is not delicate. If anything, it is sometimes reminiscent of a bulldog.

and back over the Atlantic to the United States. Here, two more hairless females were acquired by Oregon breeder Kim Mueske in 1981, bred to Devon Rexes, and included in the Sphynx programme.

TICA and FIFé recognized the Sphynx in the 1990s; in 1999 it was accepted in Australia. CFA only gave Championship status in 2002, and the GCCF began registering Sphynxes in 2006, but does not intend to register 'any other hair deficient breeds'.

OWNING A SPHYNX

The Sphynx is not truly hairless, but retains a covering of peach-like down,

LILAC AND WHITE Colours are shown in blueprint form on the skin. Exact colours can be hard to determine; FIFé, which has codes for colours, has adopted a new set for hairless cats.

sometimes a little more on the tail tip, bridge of nose, and ears. They are warm to the touch – they have been described as suede-covered hot water bottles.

Oils that would normally disperse along the hair shafts accumulate on the skin in hairless breeds, so regular bathing is a must. Injury is more likely with no cushioning coat, and for this reason, coupled with the sensitivity to cold in winter and potential for sunburn in summer, most feel these cats to be real indoor-only animals. The lack of insulation also means the Sphynx burns more calories than feeding guidelines predict for a cat of its size.

If it lives in a suitable environment, the Sphynx has a reputation as loving and playful, always ready to act the clown, and keen to curl up with its owner for warmth.

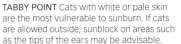

TABBY POINT Cats with white or pale skin are the most vulnerable to sunburn. If cats are allowed outside, sunblock on areas such as the tips of the ears may be advisable.

Peterbald

ORIGIN Russia (1990s)

SYNONYM None

WEIGHT 3.5–7 kg (8–15 lb)

BUILD

TEMPERAMENT

COAT CARE

COLOURS All colours in all shades and all patterns

The Peterbald has to overcome an impression that it is a mere spin-off from the Donskoy mutation; but remember, the pointed pattern was once singular enough for any pointed cat to be carelessly classed as 'Siamese'. This breed takes its name from St Petersburg, where it was first developed and gained popularity.

BLACK & WHITE   TORTIE   TORTIE & WHITE   SEAL POINT   BLUE POINT

BREED ORIGINS

The Peterbald breed has its origins in the same mutation as the Donskoy (*see* opposite). When Olga Mironova mated a Donskoy male named Afinogen Myth with an Oriental (*see* pp 224–29) female named Radma von Jagerhof in 1993, the results were different enough for a new strain to develop, and this was the start of the Peterbald.

FIFé and TICA have recognized the breed, although other registries remain cautious. The Peterbald is still outcrossed to Siamese (*see* pp 220–23) and Orientals, to increase the gene pool and develop the type.

VARIED COATS
The coat changes throughout the first few months of life. A kitten born with a short, wiry coat may be bald as an adult.

OWNING A PETERBALD

Like the Donskoy, it has a variable coat, ranging from truly bald, with a slightly rubbery, sticky feel to the skin, through a velvety fuzz, to a sparse, wiry, 'brush' coat with a definite curl. In type, it is not simply an Oriental with its clothes off. Although slender in build, with long legs, its body is not quite so svelte; it has a different head with a more blunted muzzle; and the extraordinary, large ears are set lower on the head.

The Peterbald personality, however, is all Oriental. These cats are lively, gregarious, attention-seeking, and very, very loud when they want to be.

IN DEVELOPMENT The Peterbald look is still being refined, but the head should be an Oriental-style wedge with the ears ideally broad and flaring out to continue the lines.

Donskoy

ORIGIN Russia (1980s)

SYNONYM Don Sphynx, Don Hairless

WEIGHT 3.5–7 kg (8–15 lb)

BUILD 🐈

TEMPERAMENT 🐈

COAT CARE 🖐

COLOURS All colours in all shades and all patterns

It is an old truism that you can wait an age for a bus, and then three come along at once. This is rather what has happened with hairless cat breeds: having regarded them as a rare and unfortunate oddity for a century, the cat fancy suddenly found there were three types petitioning for recognition.

BLACK SELF

LILAC SELF

TORTIE & WHITE

SEAL POINT

BLUE POINT

BREED ORIGINS

This breed was at first called the Don Sphynx, giving the false impression that it carries the same mutation as the Sphynx (*see* pp 326–27), with a Russian twist. In fact, the Donskoy story starts with a blue-cream female kitten rescued in the town of Rostov-na-Donu in Varya by Professor Elena Kovaleva in 1988. She passed on the dominant trait to her kittens. This showed it to be distinct from the recessive Sphynx mutation.

Breeder Irina Nemikina developed the Donskoy through outcrossing to European Shorthairs (*see* pp 194–95) and Siberians (*see* pp 274–75) to improve the gene pool. FIFé and TICA recognize the breed, but the GCCF does not want more hairless breeds.

OWNING A DONSKOY

This is a medium-sized cat of a moderate type. The hairlessness varies from a sparse, wiry fuzz to complete hairlessness. A safe, warm environment is vital, and like other hairless breeds this is best off as an indoor cat.

Donskoys are intelligent and friendly cats, happiest with owners who are at home and available for regular play and conversation throughout the day.

WORRY LINES Apart from the coat, the Donskoy's most striking feature is that its skin seems many sizes too large. The vertical lines on the forehead give the cat a misleadingly worried appearance.

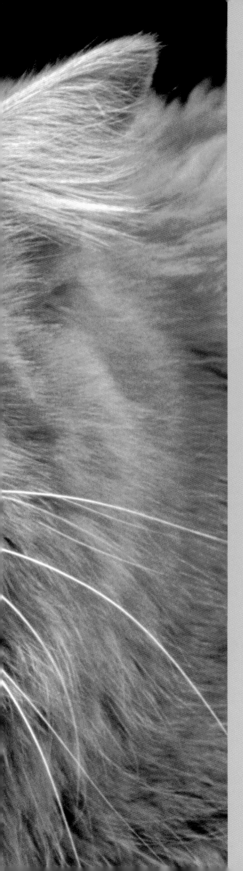

BREEDS WITH UNUSUAL FEATURES

All domestic cats with solid or pointed coats, blotched or ticked tabby patterns, or long hair are mutations. These we have grown used to; others are stranger, but not always novel. Charles Darwin recorded reports of a cat with drooping ears in China (*see* Scottish Fold, pp 346–49), cats with 'truncated tails about half the proper length' in southeast Asia (*see* Japanese Bobtail, pp 340–41), and six-toed cats (*see* Clippercat, p 358). He even said that he himself had seen 'a cat which always carried its tail flat on its back when pleased', a trait that may one day be recognized in a nascent breed called the Ringtail.

CYMRIC This is the longhaired version of the famously tailless Manx. Taillessness is a common trait, although the mutations that cause it take many different forms.

Manx

ORIGIN Isle of Man (before 1700s)

SYNONYM None

WEIGHT 3.5–5.5 kg (8–12 lb)

BUILD 🐈

TEMPERAMENT 🐈

COAT CARE 🪮

COLOURS All colours in self, tortie, bi-colour, solid, smoke, and tipped; blotched, striped, and spotted tabby patterns; pointed pattern in TICA only

If this famous symbol of the Isle of Man were to appear for the first time today, it would be unlikely to win such wide acceptance. This is a curious breed whose movements were described by one early breeder as 'a comical sight calculated to excite laughter in the most mournfully disposed person'.

BLACK SELF   BLUE SELF   BLUE & WHITE   BROWN CLASSIC TABBY   RED STRIPED TABBY   TORTIE

BLACK SELF This cat could not be shown in most associations, which demand a smooth rump, with no stub of bone large enough to feel. However, 'stumpies' with tails up to 3 cm (1¼ in) can win awards in FIFé.

BREED ORIGINS

The exact time and place of origin of the tailless or short-tailed Manx are unknown. This lack of certain knowledge has prompted plenty of speculation: some of it is plausible, some more far-fetched, and some flatly ridiculous (*see* p 335).

Because short-tailed cats are rare in Europe but relatively common in East Asia, it was often suggested in the past that tailless cats came west via very early Phoenician trade routes. Another suggestion is that tailless cats were shipwrecked on the Isle of Man. Writing about the island in 1845, Joseph Train recorded a

BROWN TABBY AND WHITE Although fairly popular in the United States, where it falls about halfway down the ranking by number, the Manx is increasingly rare in its homeland.

tradition that the first Manx 'was cast on shore from a foreign vessel that was wrecked on the rocks at Spanish Head, but at what period no one pretends to say'. Other sources state with apparently more certainty that

the cats came with the ships that gave these rocks their name, and were survivors of a ship of the Spanish Armada said to have foundered there in 1558, carrying ships' cats picked up on an earlier

not known whether this was the same mutation or a separate one. In fact, tailless mutations occur fairly regularly across the world, but almost always they simply die out.

BREED HISTORY

The first written record of the breed is from 1810, when English painter JMW Turner is claimed to have had seven; it is likely that they existed some time before this, because they are not mentioned as a novelty but a regional curiosity. Manx, which began to die out as the island's main spoken language in the early 18th century, contained no word for the cats; this could mean that they appeared no earlier than this.

BLUE-CREAM BI-COLOUR In Manx litters, the balance of female to male kittens is tilted slightly away from the feline average in favour of the females. It may be that the harmful effects of the mutation affect males more severely.

trip to the Far East. Eastern Europe and Russia also seem to be favoured as a possible source, with tales of a ship from the Baltic or populations of tailless cats in the Crimea. All these theories have at their heart a foreign, Oriental origin for the gene; the biggest stumbling block for this theory is that we know now that bobtailed Asian cats do not have the same mutation as the Manx.

The rarity or absence of the Manx mutation across the rest of Europe, and indeed the world, may mean that it is a local occurrence, and the breed is Manx through and through. Or it could be that the mutation arose elsewhere, but due to its health implications (*see* pp 334–35) survived only in the limited breeding population of an island. Similar tailless cats have been recorded occasionally in the rest of the United Kingdom: in the late 19th century, they were known in Cornwall and Dorset, and called Cornish cats as well as Manx cats, although it is

RED SPOTTED TABBY The ideal show 'rumpy' in most associations has a dimple where the tail would be, but a very small rise of bone is permitted as long as the cat still looks and feels tailless.

Manx cats were shown from the start of the United Kingdom cat fancy in the 19th century; at first there was some debate as to whether cats with short tails were 'true' Manx. Like other early breeds, they were exported and accepted by registries abroad quite early, with CFA accepting them in 1920. Pointed Manx have been developed, initially in Australia, but are accepted only in TICA; the longhaired Cymric (*see* pp 338–39) is more widely recognized.

THE MANX GENE

The Manx gene is an incomplete dominant, with varying effect. Cats may be longies (with a long, although not full-length tail), stumpies (with a short stub of a tail), and rumpies (with no tail).

The gene, sadly, is semi-lethal or sub-lethal. Homozygous kittens, with two copies of the gene, are stillborn, or die early in development and are reabsorbed. Surviving kittens are all heterozygous, with one Manx-mutation gene and one normal gene, so the Manx will always produce normal-tailed variants (called tailies). Stillborn kittens show serious neural and skeletal defects. Surviving cats occasionally have fused vertebrae and pelvic bones, which leaves them stiff and chronically constipated.

BROWN CLASSIC TABBY The Manx build is distinctive. The hind legs are longer than the front legs, and the body is short, meaning that the rump is carried high with the back gently curved.

RED CLASSIC TABBY The Manx is slow to mature, and can take four years to achieve its full potential. This young cat still has a relatively rangy build: the prized bulk comes with maturity.

Manx tales

Some of the legends about the Manx are based on the mistaken belief that an injury suffered by an animal in its lifetime can be passed to its offspring. A moment's thought tells us that we should have naturally tailless sheep and some pretty strange effects in the human population if this were true, but it was once widely believed. It led to some quaint myths, such as the tail of the Manx being trapped in the door of Noah's ark, or bitten off by a dog as it left the ark, whereupon it swam to the Isle of Man. Other stories have Vikings cutting off kittens' tails for helmet plumes, and mother cats biting off their kittens' tails.

But the most extraordinary claim of all is that the cats are 'cabbits' – the offspring of female cats and buck rabbits. This biological impossibility was firmly believed by many, including owners of the cats who saw rabbit-like traits in their behaviour, and must have looked plausible, given the breed's long hind legs, short body, and strange gait. What they never explained was just how the male rabbit would persuade the famously adept hunting Manx that it was a suitor and not dinner!

The spinal cord may be shorter than normal, leaving the cat with poor control of its bowel, bladder, and hind legs.

These problems are far from universal, but breeding to show standards did make them more prevalent. As long ago as the 1950s, it was noted that breeding two 'good' show rumpies led to more deformed and dead kittens than usual. With greater understanding of how the gene functions, responsible breeding choices have greatly reduced the casualties. Registries have become wiser: the GCCF removed references to a 'hoppity gait' from its standard, and FIFé also awards to stumpies, removing the emphasis on rumpies. This is not a problem that can be bred out of the Manx; it is an inherent part of it, and breeders must always breed wisely.

OWNING A MANX
It is vital to obtain kittens from a reputable and responsible breeder. They may make you wait until the kittens are older than in other breeds, to ensure they only sell healthy stock, because problems show up fairly early. Avoid breeders who deny any problems exist; only those who know the potential problems can avoid them.

In the home, these large cats can be surprisingly quiet. They are affectionate, and from as far back as 1902 have been described as dog-like, padding around after their owners discreetly and providing quiet companionship.

MANX (*see* pp 332–35) Genetically sound members of this tailless breed make healthy, hardy, and long-lived cats. They were traditionally prized as mousers and working cats on their native island, a heritage that has stayed with them.

Cymric

ORIGIN Canada and United States (1960s)
SYNONYM Longhaired Manx
WEIGHT 3.5–5.5 kg (8–12 lb)
BUILD
TEMPERAMENT
COAT CARE
COLOURS All colours in self, tortie, bi-colour, solid, smoke, and tipped; blotched, striped, and spotted tabby patterns; pointed pattern

The name of this breed comes from Cymru, the Welsh name for Wales. Welsh spelling and pronunciation are quirky: Cymru is pronounced (approximately) *Koomree*, with the first syllable stressed, and Cymric is pronounced *Koomrick*, although *Kimrick* is common. But there is actually nothing Welsh about this breed.

RED SELF

BLACK & WHITE

RED & WHITE

BROWN STRIPED TABBY

TORTIE

BLUE TORTIE & WHITE

BREED ORIGINS

Because this breed is simply a longhaired Manx (*see* pp 332–37), it largely shares the same origins. But with its long coat, it has the chance to pick up a little extra speculation. Where did the longhair trait come from? Some romantically believe that shaggy Norwegian Forest Cats (*see* pp 268–73), perhaps en route to Greenland or even the New World with early Viking expeditions, stopped off at the Isle of Man and engaged in a few onshore amusements, leaving longhaired progeny behind. However, the Isle of Man's ports were busy with international trading ships throughout the 18th and 19th centuries. The original mutant gene for taillessness may have arrived on one of these ships, and the longhair trait could just as easily have been brought in

COPPER-EYED WHITE The short body of the breed is in part another effect of the gene for taillessness. This can affect the vertebrae all the way up the spine, making them shorter than usual.

by ships' cats – more easily, perhaps, because it would be less remarkable, or hidden in a shorthaired cat. Some have also suggested an outcross to Persians (*see* pp 258–61) in the 1930s or 1940s, but this has always been denied.

The Cymric was first shown in North America in the 1960s. It made its first appearances under the name of Longhaired Manx, which was changed to Cymric in the 1970s. This name was chosen by Blair Wright and Leslie Falteisek, two

CREAM SELF The coat is moderately long over most of the body, and noticeably longer on the ruff, the abdomen, and the fluffy britches on the hind legs.

BROWN MACKEREL TABBY BI-COLOUR The CFA and TICA standards award only five points for colour and pattern, and the FIFé standard none. Head and body shape are more important.

In 1994, CFA dropped the name Cymric and revised the Manx standard to include both longhair and shorthair divisions, because shorthaired litters inevitably included longhaired kittens that could not be shown as Cymrics. Other associations use the two names but essentially treat the breeds as partners, with longhaired Manx automatically being classed as Cymric.

OWNING A CYMRIC
The first task if you want to own a Cymric is to find one. Cymrics are by no means common, although they are seen more frequently in North America than elsewhere. One reason why there is little pressure for the GCCF to recognize the Cymric is that the Manx languishes at the bottom of the popularity ratings in the United Kingdom, while the Manx in short and long coats combined sits about the middle of the CFA rankings.

Cymrics are essentially higher-maintenance Manx that need grooming two or three times a week. The same cautions about health apply, and they have the same peaceable nature.

Cymric breeders from Canada and the United States respectively, who were closely involved in the recognition of the breed. Blair Wright's grandmother said that she had seen longhaired, tailless cats in Wales, hence the Welsh name. The Cymric was recognized by the Canadian Cat Association in the 1970s. TICA and CFA both followed by the end of the 1980s, and FIFé finally accepted the breed in 2006. The GCCF does not recognize it, and is very unlikely to: its policies now rule against potentially harmful traits.

Japanese Bobtail

ORIGIN Japan (before 1800s)
SYNONYM None
WEIGHT 2.5–4 kg (6–9 lb)
BUILD 🐈
TEMPERAMENT 🐾
COAT CARE 🖌
COLOURS All colours in self, tortie and bi-colour; striped, blotched, and spotted tabby patterns

This short-tailed, endearing breed was something of a Japanese cultural ambassador to the United States after World War II. Although still far behind the Thai-derived breeds in popularity, Japan's traditional good-luck cat has a secure place in the hearts of the American and European cat fancy.

BLACK SELF

RED SELF

BLACK & WHITE

BROWN STRIPED TABBY

TORTIE & WHITE

BLUE TORTIE & WHITE

BREED ORIGINS

The early history of bobtailed cats is not known. There is a tradition that cats were brought to Japan in 999AD, but in fact they arrived centuries before this. In the classic *Tale of Genji*, thought to have been completed by 1021, a character obtains a Chinese cat, which is distinguished from the 'swarms' of Japanese cats and said to be more affectionate; bobbed tails are not mentioned.

Cats with shortened, kinked, and pompom tails are found throughout southeast Asia, but they are more numerous on the Japanese islands. This could be because a high proportion of the first cats to arrive were bobtailed, or because they were particularly favoured by the Japanese.

Cats were not pampered court pets in Japan – indeed for a time they were

RED TABBY AND WHITE
The first kittens imported to the United States included a red-and-white male. CFA still allows only traditional Western colours.

RED TABBY AND WHITE This breeding male has developed the typical stud jowls and a rather sturdy build; the breed standards are more favourable to female cats.

Tales of tails

The Japanese Bobtail has acquired a legend or two. The most popular is that once a cat warming itself by the fire crept too close and set its tail alight. In a panic, it raced from the house and through the streets, in the process setting fire to houses throughout the city. As a punishment, and so that such a thing could not happen again, the emperor decreed that all cats should have their tails cut short. On a happier note, the Bobtail is said to be the original Maneki Neko (see p 128).

These cats may have become popular in Japan because of another legend. It was believed that a cat could become a *bakeneko*, a monster with shapeshifting abilities and the power of speech, if it reached a certain age or size or if its tail became forked: a cat with a short tail might seem to carry less risk.

apparently an incomplete dominant. But they were not really prized until after World War II, when American service personnel brought cats home to the United States with them. Breeders Elizabeth Freret and Lynn Beck imported kittens and wrote a standard. This emphasized a more slender cat than the cobby types often seen in Japan, ensuring it was distinct from the chunky Manx, the only other tailless breed of the time. The Bobtail is now recognized by every major registry except the GCCF. The shorthair, sleek but not as flat-coated as some other Oriental breeds, was the first recognized, but carried the longhair gene within it. Only the shorthair is recognized by FIFé.

OWNING A BOBTAIL

Both the longhair and shorthair coats are silky and easy-care, unless the cat needs bathing, at which time they prove quite water-repellent. Japanese Bobtails are a healthy breed: the mutation that causes the shortened tail does not seem to have any other effects.

They are intelligent and lively cats with a reputation for enjoying carrying things in their mouths and playing fetch, like dogs, and being less averse to a dip than many breeds. Sociable and talkative, but with soft voices, they are recommended for multi-cat homes, especially if their owners are not going to be around much.

forbidden as pets, because all were needed to protect everything from scrolls and silk worms to rice stores from vermin. Bobtails are found in Japanese art from courtesans' portraits to scenes from rural life (*see* p 132). They appear not as a separate breed, but in mixed groups of cats, in all coats, although predominantly a van pattern of white with just a few areas of colour.

Bobtails were remarked on by curious Westerners for centuries, and suggested as a possible source of the Manx (*see* pp 332–37). This theory is now discounted, because this is a separate mutation, although also

TORTIE AND WHITE Called *mi-ke* in this breed, this is a prized combination, especially with the addition of odd-coloured eyes. The spots may be of mixed colours or separate.

Kurilean Bobtail

ORIGIN Kuril Islands (before 1700s)

SYNONYM Kurile Island Bobtail

WEIGHT 3–4.5 kg (7–12 lb)

BUILD

TEMPERAMENT

COAT CARE

COLOURS Western colours in self, tortie, bi-colour, smoke, shaded, and tipped; blotched, striped, and spotted tabby patterns

This breed is more likely to be spelled Kurilian in North America but, as the first major registry to recognize it, FIFé has settled on this spelling. It has also been called the Kuril Bobtail or Kurile Island Bobtail, and it first came to public attention with the upsurge in Russian cat-breeding late in the 20th century.

RED SELF

CREAM STRIPED TABBY

SILVER STRIPED TABBY

BLUE SILVER TABBY

TORTIE TABBY & WHITE

BROWN TABBY & WHITE

BREED ORIGINS

The Kurilean comes from the Kuril Islands, an archipelago connecting the northernmost point of Japan with the Kamchatka Peninsula. Ownership of the islands has been long disputed between Japan and Russia, making the nationality of this breed a political issue: currently, it is a Russian breed.

Cats with short tails were long known in this area, just as they are throughout the Far East. The bobtail mutation seems to be the same as in the Japanese Bobtail (*see pp 340–41*), and there was (and still is) some feeling that these are just stockier Japanese Bobtails. But proponents of the breed claim, with some justification, that theirs is the 'natural cat', only recently coming under the sway of human intervention, while the Japanese breed is more man-made. More contentious is the claim that the mutation spread from the north to the south, not vice versa.

Cats were brought back from the area in the second half of the 20th century. They were first shown in the 1990s, sparking interest in western Russia, and in European and American breeders who had already seen the Siberian (*see pp 274–75*). The first breeders were Lilia Ivanova and Tatiana Botcharova, who were in competition over the breed and its standard, but there are now many breeders in Russia, with a scattering in Europe and a toehold in North America. FIFé recognized the breed in 2003, and TICA has begun to register Kurilean Bobtail cats.

OWNING A KURILEAN

The breed comes in short and long coats, both of which are dense and weatherproof. Having largely lived off its wits in the sparsely populated islands, it is renowned as a hunter of quite large prey when free-ranging, and an excellent domestic mouser. Russian legend has it that Kurileans needed curled tails to hold on to riverside vegetation while they were fishing, and they are less averse to water than many cats. They are intelligent and calm, but cats of dignity, not given to instant and insistent affection.

SILVER TABBY Kurilean Bobtails are large, sturdy, well-muscled cats with a wild appearance. It is said that they differ in type from island to island throughout the archipelago.

American Bobtail

ORIGIN United States (1960s)

SYNONYM None

WEIGHT 3–7 kg (7–15 lb)

BUILD

TEMPERAMENT

COAT CARE

COLOURS All colours in all shades and all patterns

Emphatically 'born in the USA', this is a medium to large, athletic cat with a short or bobbed tail, a rolling gait, deep-set eyes, and tufted ears all combining to give a strong, wild appearance. It is not the look that was originally envisaged for the breed, but it has proved successful and very much typical of the times.

BLUE & WHITE | BROWN STRIPED TABBY | SILVER TABBY | BLUE TABBY & WHITE | LILAC POINT | BLUE TABBY POINT

BREED ORIGINS

The American Bobtail breed began with Yodi, a short-tailed, brown tabby male adopted in the 1960s by John and Brenda Saunders from Iowa. He mated with their seal-pointed cat, and there was an attempt to produce a short-tailed breed of the Snowshoe type (*see* pp 204–205) from the resulting litter. The lines became inbred, however, and largely died out. Work by Reaha Evans and Lisa Black in the 1980s and 1990s saw the breed accepted with a look based on Yodi's original appearance; it has Championship status in TICA and CFA.

There is some rivalry between this breed and the Pixiebob (*see* pp 344–45). The American Bobtail has

emphasized a wild look since before the Pixiebob appeared, but never claimed wild ancestry. It has not yet been established whether or not the dominant mutation is the same as the Manx (*see* pp 332–37); it produces similar tails, but it could be a similar, new mutation. The tail appears to be a genetic 'hotspot' in the cat, prone to such variation. No other bobtailed cats are allowed as crosses.

AMERICAN BOBTAIL HEAD The head is a strong, broad, modified wedge in shape. The eyes are typically a little rounder than almond-shaped, and rather deep set below a fleshy brow.

AMERICAN BOBTAIL LONGHAIR Unusually, this breed was recognized as a longhair first, but now comes in both coats; both are fairly easy-care, although the britches need regular attention.

OWNING AN AMERICAN BOBTAIL

This seems to be a healthy breed, without the problems of the Manx. They are reputed to be laid-back companions for children, and are good travellers, even making cabin companions for long-distance haulage drivers. They are not the most vocal cats, more inclined to trill and chirp than mew.

Pixiebob

ORIGIN United States (1980s)
SYNONYM None
WEIGHT 4–8 kg (9–18 lb)
BUILD 🐈
TEMPERAMENT 🐈
COAT CARE 🖌 🖌🖌
COLOURS Brown spotted tabby only

These brown spotted tabby cats are bred to emulate the looks of the bobcat (*see* pp 18–19), with a powerful build, shortened tail, heavily ticked coat, and a 'pouch' of loose skin on the belly. They are also the only breed accepted as a polydactyl, with more toes than normal, up to a maximum of seven on each paw.

BREED ORIGINS

The Pixiebob was first thought to be descended from the offspring of matings between barn cats and the wild bobcat, but it is accepted by TICA as 'a domestic cat with a visual similarity to the North American Bobcat' and no hybridizing is allowed.

Carol Ann Brewer of Washington state acquired and bred two such 'Legend cats' (now a trademarked term) in the mid-1980s. The result was Pixie, founding mother of the breed and origin of both its look and name. TICA accepted the breed with Experimental status in 1994, and it reached Championship status in a record-breaking four years. Unlike the American Bobtail (*see* p 343), Pixiebobs have not yet been accepted by CFA, and neither breed is well known beyond its homeland.

OWNING A PIXIEBOB

These cats are enthusiastically endorsed by their breeders as 'intelligent beyond belief', highly trainable, dog-like, and all-round ideal cats. More broadly, Pixiebobs are generally considered lively, clever, sociable cats with quiet, chirping voices. They come in two coat lengths, both easy-care.

Bobcat hybrids?

Historical references cited in support of the hybrid theory include a domestic-type cat given to Columbus on landing, descended from cats left by Viking expeditions. Since the Vikings landed in Newfoundland and Columbus in Venezuela (beyond the bobcat's range), this seems implausible. Comparisons are also drawn with matings of domestic cats and Scottish wildcats (*see* p 26). These occur where wildcats are scarce, and the progeny are intractable, and more a threat to the identity of the wildcat than potential pets. In the end, the lack of any wild genetic material has clinched the argument in the minds of most people, but the legendary origin is still held dear by many breeders.

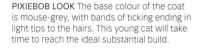

PIXIEBOB LOOK The base colour of the coat is mouse-grey, with bands of ticking ending in light tips to the hairs. This young cat will take time to reach the ideal substantial build.

PIXIEBOB FACE The head is the core of the Pixiebob breed 'look'. It is an inverted pear shape, with hooded, deep-set eyes and tufted tips to the ears.

Scottish Fold

ORIGIN Scotland (1960s)
SYNONYM None
WEIGHT 2.6–6 kg (6–13 lb)
BUILD
TEMPERAMENT
COAT CARE

COLOURS Western colours in self, tortie, bi-colour, smoke, shaded, and tipped; all tabby patterns; pointed pattern in TICA

Originally called 'lops' because their ears resembled those of lop-eared rabbits, these cats have also been likened to owls or teddy bears. They are certainly unmistakable. Although Scottish in origin, they are now an American breed: European registries are reluctant to recognize breeds with such abnormalities.

BLUE SELF   RED SELF   BROWN CLASSIC TABBY   SILVER STRIPED TABBY   TORTIE   BLUE TORTIE & WHITE

BREED ORIGINS

This is not the first known cat with folded ears: similar cats were recorded in China two centuries ago, and in the United Kingdom in the early 20th century. But today's Scottish Folds trace their parentage back to Susie, a barn cat from Tayside in Scotland. Mary and William Ross were given one of her kittens in 1963, a female they named Snooks. Her first kitten was a male, Snowball, who was bred to a white British Shorthair (*see* pp 188–93), Lady May. The resulting litter contained five folded-ear kittens, and was the start of the Scottish Fold breed.

The GCCF initially accepted the breed in 1966, but then suspended registration by 1971 due to concerns that the folded ears could give rise

BLACK AND WHITE The standards award most points to the head and the body conformation, with far fewer for the colour and pattern.

to ear-mite infestation or hearing problems. The breeding programme crossed the Atlantic, imported into the United States by geneticist Neil Todd, who was studying mutations. When the study ended, the cats were dispersed to pet homes, but one went to Manx (*see* pp 332–37) breeder Salle Wolf Peters. Soon other breeders were involved, and in 1974, the breed began to work for CFA recognition, which they achieved by 1978. The breed is also recognized by TICA, but not by FIFé or the GCCF.

BLUE-CREAM AND WHITE The earliest Scottish Folds included longhairs. However, the breeders pressed for recognition of shorthairs first, and longhairs had to wait far longer for their turn.

BLACK SMOKE AND WHITE The small ears have rounded tips and are laid against the head 'in a cap-like fashion'. The smaller and more tightly folded the ear is, the better it is for showing.

BLUE-CREAM Susie, the original Fold, had ears that simply bent forwards, and resembled an owl. Today's Folds aim for a tight 'triple fold' that lays the ear flat against the head.

FOLD PROBLEMS

From the start, many Folds had shortened, stiffened tails, and in the 1970s, x-rays of cats showed skeletal problems. The Fold gene affects cartilage beyond the ears, and recent research indicates that all cats with the gene suffer from progressive arthritis of varying degrees of severity. Homozygous cats, with two copies, invariably suffer painful and disabling abnormalities early in life, but in heterozygous cats, with one copy of the gene, the problems do not occur until much later, and some may escape symptoms entirely. For this reason, cats with folded ears are never bred together but always to straight-eared cats, and outcrossing to the British Shorthair and American Shorthair (see pp 200–203) continues.

OWNING A FOLD

It is vital to buy a Fold only from a reputable breeder following a careful and responsible breeding programme. The length and the flexibility of the tail are important as an early indicator of problems, but problems with joints are always a risk as the cat matures and ages. In character, this is a gentle, calm cat, very like its two outcross breeds.

SCOTTISH FOLD (*see* pp 346–47) Only half of all kittens will have folded ears, and a breeder has to wait at least three weeks for the fold to show. Some ears fold, then straighten, and these cats cannot be shown or bred from.

American Curl

ORIGIN United States (1980s)

SYNONYM None

WEIGHT 3–5 kg (7–11 lb)

BUILD 🐈

TEMPERAMENT 🐈

COAT CARE 🖌

COLOURS All colours in all shades and all patterns

The cat fancy is often fanciful, but something about the sweet, slightly quizzical look of the Curl spurs breeders to new heights. The founders are happy to embrace the tag of 'designer' cats for their breed, describing them as 'signed masterpieces of a humor-loving Creator'. It seems every aspect of the Curl provokes a smile.

BLACK SELF   BLUE SILVER TABBY   TORTIE   RED STRIPED TABBY & WHITE   BROWN TABBY & WHITE   LILAC TABBY POINT

BREED ORIGINS

In the summer of 1981, two stray kittens aged about six months old were taken in by Grace and Joe Ruga in Lakewood, California. Both kittens were longhaired, one black and one black and white, and both had strangely curled ears. The bi-colour kitten, named Panda, went its own way a few weeks later, but the black one, named Shulamith, stayed with the couple. She became the foundation female of the American Curl breed when she produced her own first litter of curl-eared kittens later that year.

Curls were shown for the first time in 1983, and two noted geneticists, Solveig Pflueger and Roy Robinson, were contacted to study the unusual mutation, which was established to be a simple dominant. The breed had Championship status in TICA by 1987 and CFA by 1993. Its curled ears have been 'exported' into Munchkin-derived breeds (*see* pp 354–57) and the Highlander, a lynx-

RED TABBY AND WHITE Ears can curl a little or a lot. The ears of show-quality cats must curl through a full crescent, with the tips pointing down at the skull.

like breed moving towards acceptance in TICA. It is not recognized by FIFé or the GCCF, whose registration policies exclude any new breeds with skeletal or cartilage abnormalities.

CURL EARS

The ears are straight when the kitten is born, but usually within a week they have begun to curl. First they curl tightly, then they uncurl gradually, and by four months the curl has reached its final state. The cartilage in the ears feels firm to the touch, like that in human ears, except at the very tips. Curiously, the curl of the parents' ears is no guide to how curled any kitten's ears will be, making each litter something of a lottery.

Curl-to-Curl breedings began in 1984, and there are now many homozygous Curls, who carry two copies of the gene and therefore never produce straight-eared kittens. These cats seem to suffer no health problems, leading observers to a fairly secure conclusion that this

BLUE-CREAM LONGHAIR With both longhair and shorthair Curls present from the start, this was the first breed to be fully recognized by CFA as one breed with two coat lengths.

is a benign mutation without any harmful side effects.

The Curl breed standard is based on the look of Shulamith, and the only outcrossing allowed is to non-pedigree domestic cats that closely match the breed standard. The type of the American Curl, especially the ears, varies from place to place, partly due to being kept open for outcrossing for so long. This policy has ensured a large gene pool and optimum health, but the closing of the outcross stage should bring more stability in the look.

Since the American Curl was recognized, there

BLACK SELF Shulamith was named after the princess in the *Song of Songs* in the Old Testament, but many Curl names – Curlton Heston, Pepsi Curla – owe less to poetry and more to puns.

have been several reports of cats with similar ears from across North America as well as in Australia, but whether these are related or an entirely independent mutation is not known. It may be that, like the feline tail, the ears are prone to such mutations and they have simply gone unremarked until now.

OWNING A CURL

This is certainly a breed for those who want something different and remarkable in their homes. Aside from their pixie-like ears, Curls are quite normal cats, healthy and robust, with no breed-specific problems. Both the shorthair and the semi-longhair coats are silky and sleek, requiring little or no attention day to day. In character, these are lively, busy cats, fond of play throughout their lives. Breeders say they are always ready to help you with whatever you are doing, whether you want them to or not.

AMERICAN CURL (*see* pp 350–51) Although it looks like a wildcat cub, this kitten does not have rounded ears. The distinguishing feature of this breed is that the tips of the ears are curled back, giving them a rounded outline face-on.

Munchkin

ORIGIN United States (1980s)

SYNONYM None

WEIGHT 2.5–4 kg (5–9 lb)

BUILD

TEMPERAMENT

COAT CARE

COLOURS All colours in all shades and all patterns

This breed has the legs that launched a thousand flame wars in breeder forums. Although some objections have been born of genuine concern for its welfare, others have been sheer gut reaction to its physique. Whichever side you take on this divisive issue, short-legged cats seem to be here to stay.

BLACK SELF	RED & WHITE	BROWN STRIPED TABBY	TORTIE TABBY & WHITE	BLUE TABBY & WHITE	SEAL POINT

BREED ORIGINS

Dwarfed cats were reported in the United Kingdom in the 1930s and 1940s, Russia in the 1950s, and New England in the 1970s. In 1983, Sandra Hochenedel adopted a short-legged, pregnant black cat she found living under a trailer in Louisiana, and named her Blackberry. Half the kittens were short-legged, and one of them, a male named Toulouse, was given to Kay LaFrance, who established a free-breeding colony of Munchkins, named after the race from *The Wizard of Oz*, on her plantation.

As awareness of the Munchkin grew, many other cats with this dominant mutation were found, and some were registered and added to the breeding stock. TICA gave the Munchkin Championship status in 2002, not without internal strife. It has been recognized in Australia, but CFA does not recognize it and both the GCCF and FIFé have stated their policies would not allow a new breed based on such a trait. In recent years there have been several proposed 'spin-off' breeds from the Munchkin, generally with cute names, such as hairless Minskins, curl-eared Kinkalows, and rexed Skookums. The last has been recognized in Australia and as an Experimental breed by TICA in 2006.

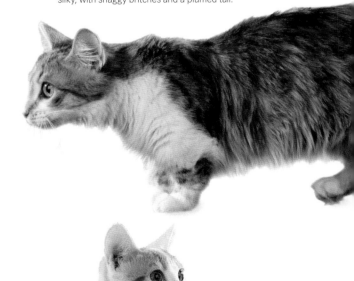

TORTOISESHELL AND WHITE The Munchkin is recognized in both shorthair and longhair versions. The long coat should be flowing and silky, with shaggy britches and a plumed tail.

CREAM AND WHITE There are no points at all for coat pattern or colour in the Munchkin breed standard. The body and head are both moderate in form.

THE MUNCHKIN CONTROVERSY

From the start, Munchkins aroused strong feelings. To their fans, they are as valid as breeds with curly hair, no hair, short tails, no tails, folded ears, or curled ears. To others, their reduced stature is a quirk too far. Where free-ranging pet cats are usual, they look cruelly vulnerable, although short-legged feral families have been recorded surviving for several generations.

There has been concern about health issues, although spinal problems caused by too much flexing of a long spine carried on short legs have not materialized. Some suffer a skeletal abnormality called thoracic lordosis, but this is also found in long-legged breeds. There are possible problems inherent in the mutation: when two short-legged cats are bred together, litters are often small, so the gene may be lethal when two copies are carried. However, it does not seem to cause other problems, unlike the skeletal abnormalities of the Manx (*see* pp 332–37) or Scottish Fold (*see* pp 346–49).

OWNING A MUNCHKIN

North America and Australia have most of the Munchkins and derivative breeds; elsewhere, they are likely to be hard to find. They can and do run, climb, and even jump, although onto chairs rather than wardrobes. An indoor life may be safest, but these cats still have a full-size need for activity and entertainment.

LILAC SELF The dwarfism in the Munchkin can cause the legs to be not only short but also slightly bowed.

MUNCHKIN (*see* pp 354–55) This quaintly named breed is the first dwarfed cat to have been recognized. It should never look like a dwarf version of another breed, but some breeders are setting out to create just that.

Clippercat

ORIGIN New Zealand (2000s)

SYNONYM Initially called New Zealand Shorthair

WEIGHT 3.5–7 kg (8–15 lb)

BUILD 🐈

TEMPERAMENT 🐱

COAT CARE ✏

COLOURS Western colours in self, tortie, bi-colour, smoke, shaded, and tipped; all tabby patterns

Clippercats are a new departure: a breed based on the trait of polydactyly, or extra toes. Rather than the five in front, four at the back standard of most cats, they can have up to seven toes on each paw. Other such breeds have been developed, but this is the first to be recognized by a mainstream registry.

BLACK SELF

RED & WHITE

BROWN CLASSIC TABBY

CREAM STRIPED TABBY

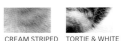
TORTIE & WHITE

TORTIE TABBY

BREED ORIGINS

Polydactyl cats are uncommon, but not very rare. They were well known in the west of England, and travelled from the United Kingdom as ships' cats. Concentrations of polydactyl cats in the United States are well known (*see* opposite), but European ships sailed to other places too.

During the 19th century, huge numbers of people arrived in Australia and New Zealand, bringing cats with them, and concentrations of polydactyls are found in the places where the ships docked.

An innovative registry in New Zealand, Catz Inc., has recognized the Clippercat as a polydactyl version of the Antipodean (*see* p 207), naming it after the clipper ships on which the cats arrived. Currently, domestic cats of the right type are still being registered, helping to ensure a wide gene pool for the breed.

BLACK SELF Historically, there was a belief among sailors that polydactyl cats would bring luck to a voyage. They were also considered to be excellent mousers.

BROWN TABBY The registration policy forbids breeding two Clippercats together, ensuring that all Clippercats registered are heterozygous, in case of unforeseen gene problems.

OWNING A CLIPPERCAT

Moderately polydactyl cats should not require any particular special care; those extra toes have been around for a long time without causing problems. In all other respects, this cat is like the Antipodean.

Other polydactyls

ORIGIN Various mutations; most development from American domestic cats

NAMES Possible breeds include Maine Poly, American Polydactyl, Polybob

BUILD Occurs in cats of all types; has no effect on type

COAT CARE 🪶 🪶🪶 🪶🪶🪶 (Extra toes may need some attention depending on number)

'Digitally enhanced' cats have been known for centuries. Naturalist Charles Darwin noted reports of 'several families of six-toed cats, in one of which the peculiarity had been transmitted for at least three generations'. At first, these toes were ignored, and most breed standards outlaw them, for fear the trait could be harmful. But recently, some have started to base breeds on polydactyly.

BREED ORIGINS

Polydactyls were popular as ships' cats, and are often found in Nova Scotia and American ports, including Boston, Halifax, and Yarmouth. The trait was common in early Maine Coons, although disallowed today. Breeders who see it as an American characteristic are seeking to create new breeds such as the American Polydactyl. Although the trait seems to have no serious side effects, there

is a tendency to seek novelty and mix it up with other mutations, as in the tailless, fold-eared, poly 'Puppykats' being bred in California. One breeder briefly touted 'Twisty Kats' with radial hypoplasia, a different, rare deformity that affects the leg bones. Although this is distinct from the usual polydactyly, it is the kind of association that makes many wary of poly breeds, especially as the same breeder continued to sell poly cats.

THUMB KITTEN Because the trait is so well known in American ports, it has been claimed to be an American trait. In fact, poly cats of all kinds have been recorded around the world.

Hemingway cats

Author Ernest Hemingway kept many polydactyl cats around his home in Key West, Florida, having supposedly been given the first cat by a drinking partner who was a sailor. About 60 cats are still maintained by the trust looking after the house today, and have been the cause of some dispute with government authorities. This colony has led to such cats sometimes being referred to as 'Hemingway cats', and that name was briefly used for a breeding programme; another American breed name used is Bigfoot. Other names include Boston thumb cats, mitten cats, and boxing cats.

HYBRID BREEDS

Once, it was believed that the domestic cat hybridized with local wild felines across the globe, accounting for regional variations of type. For a time, some also believed that it was a hybrid descendant of the African wildcat (*see* p 27) and the jungle cat (*see* p 27). Today, we know from genetic analysis that neither is true. At the same time, however, breeders are supplying what nature did not, and creating experimental hybrids such as those profiled here. Others include the part-serval Savannah under development in TICA and the similar Ashera, launched by a Californian company in 2007 – to much derision from the cat fancy – with a price tag of $22,000.

BENGAL The first and most widely accepted of the hybrid cats, this was originally created not for pet fashions or show glory, but to investigate immunity – a strange beginning for possibly the largest growth sector in cat breeding today.

Bengal

ORIGIN United States (1980s)
SYNONYM Once called Leopardettes
WEIGHT 5.5–10 kg (12–22 lb)
BUILD 🐈
TEMPERAMENT 🐆
COAT CARE 🪮
COLOURS Brown blotched and spotted tabby, or with pointed pattern over tabby

The standard-bearer for all the hybrid breeds, the Bengal has taken a long time to gain acceptance in mainstream registries and still causes some controversy. Whatever its critics say, this is a tremendously popular breed: since recognition in the United Kingdom, for example, it has soared to third place in terms of numbers, overtaking several old favourites on the way.

SNOW BENGAL Sepia, mink, and pointed patterns all appear. Snows should have an ivory to cream base coat and a 'pearl dusting'.

BREED ORIGINS

In the 1960s, there was an accidental mating between an Asian leopard cat (*see* p 25) and a black, shorthaired domestic cat at the home of breeder Jean Sugden in California. At that time, she made no further attempt to develop the hybrid offspring, but in the early 1970s, now remarried and

called Jean Mill, she received several more such hybrids from Dr Willard Centerwall at the University of California. These had been bred as part of a research project aimed at determining whether the leopard cat's immunity to feline leukaemia could be transferred to the domestic cat; as it turned out, it could not. This time, the hybrids were used to form the basis of an entirely new breed, the first intentional hybrid of a wild and a domestic cat to seek recognition. The name was taken from the scientific name for the leopard cat, *Prionailurus bengalensis*.

The early breeding programme involved ordinary domestic cats, but to develop the spotted coat, breeders soon turned to using street cats from India, chosen for their coat patterns, and Egyptian Maus (*see* pp 248–49). The breeders' aim was to replicate the look of the wild ancestry, while breeding towards a tractable domestic pet.

BREED RECOGNITION

The developing Bengal breed was presented to CFA in the 1970s, seeking recognition, but things did not go well. The cats presented were foundation cats, within three generations of original crosses to the wild cat, and not really domestic. CFA still does not recognize the Bengal. TICA began registering more

BROWN SPOTTED This was the first Bengal pattern and the first to be recognized by most associations. The spots may vary in size and shape, but large markings are preferred.

developed cats in 1983, and finally granted them Championship status in 1991. The GCCF and FIFé followed suit in Europe, together with registries in Australia and New Zealand, throughout the 1990s.

As a rule, recognition has come with the stipulation that crossing back to the wild species had to stop, and only cats from the fourth generation down from an original cross are allowed in studbooks. If

a breed is established enough to be recognized, they reason, it is established enough to need no further wild outcrossing.

However, not all breeders have been happy to pay this price for official recognition. There are still breeders who are working outside the mainstream associations and crossing to the leopard cat. They feel the coat is improved by these crosses, becoming closer to that of the wild species, with more horizontal flow to the spots or marbling.

BROWN SPOTTED The coat should have a highly rufoused ground colour of yellow, buff, golden, or orange, bearing well-contrasting markings with a crisp outline.

SEAL SEPIA SPOTTED The Bengal coat often has a glitter effect. It is caused by transparent areas at the hair tip (called mica) or along the shaft (called satin).

BENGAL LOOKS

Domestic Bengals are not as large as foundation hybrids, but still relatively large, and substantial in appearance. Originally there was just a spotted coat, but over time new variations have appeared and the status of these varies from one association to another. There are the 'snow' colours, the result of the recessive pointed gene carried in one of the domestic parents of the breed. Marbled cats, with a modified blotched tabby pattern, have also emerged, and been accepted.

More recently (and controversially) silver Bengals with a white undercoat have appeared. These are so far accepted in only a few associations; in others, breeders are worried that silvering genes may weaken the effect of the strong tabby markings.

OWNING A BENGAL

Firstly, it is important to know exactly what is meant by a Bengal. The breed name should really only be applied to what are known as F4 hybrids: that is, cats four generations down from the wild cross. Animals of earlier generations, known as foundation cats, are more like wild animals; the closer they are to the cross, the wilder they are. This means that they often need special housing, are frequently too nervous

Ethics of hybridizing

The Bengal and other hybrid breeds can be a divisive issue. Those who see the successful results are only too happy with them, but animal sanctuaries and welfare officers can see a less successful side: aiming for a domestic cat in a wild coat inevitably creates some wild cats in a domestic coat. This means there are real ethical issues raised by continually breeding back to the wild species.

Another worry is that a wild-looking cat might be a target for the fur trade. A prominent commercial fur is Lipi (also spelled Lippi), a name used only in the fur trade for a Chinese sub-species of the leopard cat, and domestic cat skins do find their way into the fashion fur market. Breeders might hope that a beautiful cat convinces people the best place for fur is on an animal, but it has not worked yet.

to integrate into a family home, and may spray abundantly (even when neutered) because they feel insecure in the restricted domestic territory. These foundation cats are not pets in the usual sense of the word, and owning them may bring legal complications. A mainstream pedigree probably carries more worth, meaning, and peace of mind in hybrids than in any other breed.

Feeding a Bengal may be a little tricky. Anecdotally, they seem to have a greater incidence than other breeds of irritable bowel syndrome (IBS), possibly because of their recent wild heritage. The cereal content in commercial cat foods (*see* pp 88–89) seems a particular irritant, and finding an appropriate food may take time if this proves a problem for your cat. Another cause of bowel problems can be microscopic parasites (*see* pp 110–11); again, anecdotal reports seem to imply the Bengal is particularly vulnerable to these, and owners in areas without chlorinated water supplies may want to take the precaution of only giving water that has been boiled.

In character, this is one breed that is not commonly described as devoted, trainable, and cute. Its breeders are adamant that Bengals are people-oriented, enjoying human company and mixing well with other pets and children, and performance on the showbench over recent years backs this up. They do stress, however, that they can also be mischievous, boisterous, and very active; this is a busybody, and not a pet-it-and-forget-it sort of cat.

BROWN MARBLED This pattern should ideally have a horizontal, rather than circular, flow, and the markings should show a darker outline and lighter middle.

BENGAL KITTENS Coats are clearly spotted at birth, but when they develop guard hairs around the age of four weeks, they take on a blurred appearance, which starts to clear again at about ten weeks of age.

BENGAL (*see* pp 362–65) Breed standards for this cat vary but all emphasize a wild look, particularly for the head. Small, rounded ears, a wide nose with 'puffed' leather, and a strong muzzle all contribute to a strong, wild face.

Toyger

ORIGIN United States (1990s)
SYNONYM California Toyger
WEIGHT 5.5–10 kg (12–22 lb)
BUILD 🐈
TEMPERAMENT 🐆
COAT CARE 🖌
COLOURS Brown striped tabby

The domestic cat has often been referred to as the tiger on the hearth, but only recently did this comparison become almost literal. The Toyger is unashamedly a designer breed, created like the Bombay (*see* pp 234–35) to emulate a big cat. With computer-generated images used to define the desired look, this is also truly a breed of the times.

TOYGER MARKINGS The coat is a modified striped tabby, and should be heavily rufoused. Flame-like, 'braided' markings on the body are ideal, as are circular markings on the face.

BREED ORIGINS

In the late 1980s, Judy Sugden, daughter of Bengal (*see* pp 362–67) breeder Jean Mill, noticed two small spots of tabby markings on the temple of one of her cats, an area usually free of darker colour. Judy saw the possibility of breeding a cat with facial markings resembling those of a tiger (*see* pp 14–15), with lines running across the face rather than back over the head. She had already urged that the Bengal should aim for a type like a leopard in miniature: now she and a few like-minded breeders turned their attention to creating a tiger in miniature.

TICA began to register the cats, under the name of California Toyger, in 1993, and accepted them for showing from 2000. In the summer of 2007, the breed finally achieved Championship status. It has also been recognized by the Waratah National Cat Alliance in Australia.

OWNING A TOYGER

Although new, this breed is on the up worldwide, with breeders in several countries including the United Kingdom already. For those who do acquire one, it is essentially a descendant of the Bengal, although more domestic bloodlines have been introduced in pursuit of the elusive markings: be prepared for an active, interested breed.

The tiger look

The aim with the Toyger is to create a tiger in miniature in every part, and this is still a work in progress. Work continues on making the ears smaller and more rounded, without the 'lynx tip' tufts so prized in other breeds, and the nose broader, especially towards the tip. The long, muscular body is carried relatively low to the ground on robust legs.

Chausie

ORIGIN United States (1990s)

SYNONYM Earlier hybrids called Stone Cougars and Nile Cats

WEIGHT 6–11.5 kg (13–25 lb)

BUILD 🐈

TEMPERAMENT 🐆

COAT CARE 🖌

COLOURS Black self, brown ticked tabby, silver tip only

Occasional natural hybrids of the jungle cat (*see* p 27) and the domestic cat have been reported for a long time: some claim that they have survived in the United Kingdom since 18th-century sailors brought wild cats home. Others were created in the 1960s and 1970s, when owning wild animals became legally restricted.

BLACK SELF

BROWN TICKED TABBY

BREED ORIGINS

Although recent DNA research indicates the jungle cat was not part of the domestic cat's origins, it is close to the wildcat, and female hybrid offspring are fertile. In the 1990s, breeders began working with deliberately created hybrids to make a new breed. Some of the early hybrids were originally known as Nile Cats, but the name Chausie won out.

The first generation of hybrids are large and vigorous, but if bred back to domestic cats a tractable, domestic type of cat eventually emerges. Thus far, the only major registry to recognize the Chausie is TICA, which began registering these cats in 1995. Whether other registries will follow suit is doubtful: the GCCF has said it wants no more hybrids.

OWNING A CHAUSIE

As with other hybrid breeds, this may be problematic. Breeders will admit that certainly earlier generations may not be reliably housetrained. This is an assertive, physically active breed that needs a lot of time and energy, not a novelty to be bought for its looks.

SPOTTED TABBY Spotted Chausies cannot be shown. Some may have been registered as 'Legend Cats' in the Pixiebob breed when this was permitted.

TICKED TABBY With its ticked and occasionally silver-tipped coat, the Chausie may be outcrossed to only one breed, the Abyssinian, and non-pedigree shorthairs.

USEFUL BOOKS AND REFERENCES

USEFUL BOOKS AND PAPERS

Bernstein, P, and M Strack. *A game of cat and house: Spatial patterns and behavior of 14 domestic cats (Felis catus) in the home.* Anthrozoös, 1996.

Biró, Zs, et al. *Feeding habits of feral domestic cats (Felis catus), wild cats (Felis silvestris) and their hybrids.* Cambridge University Press, November 2004.

Bradshaw, John. *The True Nature of the Cat.* Boxtree, 1993.

Dosa, David M. *A Day in the Life of Oscar the Cat.* The New England Journal of Medicine, July 2007.

Driscoll, Carlos A, et al. *The Near Eastern Origins of Cat Domestication.* Science, June 2007.

Engels, Donald. *Classical cats.* Routledge, 1999.

Fogle, Bruce. *The New Encyclopedia of the Cat.* Dorling Kindersley, 2001.

Fogle, Bruce. *Cats (Eyewitness Companion).* Dorling Kindersley, 2006.

Johnson, Warren E, et al. *The Late Miocene Radiation of Modern Felidae: A Genetic Assessment.* Science, January 2006.

Li, Xia, et al. *Pseudogenization of a Sweet-Receptor Gene Accounts for Cats' Indifference toward Sugar.* PLoS Genetics, July 2005.

MacLeod, Ross, et al. *Mass-dependent predation risk as a mechanism for house sparrow declines?* Biology Letters, March 2006.

Malek, Jaromir. *The Cat in Ancient Egypt.* The British Museum Press, revised edition, 2006.

Miller, Paul E. *Vision in Animals – What do Dogs and Cats See?* Waltham/OSU Symposium: Small Animal Opthalmology, 2001.

Morris, James G. *Ineffective Vitamin D Synthesis in Cats.* The Journal of Nutrition, 1999.

Randi, Ettore, et al. *Genetic Identification of Wild and Domestic Cats (Felis silvestris) and Their Hybrids Using Bayesian Clustering Methods.* Molecular Biology and Evolution, vol. 18 no. 9, 2001.

Turner, DC, and P Bateson, eds. *The Domestic Cat: The Biology of its Behaviour.* Cambridge University Press, 2000.

Say, L, et al. *Influence of oestrus synchronization on male reproductive success in the domestic cat.* Proceedings of the Royal Society of London Series B: Biological Sciences, May 2001.

Vigne, JD, et al. *Early taming of the cat in Cyprus.* Science, 9 April 2004.

Villablanca, Jaime R, and Charles E Olmstead. *Neurological development of kittens.* Developmental Psychobiology, March 1979.

Zuffi, Stefano. *The Cat in Art.* Harry N. Abrams, Inc., 2007.

REPRINTS OF OLD BOOKS

Mery, Fernand. *Just Cats.* Read Books, 2006.

Weir, Harrison. *Our Cats And All About Them: Their Varieties, Habits, And Management; And For Show, The Standard Of Excellence And Beauty.* Read Books, 2006.

Simpson, Frances, and Julia Craig-McFeely, ed. *The Book of the Cat.* Old-style Siamese Club Facsimiles, 2005.

Van Vechten, Karl. *The Tiger in the House.* Dover Books, 1996

USEFUL WEBSITES

http://www.breedlist.com – The Fanciers' Breeder Referral List, an American-based site with information on purchasing pedigree cats and contacts for breeders in North America, Europe, the Far East, and Australia.

http://www.fanciers.com – Broad-ranging American website, primarily devoted to pedigree breeds but also carrying veterinary and general care information.

http://www.koratworld.com – The history section includes slides and translations of the *Smud Khoi*, a version of the *Thai Cat Book Poems*.

http://www.messybeast.com – A vast, award-winning compendium of knowledge created by Sarah Hartwell, and widely quoted.

http://www.gla.ac.uk/companion/ownernotes – University of Glasgow Veterinary School pages with concise explanations of infectious diseases and vaccines.

http://www.ieper.be – Site for the town of Ieper/Ypres in Belgium, home of the Cat Parade.

WELFARE ORGANIZATIONS AND CHARITIES

http://www.cats.org.uk – Cats Protection, a British welfare charity.

http://www.fabcats.org – Feline Advisory Bureau, a British welfare charity.

http://www.hsus.org – The Humane Society of the United States.

http://www.rspca.org.uk – Royal Society for the Prevention of Cruelty to Animals, a United Kingdom charity that inspired many independent but similarly named charities, engaged in promoting and enforcing animal welfare legislation.

http://www.scottishspca.org – Scottish Society for Prevention of Cruelty to Animals.

http://www.ispca.ie – Irish Society for the Prevention of Cruelty to Animals.

http://www.rspca.org.au – Royal Society for the Prevention of Cruelty to Animals – Australia.

http://rnzspca.org.nz – Royal New Zealand Society for the Prevention of Cruelty to Animals.

http://www.nspca.co.za – National Council of SPCAs of South Africa.

http://www.aspca.org – American Society for the Prevention of Cruelty to Animals.

BREED REGISTRIES

NORTH AMERICA

The American Association of Cat
Enthusiasts, Inc.
PO Box 321 Ledyard, CT 06339
United States
+1 973 658 5198
http://www.aaceinc.org

American Cat Fanciers' Association
PO Box 1949, Nixa, MO 65714-1949
United States
+1 417 725 1530
http://www.acfacats.com

Canadian Cat Association/
Association Féline Canadienne
289 Rutherford Road, S #18
Brampton, ON
L6W 3R9
Canada
+1 905 459 1481
http://www.cca-afc.com

The Cat Fanciers' Association, Inc.
1805 Atlantic Avenue,
PO Box 1005,
Manasquan, NJ 08736-0805
United States
+1 732 528 9797
http://www.cfainc.org

Cat Fanciers' Federation
PO Box 661
Gratis, OH 45330
United States
+1 937 787 9009
http://www.cffinc.org

The International Cat Association
TICA Executive Office
PO Box 2684
Harlingen, TX 78551
United States
+1 956 428 8046
http://www.tica.org

The Traditional Cat Association, Inc.
PO Box 178
Heisson, WA 98622-0178
United States
http://www.traditionalcats.com

EUROPE

Governing Council of the Cat Fancy
5 King's Castle Business Park
The Drove
Bridgwater, Somerset
TA6 4AG
United Kingdom
+44 (0)1278 427575
http://www.gccfcats.org

Fédération Internationale Féline
No direct contact with offices
http://www.fifeweb.org
United Kingdom member
organization:
Felis Britannica
No dedicated offices
http://www.felisbritannica.plus.com

World Cat Federation
Geisbergstr.2
D-45139 Essen
Germany
+49 201 555724
http://www.wcf-online.de

AUSTRALIA AND NEW ZEALAND

Australian Cat Federation Inc.
Secretary: Mrs Nell Evans
PO Box 331
Port Adelaide BC SA 5015
Australia
+61 8 8449 5880
http://www.acf.asn.au

The Co-ordinating Cat Council of
Australia Inc.
No dedicated offices
http://cccofa.asn.au

CATZ Inc.
No dedicated offices
http://catzinc.org.nz

New Zealand Cat Fancy Inc.
No dedicated offices
http://www.nzcatfancy.gen.nz

SOUTH AFRICA

Cat Federation of Southern Africa
PO Box 25
Bromhof
2125
Republic of South Africa
+27 16 987-1768
http://www.cfsa.co.za

The Southern Africa Cat Council
No dedicated offices
http://www.tsacc.org.za

GLOSSARY

A

Abyssinian tabby *see* **Ticked tabby**.

Agouti The paler ground colour between the stripes of a tabby coat, where the hairs carry **ticking**; also used to mean **tabby**.

AOC (Any Other Colour) Colours or patterns not recognized for showing in a **breed**.

AOV (Any Other Variety) Cats that are members of a **breed** but not eligible for showing because of some characteristic such as their colour.

Awn Bristly undercoat hair. *See also* **Down**, **Guard hair**.

Allele Paired **genes** at a specific location on a **chromosome** controlling a particular trait, such as long hair. May be **heterozygous** or **homozygous**.

Amino acids 'Building blocks' that form animal proteins. The cat cannot synthesize these from vegetable sources.

B

Bi-colour A cat with some degree of white in its coat, as well as plain or patterned colour. This is not generally used to mean cats with just a **button** or **locket** of white.

Bite In a **breed standard**, this refers to the way the front teeth meet.

Blaze A stripe of white on the face.

Blotched tabby The name usually used by geneticists for a swirling pattern of **tabby** markings with an 'oyster' or 'bullseye' on the flank.

Boarding cattery An establishment where cats are cared for during the period of **quarantine** after import, or while their owners are away or cannot have them at home.

Booster An annual vaccination to maintain immunity after an initial dose.

Boots *see* **Gloves**.

Bracelets Refers to **tabby** markings on the legs.

Break A change in direction from the brow to the nose in profile; less defined than a **stop**.

Breeches *see* **Britches**.

Breed A type of cat with distinctive features that reproduces to **type** reliably and whose breeding is controlled and recorded in a **pedigree**.

Breed club An organization devoted to the promotion of one **breed**, usually affiliated to a larger **breed registry**. There may be several clubs representing more popular breeds within one registry.

Breed registry A large organization that maintains **pedigree** information and controls the **breed standards** and shows for many **breeds** in a particular country or, sometimes, internationally. **Breeders** may be affiliated directly to a registry, or to a **breed club**, depending on the registry structure.

Breed standard Written description of the ideal appearance of a **breed**, with a standard of points allocating marks to different aspects of the appearance.

Breeder Someone who breeds cats. They are divided into the mainstream show breeders, who work within **breed registries**, and so-called 'backyard breeders', who simply breed and sell cats without regard for show prizes.

Britches The long hair found on the upper part of the hind legs in some **breeds**. It stands out at the back of the leg, giving the appearance of old-fashioned riding britches.

Button Small spot of white on the chest or belly.

C

Calico An American term for **tortoiseshell**-and-white cats. Contrary to popular usage, not a distinct **breed**, but a coat pattern.

Cameo Name sometimes used for **shaded** cats in red colours. *See also* **Shell cameo**.

Cat fancy A general term for all the cat breeding and showing organizations.

Cat flu Term for various viral infections of the respiratory tract, which can have lasting effects.

Catnip *Nepeta cataria*, a plant containing high levels of nepetalactone, an aromatic substance that is thought to mimic a feline scent and triggers ecstatic behaviour in some cats. Not all cats are affected, and the trait is hereditary: most cats in Australia are not susceptible. Cats may become immune to the effects through constant exposure, but no harmful side effects have been reported. Other *Nepeta* plants, as well as valerian, contain lower levels of the substance.

Championship status In most registries, the final stage of **recognition**, where a cat can be shown and compete against other breeds at all levels of competition. *See also* **Experimental**, **Miscellaneous**, **Preliminary**, **Premiership**, **Provisional**.

Chinchilla *see* **Tipped**.

Chromosome Structure within a cell made up of **DNA**

and carried in pairs (one from each parent), cats having 19 pairs. All are X-shaped, apart from the male gender chromosome which is Y-shaped. *See also* **Gene**, **Allele**.

Class A showing category based on the **breed**, its **recognition** status, and other factors such as age or colour.

Classic tabby The name usually used by **breed registries** for a **blotched tabby**.

Cobby Sturdy build, usually compact in length, and broad with a rounded head. *See also* **Foreign**.

Colourpointing *see* **Pointed**.

Conformation *see* **Type**.

Congenital A trait, usually a health problem, present at birth and resulting from either **genes** or influences during pregnancy.

Crossbreeding The mating of cats from two different **breeds** or a breed and a non-pedigree cat, usually to create a new breed. *See also* **Hybridizing**, **Outcrossing**.

D

Declawing The surgical removal of the claws and attached bones. It is illegal or against the rules of the professional veterinary bodies in many countries.

Dilute Paler shades of coat colours, controlled by a **recessive** gene.

DNA Deoxyribonucleic acid, a long, chain-like molecule containing the 'instructions' used by all organisms to build new cells and function. Often described as the blueprints for an organism. *See also* **Chromosome**, **Gene**.

Domestic cat A non-pedigree, domesticated cat. The domestic class or household pet class at cat shows allows domestic cats to compete against each other.

Dominant A **gene** that will be shown or expressed if one copy of it is carried. *See also* **Epistatic**, **Recessive**.

Down Soft, shorter, insulating undercoat hair. *See also* **Awn**, **Guard hair**.

E

Entire Unneutered or unspayed cat, still capable of reproduction.

Epistatic A **gene** that suppresses the appearance of genes at other locations. For example, the gene for a white coat is not thought to be in the same locus as other colour genes, but when white is carried by a cat, the other colours are hidden beneath it, and it is known as epistatic white, in contrast to **white spotting**. Some **tabby** genes may be epistatic. *See also* **Dominant**, **Recessive**.

Eumelanin Component of **melanin** responsible for black and related colours in the skin and coat.

Experimental A breed category within TICA for the newest **breeds**. *See also* **Championship status**, **Miscellaneous**, **Preliminary**, **Premiership**, **Provisional**.

F

Fault A significant departure from the **breed standard**. May result in a loss of points or disqualification.

Felidae The cat family, including all feline species from the big cats to the **domestic cat**.

Feral A domesticated species living independently, not in a domestic situation. Feral cats are also called alley cats, stray cats, or street cats.

Flanks The sides of the body.

Flehmen A grimace seen in cats when sampling scents, usually sexual. The upper lip is raised.

Foreign Generally lean build with a wedge-shaped head. The original name for Oriental breeds in the United Kingdom. May also be described as Oriental, although this word often implies a more extreme **type**. Cats of more moderate type are sometimes described as semi-foreign.

Free breeding Cats that breed without human control or intervention.

Frost Name sometimes used for the colour lilac.

Frown lines Refers to **tabby** markings above the eyes.

G

Gauntlets *see* **Gloves**.

Gene A section of **DNA** within a **chromosome** carrying the instructions for a particular trait or process. A single pair of genes or **allele** controls many simple **dominant** or **recessive** traits. Others are **polygenetic**.

Gene pool The potential genetic variation of any group, from a **breed** to a **species**. A small number of potential breeding partners means a limited gene pool, and can lead to a higher incidence of **congenital** disorders.

Genotype The genetic make-up of an organism. *See also* **Phenotype**.

Ghost markings Faint **tabby** markings seen in a **self** cat.

Gloves White paws, sometimes also called mittens or boots (on the hind paws).

Guard hair Long, relatively coarse hairs making up the top layer of the coat. *See also* **Awn**, **Down**.

H

Hairball Dense mass consisting of hair ingested while grooming and usually fats from the diet.

Haw The third eyelid or nictitating membrane, not usually seen in healthy cats.

Heat *see* **Oestrus**.

Heterozygous Having one copy each of two differing **genes** at an **allele**. In most cases, this results in the **dominant** trait being shown or expressed; in the case of a **tortoiseshell** cat, it gives a mixed appearance.

Himalayan Refers to **pointed** Persian cats; also an old name for the pointed pattern.

Homozygous Having two copies of the same **gene** at an **allele**. This is essential for **recessive** traits, such as long hair, to be shown or expressed. Some genes are lethal if two copies are carried.

Hybridizing Usually used to mean crossing two distinct **species**, but sometimes loosely used to mean crossing two distinct **types** or **breeds** within a species. *See also* **Crossbreeding**.

I

Inbreeding The mating of closely related animals. Used to ensure consistent reproduction of desired traits, but always with a risk of increasing **congenital** abnormalities. Also sometimes called linebreeding.

J

Jacobson's organ A specialized organ of taste and smell, used in **flehming**. Also called the vomeronasal organ.

K

Kitten A cat under the age of 12 weeks. In showing **classes**, cats may be regarded as kittens for far longer, varying by **breed registry**.

Kitten cap Dark hairs often seen on the heads of white **kittens**, disappearing with age.

L

Lavender Name sometimes used for the colour lilac.

Locket Small spot of white on the chest or neck.

Lordosis The position of a **queen** soliciting mating, crouching with the hindquarters raised.

Lynx American term for **tabby** markings in the **pointed** pattern.

M

Mackerel tabby The name usually used by **breed registries** for a **striped tabby**.

Marbled A modified **blotched tabby** pattern, with the markings spread more horizontally along the **flanks**.

Mascara lines Refers to **tabby** markings around the eyes, specifically extending from the corners of the eyes.

Mask Dark colour on the face of a **pointed** cat.

Melanin Pigment that gives skin and coat their colours. Made up of **eumelanin** and **phaeomelanin**.

Mink A pattern halfway between **pointed** and **sepia**, shown by **heterozygous** cats carrying both patterns.

Miscellaneous The first category of showing in CFA, where cats may be exhibited but not judged in competition. *See also* **Championship status**, **Experimental**, **Preliminary**, **Premiership**, **Provisional**.

Mittens *see* **Gloves**.

Moggie Term for a **domestic cat**, used in the United Kingdom with affection. Not always perceived as affectionate elsewhere.

Mosaicing The mingled colour pattern of a **tortoiseshell**.

Mutation Change in a **gene** resulting in a different form of a trait from the original.

Muzzle The nose and jaws.

N

Natural breed A **breed** that appears through natural selection pressures or geographic isolation, without human intervention.

Necklaces Refers to **tabby** markings around the neck.

Neutered Unable to reproduce due to removal of the reproductive organs.

Non-agouti *see* **Self**.

Nose leather The toughened skin around the nostrils.

O

Oestrus The time when a female cat is in **heat** or calling for a mate.

Oriental *see* **Foreign**.

Outcrossing Crossing a cat of one **breed** with that of another or a **domestic cat**, not to create a new breed but usually to maintain a sufficiently large **gene pool**. *See also* **Crossbreeding**.

P

Parasite An animal that attaches itself to another and lives off it. May be internal or external.

Patched tabby A term used in some American registries for a **tortie tabby**.

Pedigree A record of the parentage of a cat. A paper pedigree or registration document is usually part of the purchase price for any pedigree cat. **Breeder** records in many cases go back to the foundation of the **breed**.

Pet quality A **kitten** of a **breed** that does not meet the **breed standard** well enough for showing, and so is sold as a pet.

Pinna The external, pointed flap of the ear.

Phaeomelanin Component of **melanin** responsible for red and related colours in the skin and coat.

Phenotype The appearance of any organism. This can differ from the **genotype** because **recessive** traits may be carried but not seen.

Platinum Name sometimes used for the colour lilac.

Pointed Pattern in which the body is light and the face, paws, and tail are dramatically darker. *See also* **Mink**, **Sepia**.

Polydactyl Having more toes than normal.

Polygenetic Traits controlled by more than one **gene**, and so difficult to reproduce consistently. *See also* **Dominant**, **Recessive**.

Preliminary The first stage of **recognition** within the GCCF, where cats are exhibited and all that meet the standard can receive a merit certificate. Also a stage of recognition with TICA roughly equivalent to **Provisional** in other associations. *See also* **Championship status**, **Experimental**, **Miscellaneous**, **Premiership**.

Premiership A class within CFA for **neutered** cats.

Provisional Intermediate stage of **recognition** in several **breed registries**, where cats can compete for Best of Breed but not against other **breeds**. *See also* **Championship status**, **Experimental**, **Miscellaneous**, **Preliminary**, **Premiership**.

Q

Quarantine Separation of an animal from others for a period until it is shown to be free from infectious diseases. Often imposed when entering a country, and spent at a **boarding cattery**.

Queen An **entire** female cat.

R

Random breeding *see* **Free breeding**.

Recessive A trait that will only be expressed if two copies of the **gene** for it are carried, without a copy of a **dominant** form in the **allele** to mask it; for example, long hair. *See also* **Epistatic**.

Recognition, The acceptance by a **breed registry** of a **breed** or a new trait within an existing breed. Usually has several stages. *See also* **Championship status**, **Experimental**, **Miscellaneous**, **Preliminary**, **Premiership**, **Provisional**.

Registration The recording of parentage with a **breed registry** for a **pedigree**.

Rex Any mutation causing a curly coat.

Ringworm A fungal infection, resulting in inflamed or flaking circular patches on the skin.

Rosettes Spots grouped into rings, or ring-like **tabby** markings.

Ruff Long hair around the neck and on the chest.

Rufousing Reddish tones to a coat.

S

Selective breeding Human intervention in breeding to achieve a desired **type** of animal. The opposite of **free breeding**.

Self A solid colour without markings. Also called **solid**.

Semi-longhair A genetically longhaired cat with a coat that is finer and shorter than most longhairs.

Sepia Pattern in which the body is subtly lighter than the face, paws, and tail. *See also* **Mink**, **Pointed**.

Shaded A coat with white for some distance along all hairs, giving a white undercoat with a darker colour laid over it. Always genetically a **tabby**, but not showing its markings like a **silver tabby**. *See also* **Smoke**, **Tipped**.

Shell cameo Name sometimes used for **tipped** coats in red colours. *See also* **Cameo**.

Shock Collapse due to sudden loss of blood pressure or circulatory failure.

Silver tabby A cat with white for some distance along all hairs, like a **shaded** cat, but showing **tabby** markings in the coloured part of the coat. Lighter parts of the tabby pattern are cool and silvery in tone. *See also* **Smoke**, **Tipped**.

Silvering The suppression of colour production giving **smoke**, **shaded**, and **tipped** coats.

Smoke A coat with white at the roots of the hairs, giving a white undercoat just showing under darker colour. Always genetically a **self**. *See also* **Shaded**, **Tipped**.

Snip A small area of white on the face.

Snub nose Profile with a dramatic **stop** and very short **muzzle**, as in the modern Persian.

Solid *see* **Self**.

Spayed *see* **Neutered**.

Species A group of animals (or any organisms) that naturally reproduce true to a **type**, and do not naturally interbreed with others of a different type. Often, the offspring of any **hybridizing** with another species will be sterile or have markedly reduced fertility. Cat **breeds** are not species. Whether the **domestic cat** is now a separate species from the **wildcat** is debatable.

Spectacles Refers to **tabby** markings around the eyes.

Spotted tabby A **tabby** with spots rather than stripes of any kind.

Standard *see* **Breed standard**.

Stop A definite, sometimes abrupt, change in direction between the brow and the nose in profile. *See also* **Break**.

Striped tabby A **tabby** with vertical bars or lines on the **flanks**.

Stud jowls Enlarged, heavy jawline that develops in **entire** male cats with age.

Stud tail Greasy area on top of the tail found in **entire** male cats.

T

Tabby A cat with a pattern on the body made up of solidly coloured, darker lines, and lighter-coloured **agouti** areas.

Territory The area within which a cat lives (the core of it) and hunts (a wider perimeter).

Ticking Banding of alternately light and dark areas on a hair, seen in the lighter **agouti** areas of a **tabby** coat.

Ticked tabby A **tabby** with **agouti** striped hairs all over the body, although solid **necklaces** and **bracelets** may still be seen.

Tipped A coat with white for almost the entire length of the hairs, giving a white coat with darker coloured tips. Always genetically a **tabby**. *See also* **Shaded**, **Smoke**.

Tom An **entire** male cat.

Torbie *see* **Tortie tabby**.

Tortie tabby Cat with **tortoiseshell** and **tabby** markings.

Tortoiseshell Cat with patches of **eumelanistic** and **phaeomelanistic** colour. On its own, the word means black and red; other colours are referred to as, for example, chocolate tortie.

Type The typical appearance of a **breed** (or **species**), mainly meaning the head and body shape.

V

Vetting-in Checking of a cat's health prior to a show. Not carried out by all **breed registries**.

Vibrissa Whisker or other sensory hair.

Vomeronasal organ *see* **Jacobson's organ**.

W

Weaned Eating solid food and no longer suckling.

White spotting Patches of white on a coat, resulting in a **bi-colour**. Genetically different from **epistatic** white.

Wildcat A group of related small wild cats, with the **domestic cat** being descended from the African type. They were classified as one species, *Felis sylvestris*, with several geographical sub-species. More recent classifications have them as separate species.

INDEX

ACKNOWLEDGEMENTS

Many thanks are due to Jennifer Close and Sharon Rudd at Studio Cactus, not just for the professional expertise they brought to the project but for their speed, responsiveness, a remarkable ability to pull rabbits (or cats) out of hats, and an unfailingly optimistic approach. They made it all look far easier than I know it was.

I am of course hugely indebted to all the club secretaries and breeders who devote so much of their time to providing information about their breeds and the world of cats in general to nosey people like me. They are far too numerous for me to attempt a complete list, but the seemingly inexhaustible knowledge of Julia May of Palantir in the United Kingdom has been particularly useful, as has the messybeast website run by Sarah Hartwell.

On a more personal note, I would like to thank Dr Bruce Fogle for the generosity of his encouragement and advice, without which I never would have taken on this project. I also owe thanks to all of my family who put up with an unusually feline-filled 2007. I would like to be able to thank my own cat for his patience and understanding when I was busy, but of course he never showed a jot.

Studio Cactus would like to thank Sharon Rudd for design work; Sharon Cluett for original styling; Jennifer Close for editorial work; Lindsey Brown for proofreading; Penelope Kent for indexing; Robert Walker for picture research; Peter Bull for anatomy and first aid illustrations; R & K Photographic for scanning; and Northgate Cattery (www.northgate-cattery.co.uk) for invaluable advice and photography. Special thanks to the Marc Henrie Picture Library for his advice and knowledge of cat breeds.

PICTURE CREDITS

The publishers would like to thank the following for permission to reproduce copyright material:

Abbreviations: a = above, b = bottom, c = centre, l = left, r = right, t = top

aceshot1 80 (l), 98 (b); Agphotographer 168 (t); Mohd Faizal Ahmad 377; akva 275; Gregory Albertini 103 (c); Trevor Allen 117 (b); Gail Anderson 344 (l); Ryan Arnaudin 108 (b); Carlos Arranz 56–57; Marilyn Barbone 138, 366–67; Heather Barnhart 35 (b); Galina Barskaya 33 (t), 85 (b); Mario Beauregard 96 (b); Hagit Berkovich 27 (b); Vitaliy Berkovych 30 (t); Dm N Bir 39 (b); Black Ink Designers, Corp 114 (bl); Graham Bloomfield 12 (br); Eugene Bochkarev 173 (clb); Dan Briski 73 (t); Joy Brown 62 (b); Gordon Cable 136 (c); Gorna Cakmazovic 62 (t); Tony Campbell 49 (cc), 49 (bl), 105 (b), 158 (bl); Claudia Carlsen 272–73; Ronald Caswell 316–17; Sarah Cates 38 (t); Richard Chaff 121; Norman Chan 47 (t), 52 (b); Chanan Photography/Richard Katris 210, 286, 328 (t); Ekaterina Cherkashina 160 (t), 227, 355, 356–57; Tan Chuan-Yeun 94–95; Jeff R Clow 50 (t); Condor 36 149 (t); Corbis 97, 112, 113 (b), 211, 253, 329; Waldemar Dabrowski 141 (l); Lindsay Dean 150 (t); Geoff Delderfield 181; Anna Dickie 59 (l); Jason Ding 72 (t); Tiberius Dinu 173 (tl); Pichugin Dmitry 84 (t), 103 (b); Andreas Doppelmayr 14; Sebastian Duda 51 (b); Anna Dzondzua 74 (b); Elen 120 (t); Stuart Elflett 115 (t); Meelis Endia 61 (t); Anita H Engebakken 255 (t), 255 (b); Stephen Finn 34 (t); Indigo Fish 154 (t), 274 (t); Babusi Octavian Florentin 38 (b), 120 (b); reprinted with permission from Drs Foster and Smith, Inc 71 (l), 82 (t); Lakis Fourouklas 128–29; Anthony Fransella 73 (b); Justyna Furmanczyk 150 (t); Daniel Gale 35 (t), 45 (b); Alex Galea 141 (br); Alexander Garanin 192–93; GeoM 50 (b); Vladimir V Georgievskiy 115 (b); Getty Images 29, 126 (b), 131 (b), 140, 173 (crb); Johanna Goodyear 91 (t), 105 (t); Derek Gordon 31 (b); Terry Goulden 254 (br); Meryleen Greenwood 207, 258 (t), 358 (b); Liudmila Gridina 122; Ilya D Gridnev 28 (t), 123 (b); Jerko Grubisic 104 (b); Natalia V Guseva 282 (r), 284–85; Rami Happonen 30 (b); Khafizov Ivan Harisovich 101; Tim Harman 66; Joshua Haviv 13 (bl); Brandon Heiss 43 (b); Ben Heys 63 (b); Shawn Hine 383; Jay Hocking 100 (t); Ronnie Howard 15 (t), 18 (r); iconex 12 (t); iofoto 84 (t); Peter Ivanov Ishmiriev 110 (t); Eric Isselée 44 (bl), 79 (tl), 114 (tl), 114 (tr), 143 (t), 145 (br), 172, 173 (tc), 196, 197 (t); Jim Brown Photography 287, 328 (b), 341, 368, 369 (t), 369 (b); Judy Ben Joud 32 (t); Julie Keen 91 (t); Tan Kian Khoon 35 (b); Graham S Klotz 149 (b); Devin Koob 308; Dimitry Kosterev 167 (bl); Vassiliy Koval 13 (tr); Nadezhda V Kulagina 144 (t); Arnold John Labrentz 22 (t); Erik Lam 155; Gillean Lazelle 123 (t); Michael Ledray 10 (t), 131 (t); RJ Lerich 113; Nir Levy 55 (t); Hannu Liivaar 72 (t); Khoo Si Lin 70 (t); Polina Lobanova 90 (t); Elisa Locci 371; Ovidiu Lordachi 148, 191 (b); Irving Lu 165 (b); Mircea Maieru 69 (b), 159 (b); Markabond 102; Gill Martin 40 (b); June Mateer 206 (t), 206 (b); Sandy Maya Matzen 46 (b); Sharon Meredith 78 (b); Suponev Vladimir

Mihajlovich 68 (b); Stanislav Mikhalev 43 (t); Anna Modzelewska 53 (b); Tatiana Morozova 261; Richard P Nathanson 93 (b); N Joy Neish 41 (b); Sean Nel 126 (t); Heath Newman 166 (b); NHPA 2–3, 4–5, 6, 12 (bl), 13 (br), 21 (t), 24, 25 (b), 25 (t), 64 (t), 89 (tl), 90 (b), 111 (tl), 112 (t), 117 (l), 176 (t), 177 (b), 178 (b), 200, 201, 202–203, 223, 213, 214 (t), 215, 216–17, 228–29, 232, 233, 237, 238-39, 244–45, 248, 258, 298–99, 315, 321, 314 (t), 314 (b), 320, 330, 344 (b)345, 350, 351 (t), 351 (b), 354 (b); Gary Nugent 104 (t); Nikolay Okhitin 71 (b); Kevan O'Meara 127 (t); Alvaro Pantoja 21 (b); Zoltan Pataki 90 (c); Irene Pearcey 20; Scott Pehrson 108 (c); Vuksan Pejovic 87 (b); Perrush 107 (b); Patricia Peters 343 (t), 343 (b); Michael Pettigrew 76–77, 145 (bl); Photo Intrigue 48 (t); Photos.com 69 (t), 75 (b), 173 (cb); Andreas Pidjass 58 (b); Alyssa Plano 360; plastique 75 (t); Vova Pomortzeff 15 (b), 26; Svetlana Ponomareva 342; Anita Price 234 (b); Hashim Pudiyapura 100 (b); Robert Redelowski 33 (b); Styve Reineck 384; Tina Rencelji 78 (t), 86 (b); Rex Features 134–35; rgbspace 167 (br); Nicholas Rjabow 41 (t); Robynrg 19, 46 (t), 49 (cl), 60 (t), 63 (t), 88 (b), 156–57, 163 (b), 177 (t), 336–37, 352–53, 359, 364 (b); Mostakov Roman 61 (b); Ronen 79 (b), 169; Michal Rosak 118; Mario Savola 65 (b); Pavel Sazonov 65 (t); Jeff Schultes 23; Jean Schweitzer 86 (t), 173 (cra); Kristian Sekulic 12 (tr); Jennifer Leigh Selig 170–71; Gleb Semenjuk 79 (tc); Jacqueline Shaw 99 (t); Olga Shelego 42; Elena Sherengovskaya 85 (t); Shutterstock 28 (t) 16–17, 49 (t), 55 (b), 51 (t), 79 (tl), 88 (b), 153, 151 (t), 173 (ca); Jo-Anne Simpson 332 (b), 335 (l); Edwina Sipos 323 (r); Floris Sloff 266–67; Carolina K Smith 13 (tl), 18 (l); Dwight Smith 173 (cla); Forest L Smith, III 53 (tr); solos 179 (t); SouWest Photography 27 (l); Wally Stemberger 22 (b); Michael Stokes 106; Andrey Stratilatov 68 (t); Studio Cactus 39 (t), 48 (t), 40 (t), 70 (t), 80 (r), 81, 82 (b), 83 (t), 83 (bl), 83 (br), 87 (tl), 87 (tc), 87 (tr), 88 (t), 88 (c), 92 (all), 93 (t), 93 (tr), 96 (t), 98 (t), 99 (c), 99 (b), 107 (t), 108 (cl), 108 (cr), 110 (b), 111 (b inset), 114 (br), 117 (t), 130 (t), 133 (t), 137 (b), 290–91; Juan David Ferrando Subero 137 (r); Olga Sweet 161 (b); Magdalena Szachowska 179 (b), 182, 242 (b); Ferenc Szelepcsenyi 49 (bl), 49 (bc), 58 (c) , 151 (c); Denis Tabler 112 (b), 116 (t); Sherrianne Talon 151 (b); Naomi Taylor 254 (bl); Christophe Testi 136 (t); Richard Thornton 45 (r); Jamie Thorpe 127 (b); Jeff Thrower 74 (t); Nikolay Titov 54 (b); Nikita Tiunov 52 (t); Taras Tsyurka 348–49; Suzanne Tucker 44 (br); H Tuller 8–9; April Turner 64 (b); UltraOrto, S.A. 31 (t); Jiri Vaclavek 47 (t); Simone van der Berg 32 (b); Krissy VanAlstyne 54 (t); Alberto Perez Veiga 116 (b); Victorian Traditions 136 (l); Chepko Danil Vitalevich 168 (b); Bannykh Alexey Vladimirovich 130 (l); Diane Webb 362; Ivonne Wierink 124–25; Monika Wisniewska 111 (b); Dusan Zidar 36–37 All other images © Marc Henrie, ASC

COVER IMAGES front cover top from left to right: Geoff Delderfield (1), Lakis Fourouklas (2), Magdalena Szachowska (3), Tatiana Morozova (4) Photos front cover bottom from left to right: Heath Newman (1), NHPA (2 & 3), Studio Cactus (4) Photos back cover top from left to right: NHPA (1 & 3), akva (2), Alexander Garanin (4) Photos back cover bottom from left to right: Marc Henrie, ASC (1), NHPA (2 & 4), Claudia Carlsen (4)